FROM CAMEROON TO PARIS

From Cameroon to Paris

MOUSGOUM ARCHITECTURE IN & OUT OF AFRICA

Steven Nelson

THE UNIVERSITY OF CHICAGO PRESS
Chicago and London

STEVEN NELSON is assistant professor of African and African American art history at the University of California, Los Angeles.

The University of Chicago Press, Chicago 60637
The University of Chicago Press, Ltd., London
© 2007 by The University of Chicago
All rights reserved. Published 2007
Printed in the United States of America

MM Publication of this book has been aided by a grant from the
Millard Meiss Publication Fund of the College Art Association.

16 15 14 13 12 11 10 09 08 07   1 2 3 4 5

ISBN-13: 978-0-226-57183-6 (cloth)
ISBN-10: 0-226-57183-1 (cloth)

LIBRARY OF CONGRESS CATALOGING-IN-PUBLICATION DATA
Nelson, Steven, 1962–
  From Cameroon to Paris : Mousgoum architecture in and out of Africa / Steven Nelson.
      p. cm.
  Includes bibliographical references and index.
  ISBN-13: 978-0-226-57183-6 (cloth : alk. paper)
  ISBN-10: 0-226-57183-1 (cloth : alk. paper) 1. Architecture, Domestic—Cameroon.
2. Vernacular architecture—Cameroon. 3. Musgu (African people)—Dwellings—
Cameroon. 4. Musgu (African people)—Ethnic identity I. Title.
  NA7467.6.C3N45 2007
  728.096711—dc22

                                          2006018112

∞ The paper used in this publication meets the minimum requirements
of the American National Standard for Information Sciences—
Permanence of Paper for Printed Library Materials, ANSI Z39.48-1992.

My late grandparents, Lloyd and Mary Randolph, who went to East Africa in 1972 and spent the rest of their lives talking about the experience.

The late Azao Dogo of Pouss, Cameroon, for his guidance, wisdom, wit, and generosity.

CONTENTS

NOTE ON LANGUAGE AND ORTHOGRAPHY

Munjuk, the language of the Mousgoum, is a Chadic language with five dialects. In this book I have followed the dialect called *Mpús*, which is spoken in and around Pouss. There have been a number of articles about and dictionaries of the language, chief among them being those by Henry Tourneux (1978, 1991), Johannes Lukas (1941), and Heinrich Barth (1862).

Given my own lack of linguistic training as well as Tourneux's expertise in Munjuk, I have generally followed his work in the orthography of the language. However, in cases where I did not have typographic access to certain characters, I followed Lukas's model. For the spelling of proper names, I deferred to my research assistant Hamat Gring. I have not differentiated between long and short vowels. The pronunciation of certain letters in Munjuk is as follows:

a is pronounced as in *eye* and as in *ha*
e is pronounced as in *meat* and as in *met*
i is pronounced as in *see*
o is pronounced as in *low*
u is pronounced as in *moon*
ŋ is pronounced as in *sing*
s is pronounced as in *tsar*
th is pronounced as in *bat*

Munjuk is a tonal language. Like Tourneux, I have used a grave accent (`) to designate a low tone; an acute accent (´) to designate a high tone. Most commonly, tones are used in order to designate verb tense. A low tone signifies something done in the past; a high tone signifies all other tenses. Tones also differentiate between certain words. For example, *fètiy* means "route;" *fétiy* means "sun." In the case of verbs, where the tonal mark determines the meaning of a word, I have used it. A number of nouns that are single words in English are compound in Munjuk. For example, a Muslim in Munjuk is called *dif zi sala*, which literally means "man who prays." This makes for a vocabulary that is rich in its combinations, quite precisely defining many different classes of objects and people. Munjuk nouns are divided into masculine and feminine categories; in cases where a noun has both a masculine and a feminine construction, the feminine is normally the diminutive form. Unless otherwise noted, Munjuk nouns in the text are singular; verbs are infinitives. In the case of nouns that have both masculine and feminine forms, unless otherwise noted, the masculine is used.

In the following chapters I look at the Mousgoum teleuk in particular and Mousgoum architecture more generally from number a of different vantage points, which have been affected not only by the written materials I have amassed over the past decade, but also by field research and observation I had performed in Cameroon and Chad during the 1995–96 academic year. After a preliminary trip to Cameroon in 1994 and with the advice of people there and in France, I chose Pouss as my location for research, as there are today more teleukakay standing in the village and its vicinity than anywhere else. As such, it was the most promising place to carry out research. Although I do not think of the built environment as a "text" per se, following Suzanne Preston Blier and Jean-Paul LeBeuf, I have proceeded with the understanding that one can in fact read the built environment; the combination of my readings and those garnered through field interviews and travelers' accounts have very much affected the form of this project.

Interviews were most often conducted in the homes of those being interviewed. With men, these interviews would take place over tea or a small meal. Given the still strong prohibitions on women eating in the presence of men, interviews with women did not generally involve food or drink. As a token of appreciation, I took tea and sugar to all of those interviewed. Interviews, which ranged from thirty minutes to over two hours, were conducted in French and Munjuk. After they were recorded, my research assistant Hamat Gring transcribed them into French. Important interviews were transcribed two or three times. In this period, I took hundreds of photographs and explored archival materials as well as Mousgoum ephemera in Cameroon. I also gathered cartographic materials and drew plans of enclosures. I explained to Lamido Mbang Yaya Oumar of Pouss in 1994 that I had come to write a book about the teleuk and its relation to Mousgoum life; when I returned the following year, Mousgoum people were very amenable to such an idea as many people in the region were generally concerned about cultural loss. For many Mousgoum, the few teleukakay that remain are a metaphor for those things in Mousgoum culture-at-large that had already, in some minds, been lost.

As this book has involved research on four continents, it would have been an impossible feat without an incredible amount of help and support. First and foremost, I am enormously indebted to the Mousgoum people who live in and around Pouss, Cameroon. I was welcomed into their homes, and they were generous with their time, sharing their knowledge, stories, food, and lives with me during my stay. I would like to specifically thank His Majesty Lamido Mbang Yaya Oumar for facilitating my research in Pouss. I owe much to Hamat Gring, who served as my research assistant. From logistics to sharing his valuable insights, Hamat played an integral role in the success of my work in the field. Salman Mbang Oumar and the late Azao Dogo were also instrumental during my research, and I thank them for their support. El Hadji Youssoufa Bourkou Manda, his nephew Oumar Abedi, and their family gave me a home in Pouss; more than providing shelter, they brought me into their family, and for that I am grateful. I would also like to thank Hamat's mother, Mme. Awafalakaye Évélé, who also opened up her home and treated me as a member of her own family. I also thank her for giving me the Mousgoum name "Alouakou." I hope that this book does justice to the complexities of Mousgoum cultural identities and concerns as they are articulated through the built environment.

I am very grateful to Dana Goodhue, who was a United States Peace Corps volunteer in Pouss from 1993–96. She was a wonderful sounding board and a great help on every conceivable level. She saved me months of work in the field, and she was indispensable to the fruition of this project.

I would like to thank Emmanuel Gwan, professor of geography at the University of Yaoundé, who served as my academic sponsor during my stay in Cameroon. Henry Tourneux of ORSTOM helped with Munjuk as well as logistics in northern Cameroon, and for that I thank him. I also express my gratitude to the United States Information Agency and the United States Embassy in Yaoundé as well as the United States Peace Corps; they were invaluable sources of information and logistical aid.

This project began as my Harvard doctoral thesis, and I owe a great deal to my primary advisor, Suzanne Preston Blier, who not only suggested this topic to me but also has been and continues to be intellectually and personally supportive. I am also extremely grateful to the other members of my dissertation committee, Norman Bryson and Gülru Necipoglu, for their critical insights and intellectual stimulation as well as their enthusiasm for this topic. It is in large part due to Suzanne and Gülru that I decided to become an Africanist art historian, and for that I thank them. I wish to extend my special appreciation to David Joselit, who accompanied me on my first trip to Cameroon in 1994. I have benefited greatly from his continued advice, encouragement, and friendship.

This project has been immeasurably enriched by the valuable insights, generosity, and support of a number of current and former faculty members of the Department of History of Art and Architecture at Harvard University, and I extend my sincere thanks to them. They are Yve-Alain Bois, Ewa Lajer-Burcharth, and Irene Winter.

I am much indebted to my former colleagues in the Department of Art and Art History at Tufts University for their unyielding support. In particular, I would like to thank Cristelle Baskins, Eva Hoffman, Ikumi Kaminishi, Andrew McClellan, Eric Rosenberg, and Judith Wechsler. I also express my gratitude to my current colleagues in the Department of Art History at the University of California, Los Angeles, for their unconditional encouragement, critical insights, and practical advice. Most notably, I would like to thank George Baker, Irene Bierman-McKinney, Susan Downey, Cecelia Klein, Miwon Kwon, Saloni Mathur, Z. S. Strother, Charlene Villaseñor Black, and Lothar von Falkenhausen. Other colleagues at UCLA have also been wonderfully supportive and have helped shape this book. They are Andrew Apter, Marla Berns, Donald Cosentino, Amy Futa, Aamir Mufti, Allen Roberts, Mary Nooter Roberts, and Doran Ross. I also extend my gratitude to my graduate students, whose insights have made important contributions to this book. In particular, I give thanks to Sean Sheridan Anderson, Aliaa El Sandouby, and Susan Gagliardi. I also thank my research assistants, Doris Chon, Ross Elfline, Shanna Kennedy-Quigley, and Heather Sexton, who made my life easier during the course of this project.

I am extremely fortunate in having had an extraordinary community of colleagues, peers, and friends during the life of this project; they have been generous with their conversation and intellectual engagement (and, at times, shameless validation), which have profoundly affected the shape of this volume. They continue to be my sustaining influence. They are Jülide Aker, Emily Apter, Aimée Bessire, Mark Bessire, Judith Bettelheim, Steven Biel, Randall Bird, Ryan Chavez, Andrew Cohen, Roger Conover, Margarita Crocker, Allan deSouza, Lauri Firstenberg, Christraud Geary, Maria Gough, Jonathan Hansen, Tim Hartley, Lindy Hess, Branden Joseph, Jane Kamensky, Geoff Kaplan, Juliet Koss, Pamela Lee, Jessica Levin, Michael Lobel, Elizabeth Mansfield, Christine Mehring, Laurie Monahan, the late Ernest Pascucci, Joseph Quirk, Jonathan Reynolds, Felicity Scott, Gary Shaffer, Miriam Stewart, Anthony Vidler, Cécile Whiting, Sarah Whiting, Bill Willard, and Andrés Zervigon.

Joan Beardsley, Peter Beardsley, Nicholas David, Bernard Gardi, Dominique Malaquais, and Louis Perrois helped me in locating materials and aided in the planning of my research abroad, and I extend my sincere thanks to them. My thanks also go to Karin Lanzoni and Patricia Morton, who shared their knowledge of the Getty Research Institute's Special Collections and the intricacies of rights and permissions.

I am grateful for the research, writing, and publication grants I received. Funding provided by two grants from the Mellon Foundation, a Charles Eliot Norton Travel grant from the Department of History of Art and Architecture at Harvard, and a research fellowship from Tufts University enabled the research and writing of the dissertation. I also appreciate the funding for photographic equipment, supplies, and reproduction provided by Tufts. A Tufts faculty Summer Travel Award and Faculty Research Award facilitated further research in archives in France and the United States. A J. Paul Getty Postdoctoral Fellowship in the History of Art and Humanities enabled the preparation of the book manuscript. A UCLA Faculty Senate Grant (Assistant Professor Initiative) further enabled the preparation of the manuscript, and a Millard Weiss Publication Grant furnished by the College Art Association aided in the production of the present volume. I would also like to thank Anthony Burton, Michael Koplow, and especially Susan Bielstein at the University of Chicago Press for their hard work on and enthusiastic dedication to this project.

Parts of this project were previously given as presentations at the Arts Council of the African Studies Association's 1998 Triennial Conference, Cornell University, Pomona College, and Yale University. An earlier version of chapter three was published in the *Annals of Scholarship;* an earlier version of chapter four appeared in *African Arts.* Any errors or inaccuracies in this book are my own.

Finally, I would like to express my deepest gratitude to my partner Dana Peterman, and to my parents, Joan and the late Raphael Nelson, for their guidance, for their confidence in my abilities, and, most importantly, for their unconditional love.

Los Angeles, California
October 2006

Introduction

If one builds a teleuk it is because it is that which is most noted amongst Mousgoum cultural elements. HAMAT GRING

Over a breakfast of runny eggs, undercooked bacon, and really bad coffee in the gorgeous Green Mountains of Vermont in August 2005, I was telling my friend Allan about the Mousgoum domed house, or *teleuk* (*teleukakay*, pl.), and how I explore the structure in my about-to-be-completed manuscript. I had to give away my fabulous new nugget (fig. 1). I went on and on about how I was surfing the Internet a few days before, and saw that the Cameroonian government had erected a huge reproduction of a teleuk in Expo 2005, a World's Fair in Japan.

"So you're going, aren't you?" said Allan.

"I don't have time," I muttered.

"You have to go."

Six weeks and 6,600 miles later, as I make my way through the hoards of people, undoubtedly also ordered by Allan to go to Expo 2005, the skies quickly darken, becoming that particular shade of gray that orders you to take cover. Ten feet from the buildings that house the fair's African pavilions, downpour. Wet, jet-lagged, and more than a little bit cranky, I walk around, dodge, bump into, and trip over people who are seeing, looking, oooing, aaahing, and buying things African. I say, "Excuse me," and I feel really inadequate because the only word I know in Japanese, which Zoë taught me right before I left Los Angeles, is "arigato." Thanks, Allan.

Turning the corner, I pass a bunch of African pavilions, all of them small, all of them low-tech, particularly when measured against the pavilions and exhibits of wealthy nations, and all of them, while relatively nondescript, are still a tad creepy in the way that the "It's a Small World" ride at Disneyland or the American Indian mannequins at Chicago's Field Museum, while relatively nondescript, are a tad creepy. I near another turn, and, opposite the Ghana exhibit, where you can dress in Kente cloth and be photographed like a "tribal African," I see it: the Japan teleuk (plate 1). Consisting of a hollow wooden frame covered with plaster, the structure is painted in a dark, grayish shade of brown. Above its very high doorway you read, if you read Japanese, the words "Republic of Cameroon."

FIGURE 1. Mousgoum village, 1912. Source: Musée de l'Homme.

Once you walk through the exhibit's doorway, you see two mini teleukakay with a very cheesy 8½ × 11 inch mass-produced drawing depicting Mousgoum life in a huge vitrine, art objects from the Cameroon Grasslands, products made in Cameroon, masks, posters of Cameroon's most famous soccer stars, and a photograph of Paul Biya, Cameroon's president, flanked by two Cameroonian flags. The inside wall of the dome, papered with large-scale images of Cameroonian life (one of which was photographed among teleukakay), looks like a blown-up and concave travel poster. As you leave the exhibit, you can have your Expo passport stamped with a seal of Cameroon. As an almost full participant in the Expo, I bought one of the copies of the tacky Mousgoum picture (fig. 2).

As one of thousands of things on display from the Expo's 115 participating nation-states, in 2005, the teleuk is not only most noted among Mousgoum cultural elements, but Cameroonian ones as well. The teleuk is an architectonic ambassador, it is that thing that distinguishes Cameroon from its African neighbors—and it does so quite successfully in Expo 2005—and, today, it is a form that highlights Cameroonian ingenuity in the world arena. Moreover, as a structure literally molded from a mixture of soil, grasses, and animal dung, the teleuk fits perfectly into Expo 2005's theme: "Nature's Wisdom." The house is environmentally friendly, leaves no waste in its construction, and if it falls, the materials are completely biodegradable and totally reusable. In both Japanese and English, visitors to the Cameroon exhibit learn that nature, specifically the anthill, is indeed the house's inspiration, that the form exists in Cameroon's Sudanic-Sahel region, and that it's quite cool inside even when temperatures outside are quite hot. The Internet gives a bit more detail. In the cyberexpo, Cameroonian organizers depict the ingenuity behind the teleuk as based in the shape of the dome, as derived from the termite hill, and in the thermal advantages of the materials used in the house's construction. Furthermore, the organizers suggest that the Mousgoum build these houses "just like termites do." Not ignoring the commercial issues that have always underscored world's fairs, the rhetoric surrounding the Mousgoum teleuk's earth-friendliness as well as its architectural and cultural singularity suggests that it's the eco-tourist attraction par excellence. Perhaps visiting Cameroon in Japan will encourage tourists to see the real thing in Africa.

The presence of the teleuk in Expo 2005 and its status as eco-friendly architecture may seem somehow very, very new, somehow very, very hip. Yet known outside of Mousgoum country since at least Heinrich Barth's journey to North and Central Africa during the 1850s, the teleuk's appearance in this exhibition, Cameroonian agency notwithstanding, is merely the latest installment of an ongoing chronicle in which international fascination with the building takes center stage. In that sense, the Japan teleuk and the impetus around its creation are very, very old. Alongside of and in tandem with international fascination the Mousgoum teleuk, along with Mousgoum culture more generally, has undergone massive transformations since the advent of European colonialism in the late nineteenth and early twentieth centuries. Once an element of a larger family compound, a stage for the performance of quotidian life, many Mousgoum today understand the teleuk as the preeminent sign of their culture, one that trig-

FIGURE 2. Drawing of a Mousgoum family enclosure.

gers memories of a Mousgoum past and symbolizes Mousgoum cultural survival in an ever-changing world.

The teleuk has always had the capacity to become more than itself or something other than itself. Aside from its vital role as architectonic repository of cultural heritage, the domed house also illustrates the unique nature of the Mousgoum people to themselves as well as to the outside world. Outside of Mousgoum country, people have made much of the structure. Barth saw the teleuk as a somewhat primitive structure, albeit one bearing traces of "art" and "civilization."[1] During his 1911 visit to the Mousgoum village of Musgum (Chad), the German anthropologist Gunther von Hagen compared the teleuk to the domes of the Kremlin.[2] In 1926, André Gide, visiting the same village, described the teleuk as both Etruscan tomb and prime number.[3] Following Gide's lead, Amedée Ozenfant, from his desk in Paris, placed the teleuk on a par with Roman architecture.[4] In the 1941 Hollywood movie *Road to Zanzibar* Bob Hope and Bing Crosby found themselves in a deserted village littered with teleukakay and human skeletons (fig. 3). Unannounced guests at the home of overfed African cannibals, the two men, noting that beavers probably had not built what seemed like a graveyard to

FIGURE 3. Bob Hope and Bing Crosby in a village of Mousgoum teleukakay, *Road to Zanzibar*, 1941. © 1941 Paramount Pictures, Inc. Courtesy of Universal Studios Licensing LLLP.

them, narrowly escaped becoming the daily catch. The architect Eduard Sekler, in a far more serious vein, in 1965 claimed that the teleuk makes, in his words, "an unequivocal tectonic statement."[5]

Aside from these few examples of a vast array of descriptions, the Mousgoum teleuk has appeared on French colonial and Cameroonian postage stamps, on Cameroonian currency, on Cameroonian and European travel posters, in travel guides, in Sunday newspaper travel sections, in at least four twentieth-century French World's Fairs, as the subject of tourist art (and kitsch) throughout Cameroon, and, most recently, on the Internet and here in Aichi, Japan. The list goes on. Images and textual accounts of the teleuk are remarkably easy to find, and they all beautifully illustrate the architectural historian Geoffrey Scott's 1924 dictum: "We have transcribed ourselves in terms of architecture."[6]

From Cameroon to Paris to Hamburg to Hollywood to Japan to my own Macintosh screen the Mousgoum teleuk has functioned in a vast array of discourses, and thus it has not one history, but many. With that understanding, *From Cameroon to Paris,* in looking at the house in a number of seemingly disparate venues, investigates how these various histories not only situate the Mousgoum teleuk as a complex structure, but this project also explores how the reception of the Mousgoum house complicates our comprehension of the relations between architecture and human experience. The various interpretations of the Mousgoum teleuk directly point to the many differences of those making their claims, but what ties all of these ideas, buildings, and images together—besides their obvious connections to the house itself—are the modes used to ascribe meaning and importance to the built environment more generally and how architecture ascribes psychological meaning to self and non-self. Along such lines Sekler's description of the teleuk and Scott's insistence on the centrality of architecture to human experience provide what is perhaps the device of paramount importance in making meaning out of built environments: tectonics.

Quite simply, tectonics is the means through which the architect can make the intangible tangible (or the invisible visible), and through this operation, architecture is given the ability to produce meaning.[7] It is in this fashion that Mitchell Schwarzer interprets Kenneth Frampton's analysis of tectonics, noting that for Frampton, tectonics is "a condition of knowledge." Schwarzer goes on to insist, "Tectonics is at once total experience and splintering representational tale."[8] Similarly, tectonics is intimately related to the ways in which architecture can be a template for the representation of self and non-self. Heinrich Wölfflin was quite explicit on such a point, explaining:

> We read our own image into all phenomena. We expect everything to possess what we know to be the conditions of our own well-being. Not that we expect to find the appearance of a human being in the forms of inorganic nature: we interpret the physical world through the categories . . . that we share with

it. We also define the expressive capability of those other forms accordingly. *They can communicate to us only what we ourselves use their qualities to express.* (emphasis in original)[9]

Tectonics is thus the mode through which construction becomes structure. It is the mechanism that transforms architecture into art. It is the device that, for Sekler, changes a "hut" into a nearly perfect building. It is the method that allows us, following Scott, to transcribe ourselves into architecture. As such, tectonics allows architecture to become not only a mirror but also a lens through which we see the world. As Julian Patrick has noted, tectonics, as "authentic representation" is structured by chiasmus, defined by Detlef Mertins as the struggle "to bridge the unbridgeable gap between self and other, known and unknown, conscious and unconscious in order to stabilize representations prone to coming apart."[10]

In grounding perception in tectonics, those in contact with the teleuk tap into the rhetoric of ancient culture espoused by architectural thinkers since the nineteenth century. Scott Wolf observes that nineteenth-century archaeologists took the term "tectonics" from the Greek "tekton," and it would come to signify the perception of architecture as a structural system whose elements served pragmatic and aesthetic functions.[11] While tectonics was understood in a number of different ways, it was firmly rooted in the notion that cultural artifacts (as well as modern buildings) contained and articulated a psychological perception, what Wolf calls a "new *Anschauung*."[12] As this perception gained currency, it gave new connotations, rooted in the ability of architectural forms to speak, as it were, to the built environment in ancient and modern Europe. Moreover, this notion of architecture was exported, and it became a tool to represent the non-Western other. Conversely, through tectonics, the Mousgoum can represent themselves. In this fashion, tectonics was used as a tool not only of ethnography but also of what one might call ethnoarchaeology. In northern Cameroon itself, tectonics is a tool for the construction of subjectivity.

In his analysis of tectonics, Sekler writes about the concept in terms of a "tectonic statement." In his words:

> Through tectonics the architect may make visible, in a strong statement, that intensified kind of experience of reality which is the artist's domain—in our case the experience of forces related to forms in a building. Thus structure, the intangible concept, is realized through construction and given visual expression through tectonics.[13]

Sekler gives a number of examples of tectonic statements, and for him, the most accessible is that of the Gothic cathedral:

We have learned that in the experience of a High Gothic cathedral it is the tectonic statement which shares with space and light the task of conveying a analogical meaning. In order to direct the beholder's mind spiritually upward, a play of forces is enacted most dramatically and appeals directly through empathy, even though what goes on behind the scenes of ribbing and shafting may be different from what we are led to believe.[14]

Although the forms of the High Gothic cathedral constitute the statement that allows the mind to be thrust heavenwards, the architectural pieces cannot perform such a feat alone. Sekler suggests that one has to have empathy to be able to comprehend the tectonic statement of the structure. What this in turn requires in the viewer or resident is the ability to identify with the architectural forms, for it is only through this identification that the otherwise mute building can speak. Such views also highlight architecture's psychological power.

Sekler understands this notion of empathy, that ability to identify with the built environment through his reading of Wölfflin's 1886 dissertation *Prolegomena zu einer Psychologie der Architektur.* Here, Sekler explains that in Wölfflin's thought tectonics was a manifestation of empathy in architecture. This formulation illustrated Vitruvius's analogy between humans and architecture by corroborating it through psychology. Ultimately, in the course of coming to terms with the relationship between the two, empathy is really a psychological projection, one that allows the constitution of an architectural language.[15] Hence, the forms themselves constitute a mirror, a way to see the self. Wölfflin would have agreed with such a premise, recognizing that "we supposit [*sic*] our own image under all appearances."[16]

If architectural forms can speak and we can, through identification, understand them, architectural form is its own language and the empathetic observer its translator. Sekler shows how tectonic language transcends those merely spoken. On the Mousgoum teleuk, he writes:

There are those rare cases when a building is an almost perfect realization of a structural principle in terms of a most appropriate and efficient construction while at the same time a clearly related unequivocal tectonic statement is found. At one end of the scale such buildings may occur in anonymous architecture, as in the corrugated, beehive-shaped mud huts of the Mousgoum tribe from Lake Tchad, so often illustrated in recent years. Their shape, conditions of climate apart, is governed by the plasticity of the available building material and by the necessity to create a vault of statically favorable cross section . . . the striking corrugations not only strengthen the comparatively thin curved surface but they also prove useful at times of torrential rain and as a kind of permanent scaffolding.[17]

As empathy is based in the ability of a person to identify with someone or something else, it also posits that that identification allows the empathizer (almost exclusively a Westerner) not only to understand and to know meaning, but also to tap into the language of building itself.

Alongside a consideration of tectonics, notions of time underlie the cacophony of meanings attached to the Mousgoum teleuk. From the historic building and destruction of teleukakay to its present status as symbol of a Mousgoum past, time has served as a conscious and unconscious ingredient in the interpretation of the dome. Although many Mousgoum people understand the teleuk as a contemporary thing, one that merges the past with contemporary concerns, many Western tourists and scholars continue to depict the structure as a relic, as a mark of an irretrievable, non-Western past. For example, in 1991 a photograph of a Mousgoum teleuk was included in an encyclopedia of architecture as a living example of humankind's earliest architecture.[18] In Dennis Sharp's seamless (and racialized) conflation between a contemporary Mousgoum teleuk and a primordial hut, the non-Western house is deployed to connect the British architect to a past that he can recoup only through the projection of his desire onto the dome. This imagined and romanticized past recalls notions of "vernacular architecture" put forth by Bernard Rudofsky in his 1964 Museum of Modern Art exhibition Architecture without Architects. In the catalogue that accompanied the exhibition Rudofsky insisted, "Vernacular architecture does not go through fashion cycles. It is nearly immutable, indeed, unimprovable, since it serves its purpose to perfection."[19] According to this mythic ideal, the producers are incapable of (and uninterested in) innovation, implying that they have been frozen in the past; furthermore, such an ideal enables the author to conjure up other stereotypes as well. Rudofsky sentimentally insists, "In civilizations less ponderous than ours, enclosures made from woven matting are considered fit for kings."[20] Consequently, Sharp and Rudofsky's construction of a past through the built environment neatly illustrates the contemporary validity of Peter Brooks's assertion that to leave Europe—physically or mentally—is to go back in time.[21] Along such lines, time, like geographic distance and mental and racial difference, serves as a distancing mechanism. Thus, things like the teleuk, in their reception, become icons of a past, one that can accommodate, as we will see, various and seemingly contradictory agendas.

Within the literature of anthropology, tourism, and museum studies, writers have commonly thought about time in the construction of meaning. However, outside of preservation and heritage architecture, the importance of time has rarely been understood outside of attempts to actually represent it in space. In its connection to these arenas, and in the various ways in which the building has been interpreted, rebuilt, and represented, the Mousgoum teleuk allows for an opportunity to think about the connection of time and architecture and to postulate time itself as being a critical element in the making of architectural meaning.

Quite simply, the Mousgoum teleuk moves into, out of, back into, and back out of Africa, and such movement says much about the relationship of architecture to different groups of people. Chapter one explores what can best be called historic Mousgoum architecture and serves as a foundation for better understanding the massive changes in meaning that have taken place with respect to the dome over the course of the twentieth century. Looking at the relationship between architecture and language as well as that between architecture and dance, this book teases out the intricate links between the built environment and other forms of communication. Moreover, this chapter is aimed at gaining a better comprehension of the historic role of the teleuk in the larger family homestead, for a close examination of the house in the historical context of the homestead reveals that the teleuk was not always the most highly regarded of Mousgoum residential forms.

Chapter two examines the encounters between the Mousgoum teleuk and the travelers Heinrich Barth, Olive MacLeod, André Gide, and Marc Allégret, exploring how such encounters force the travelers, if only momentarily, to question their preconceived notions of "the primitive." Considering Barth's extensive travel experience, education, political sympathies, and understanding of architecture as being one of the paramount tools for defining cultural advancement, this text demonstrates how the familiar and strange begin to oscillate in a fashion that threatens to make the explorer's perceived differences between "civilized Europe" and "savage Africa" collapse. For MacLeod, a similar oscillation occurs, but her 1910 encounter with the teleuk also allows for an analysis of the ways in which a female traveler uses architecture to validate her voyage and to be taken seriously as a traveler, one on a par with her male counterparts. We then turn to Gide and Allégret's 1926 visit to Mousgoum country, showing how their encounter with the dome reveals a reflexive move, one that serves as a detailed rumination on themselves in particular and on an understanding of modernity more generally.

Chapter three investigates the appropriation of the Mousgoum teleuk for the French Equatorial Africa Pavilion at the 1931 International Colonial Exposition in Paris. France's goal in displaying its colonies and the ways in which the French used the Mousgoum dome for the pavilion invites an investigation into the meeting of the "primitive" and the "modern," showing how architecture—as representation of the civilizing mission—became an integral part of the construction of France's imperial identity.

Chapter four takes us back to Cameroon, where contemporary Mousgoum teleukakay and wall murals take center stage. This examination demonstrates the ways in which these objects and structures address the importance of Mousgoum agency and ingenuity. Moreover, the text considers how indigenous values, Western perception and tourism, and religious conversion have come together, creating syncretic narratives that have been projected onto the teleuk by Mousgoum people, Westerners, and Cameroonian government officials alike. This chapter also explores the new appearance of figural motifs on the outer walls of private homes during the 1990s, analyzing how this has changed the symbolic force of Mousgoum architectural decoration. Ultimately, the meeting of Mousgoum and Western understandings of the teleuk has transformed the structure from a house to an architectonic repository of Mousgoum (and Western) cultural history, memory, and experience.

A Brief History of the Mousgoum

The Mousgoum make their home in the Sudanic-Sahel climatic region approximately eleven degrees north of the equator, in an area that straddles the border between the central African nation-states of Cameroon and Chad (fig. 4). About 300 meters above sea level, this nearly treeless plain, about 125 miles south of Lake Chad and bordered on the west by the Mandara Mountains, extends eastwards over the Logone River to the banks of the Chari (fig. 5). Temperatures here vary from about 78 degrees Fahrenheit during the cool season to upwards of 130

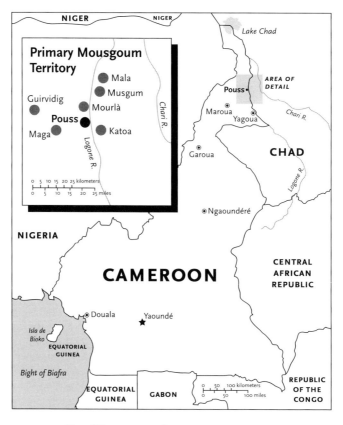

FIGURE 4. Map of Mousgoum region.

FIGURE 5. Region around Musgum, Chad, 1911. Photographer: Ernst M. Heims.
Source: Friedrich, *From the Congo to the Niger and the Nile*, 1913.

degrees Fahrenheit during the hot. From November to January, the weather is
relatively cool and dry. The hot season stretches from February to May, and during this time the humidity increases. The rainy season lasts from June to October. What the Mousgoum themselves call "small hot season" extends from October to mid-November.

The Mousgoum are generally believed to have been in this region since at
least the sixteenth or seventeenth century and are said to have migrated here
from the east and northeast. Many Mousgoum today tell of origins in Sudan or
in southern Chad. According to Christian Seignobos, the Mousgoum and the
neighboring Massa seem to be the descendants of the Paleo Munjuk, who lived
near the banks of the Chari before the two cultures migrated to the Logone.[22] The
Chadian village of Musgum, historically one of the best-known Mousgoum villages to Western travelers, was likely founded by the seventeenth century.[23]

Most histories of the Mousgoum emphasize the interweaving of migration
and warfare. The German explorer Gustav Nachtigal suggests that the Mousgoum and other non-Islamic groups had been human booty for the Islamicized
Bagirmi kingdom for centuries, noting that the Bagirmi kings had made a point
of raiding the area since the first half of the seventeenth century.[24] While recit-
ing a history of the Bagirmi, Nachtigal mentions two seventeenth-century raids
made on the Mousgoum, who, according to him, lived between the Chari and
Logone Rivers. In a raid that took place in the mid-seventeenth century under
the Bagirmi ruler Burkomanda (1635–65), the traveler also mentions the village
of Musgum.[25] Nachtigal also notes that in 1846 the Bagirmi ruler Abd el-Qadir
"ravaged various sections of the Musgo [*sic*], whose walled town of [Musgum],
among others, he found . . . necessary to besiege."[26]

During the nineteenth century both the Bagirmi and Bornu kingdoms posed
a constant threat to the Mousgoum. Barth writes that the Mousgoum were often

the victims of bloody slave raids. The explorer specifically described an attack by the Muslim Kanuri, which he himself had accompanied. Throughout this period, chiefs in the eastern part of Mousgoum country paid tribute to the Bagirmi rulers. In the western part, things were more in flux. The Foulbe attacked many of the Mousgoum in what is now the Mousgoum sultanate of Guirvidig. At the same time, the Mousgoum themselves were said to pose a threat to smaller and weaker groups that lived outside of the Bagirmi kingdom, near the western shores of the Chari. Von Hagen suggests in 1912 that the walled villages of Musgum and Mala were built to keep out the continuing "plundering raids of the Kotoko, the Bornu, the Bagirmi, and the Foulbé."[27] The Mousgoum were subjugated by the Germans and French during the early and mid-twentieth century.

As the literature suggests, the Mousgoum have spent the better part of the past three centuries warding off and evading political oppression by stronger forces while also attacking weaker neighbors. Not surprisingly, many of the stories recounted to me during my stay in Pouss were also concerned with warfare, a theme that also finds expression in architecture. Similarly, body scarification in Mousgoum country, according to a number of interlocutors, was seen by some as a means of discouraging slave traders from abducting Mousgoum women.

The principal Mousgoum town of Pouss was populated by Mousgoum inhabitants at least by the nineteenth century, and given its proximity to Musgum and Mala, it may have been established earlier. Barth relates that during his visit to the court of the Mousgoum chief A'dishén "we heard a native chief, of the name of Puss or Fuss, mentioned in a manner that assured us our friends [the Kanuri] were afraid to attack him." During the Kanuri slave raid that Barth accompanied, he noted, "This fertile district, which is enclosed by the River of Logón on the east, and by the narrow, channel-like water-course on the west side, seems to be that very dominion of 'Fúss,' the power of which, as I related before, was greatly dreaded by our friends."[28] These references are about a chief, but it would not be out of the ordinary to see the name of a person and place conflated (the village of Musgum is a prime example). By the late nineteenth century, many of the villages that stand today were already established, and among these villages, Nachtigal writes, lay "the town of the chief of Puss or Fuss."[29] The present Mousgoum sultanate of Pouss dates to 1911 when Mbang (Sultan) Mati (r. 1911–31), leader of the Siakou family, migrated to Pouss in order to escape both the domination of the Bagirmi and the oppression of the French.[30] (By moving across the Logone, the sultanate remained under German jurisdiction, which was thought to be more benign.) It is extremely likely that Mbang Mati installed his court in an already populated village, taking it under his dominion. The palace of Lamido Mbang Yaya Oumar of Pouss (plate 2), built around 1911, is derived from the architecture of the Islamicized Bagirmi kingdom and stands as an excellent architectural example of Islam's introduction to the region. With Islamicization also came the creation of Mousgoum royalty who in turn established the sultanates of Guirvidig and Pouss.[31]

While the area surrounding of Pouss was likely Islamicized directly through Mbang Mati's arrival, Guirvidig (approximately twelve miles west of Pouss) and its environs appear to have been converted through the influence of the neighboring Foulbe kingdoms as much as 150 years earlier.[32] Before the advent of independence, Mousgoum sultanates, like the French colonists, followed a policy of forced labor, using non-Muslim village residents to work the royal fields and to build royal residences.

The Mousgoum today tell a myth of origin that involves the Kotoko, who neighbor the Mousgoum to the north, and the Massa, who border them to the south. According to this myth, the Kotoko sultan of Carnak often waged war on the Massa for purposes of plunder and the expansion of his dominion. The Massa in turn fought back. When the sultan's son Prince Héritier came of age, he was sent to a place between the regions of the Kotoko and the Massa in order to found a new village. In this village, where it was assumed there would be much carnage between the two cultures, there was none, and the two groups gradually learned to respect one another. In one account:

> When Prince Héritier died his son succeeded him. When this son decided to find a wife, after looking at all of the Kotoko women in the region, he decided to marry a Massa woman who was renowned for her beauty. He then went to her, dressed in his finest royal clothing, and he asked for her hand in marriage. She spurned him and later sent him a message through her mother that in order to prove his worthiness, the young chief would have to be clad in the traditional costume of the Massa, which consisted of a simple, small goat skin covering tied around his midsection. This was the only way that she could know that the young ruler was indeed beautiful. The woman's mother relayed this message to the young chief. He obliged. The newly wed Massa woman and her Kotoko husband then followed the customs of the Massa, and it was in such a union that the Mousgoum were born.[33]

What is clear in both the myth of origin and the work of Seignobos is the long-standing contact the Mousgoum have had with their neighbors; furthermore, such a fact is reflected in Mousgoum language, religion, and many customs. Mousgoum syncreticism is also a distinguishing characteristic of their architectural practices.

Social and Economic Structure

Agriculture and fishing are the primary Mousgoum economic resources. Fish and rice are the region's largest exports. Both men and women fish. Mousgoum men have long been known to be expert fishers, throwing large nets into the Logone from *pirogues* (canoes) made from the hollowed-out trunks of trees; women, by contrast, stand in the river or in a shallow pond, using a sturdy net with a frame to capture fish as they swim by. Both men and women conduct agricultural work, cultivating the region's main staples: red millet and rice. Whereas in the past, many people cultivated crops adjacent to their homes, today the millet fields are quite distant, and rice is now grown on the irrigated plains owned by SEMRY (Société d'Expansion et de Modernisation de la Riziculture de Yagoua).[34] Before the adoption of Islam on a large scale, a fairly large number of people grew tobacco by their family compounds. Cattle herding was historically a common Mousgoum undertaking.[35] In the past, men who specialized as masons built teleukakay for others in their villages. Today—as in the past—women make pottery that they vend in the market. Some women also earn money by brewing millet beer, which they sell on market day (Tuesday).

Mousgoum family structure is patrilineal and in large part polygamous.[36] Today, many Mousgoum men have two to four wives; the number usually depends on one's wealth. Mbang Mati was said to have had one hundred wives.[37] While the husband is the head of the household, the first wife generally controls the family's domestic life. Naming reflects the patrilineal orientation of family structures: a man's children take his first name as their surname. Fathers are charged with making their sons into men; mothers raise their daughters to be desirable wives and mothers. The eldest son is highly esteemed and has considerable power over his siblings, thus putting him in a psychological and, in many cases, financial advantage within the family. Girls are generally married by age fourteen, and a successful suitor must pay a dowry to her parents. In the past, this was paid in cows or other livestock: today it is usually paid in cash.[38]

In the Mousgoum family homestead, which is also very much a reflection of the familial unit, the head of the family (unless he is very poor) has his own house. Each wife has her own as well. Young children live with their mothers. Girls remain with their mothers until married; older unmarried boys often have their own houses. These domestic living arrangements allude to the intricate relationship that architecture has to Mousgoum hierarchy, and architecture helps to define the place of each individual within this social structure.

In the same way that the private home is a vital link to one's place in the world, the village plays an important role with respect to group identity. As the names of individuals are derived from the father, so too the names of various Mousgoum groups are derived from those of the villages and towns where they live. For example, *Mapasay* literally means "people of Pouss"; *Mamalakay* translates as "people of Mala"; *Muskomay*, "people of Mousgoum"; and *Monjokay*, "people of Guirvidig." There is a "Mousgoum" culture per se; but the name itself is not unitary and encompasses a number of smaller groups. More broadly, the Mousgoum on the Cameroonian side of the Logone still use the term "Mousgoum" to identify themselves; those on the Chadian side are known as "Moulouli" or "Massa Moulouli."[39]

Religion

Although it is almost impossible to ascertain when religious conversion began in Mousgoum country, today most Mousgoum families have been Muslim for at least a generation. About 10 percent are Christians. A Lutheran mission existed in Pouss from around the beginning of the twentieth century until about 1968. A Catholic mission is located in the Mousgoum village of Maga. Nowadays, when elders who follow traditional Mousgoum religion die, already-converted descendants often will give the deceased family member a Muslim or Christian name.

Traditional Mousgoum belief centers on a supreme god named Alaw, who created both the earth and the mantle of spirits who govern it.[40] All of these spirits, or what we might think of as nature deities, have a role in protecting the Mousgoum. Zigla, the goddess of fertility, is responsible for providing children. People also make sacrifices to Zigla to ensure the well-being of newly born children. Bangui is the god of the sky and is associated with the pole star. Golo Agonan explains, "When you go out at about four o'clock in the morning, you see a star that shines in the east. That is Bangui." Mme. Abezidi Wendi claims that Bangui can protect one from illness but can also attack one's sight. Not knowing why this is true, she insists, "I have only one eye, and it was Bangui who attacked me." Mme. Djaoro Abourgadaï, along similar lines, explains that one makes sacrifices to Bangui to protect the eyes. Math is the god of the wilderness, and one makes sacrifices to him for protection while traveling. Maana is the goddess of water and has the power to provide good fishing or to ensure that there is no catch. She can also bring illness. Gangan, her husband, or complement, is the god of water. Sacrifices are usually made to Maana and Gangan at the same time; however, a person sometimes may pray and make sacrifices solely to Gangan for luck in fishing or protection from the hippopotami that inhabit both the Logone and Lake Maga. It is said that one must be careful in making sacrifices to Maana and Gangan, for if they are not treated equally, and one of the spirits feels slighted, the slighted spirit may become jealous and undo the benefice provided by the other.[41] Still another deity is Yaye, the local god of Pouss. He protects the village and ensures a successful harvest. Today, in an Islamic context, many of the younger Mousgoum know the names of these deities and their roles, but if there is any religious affiliation with them, they are often thought of as jinn, that is, Islamic spirits. Nonetheless, the Mousgoum express their concern with and attachment to these gods in the construction and maintenance of the family enclosure.

Architecture and Mousgoum Cultural Change

In 1911 Ernst Heims, a German artist traveling with the exploration party of Adolph Friedrich, writes, "On the twentieth of January we reached the town of Musgum, in which all of the houses resemble bee-hives."[42] Mere decades later, in

FIGURE 6. View of Pouss, October 1995.

the small amount of literature about the Mousgoum and the teleuk, the building was said to be on the brink of extinction by 1952.[43] While the Mousgoum are today reconstructing the teleuk, the structure is no longer a common part of the region (fig. 6). Some believe that the teleuk began to disappear as early as the first decades of the twentieth century. Others see the beginning of this process as having begun in the 1930s. Still others give dates as recent as the 1960s.

Although there are a host of different dates given by Mousgoum people themselves with respect to the disappearance of the teleuk, generally they are tied to periods of intense cultural change and upheaval. Often they emphasize warfare and oppression at the hands of other African cultures, the Germans, or the French colonials. All of these, as well as the tyranny of the sultanate of Pouss itself in the 1930s, led to a mass northward exodus of Mousgoum.[44] In the 1960s, rice production began on a large scale; moreover, a disastrous cholera epidemic hit the region. Furthermore, members of other cultures moved into what were historically Mousgoum villages, bringing their ways of building with them. With the exposure to these new types of homes, some local residents simply preferred them to teleukakay. These new houses, which were constructed from mud brick with roofs of straw, were also much easier to build and maintain. The teleuk needed almost constant attention, and it took between three and six months to construct. A mud brick house with a straw roof, in contrast, could be built in a little over two weeks. With the advent of large-scale rice agriculture in the region, more and more people cultivate the grain for longer periods each year. In other arenas, Mousgoum people began to have less and less time to devote to building homes; as a result, fewer and fewer teleukakay were made. Alongside of these changes, likely a result of them, decreasing numbers of men chose to become masons.

What is important, however, is not whether the dates or reasons given are right or wrong, but rather what these responses reveal about the intricate relationship between the teleuk and daily living for the Mousgoum and how their discussions of the teleuk's disappearance, no matter what the date or reason given, are tied to individual experience. Hence, the symbiotic relation between the teleuk and those who live in it or even recall it is reflected in the manner in which people—Mousgoum or otherwise—talk about the house.

Performing Architecture

I want to suggest that the concept of home seems to be tied in some way with the notion of identity—the story we tell of ourselves and which is also the story others tell of us. *(emphasis in original)* MADAN SARUP, "HOME AND IDENTITY"

1

To build a home is to build a discrete world, a stage for all of life's phases. As Madan Sarup insists in the epigraph, home is inextricably tied to a sense of self, and it is the source of the tales that we weave and the ways in which they are retold. In this sense, home is the source of autobiography. Home also becomes a framing device not only in our orientation to the subject at hand, but also to the ways in which that subject is put into writing. Thus, much of our intellectual endeavor is, in the sense of James Clifford, "ethnographic allegory."[1] While we interrogate, investigate, and analyze, we unconsciously tell stories of ourselves, and our work becomes, in large part, a product of the meeting between the researcher's life experiences and the world that is the intellectual project.

In the present discussion, my concerns meet with the thoughts and observations of the people I interviewed. Thus, what emerge are the voices of Mousgoum people that are mediated by my position as a Western researcher. This chapter is the explicit mixing of voices and interpretations from a number of different positions and arenas. Where I believe these strands come together is in a shared interest in the Mousgoum built environment and the ways in which it articulates a Mousgoum home.

In the space that constitutes the home, major life events such as births, marriages, and deaths are those times when the relationship between the house and its residents is most clearly articulated. The Mousgoum homestead is no different. It is the arena in which these events take place, it is the setting in which lives mature and change, it is the sphere in which one unconsciously learns one's place in the family unit and Mousgoum culture-at-large. People become socialized not through the major events, but more often through those of quotidian life, and the architectural environment constantly reinforces those social, cultural, and religious values deemed to be important and desirable by the larger world. The roles played by the microcosm defined by domestic architecture in this way subliminally amplify and buttress the more conscious forms of socialization based in a parent's teachings, a religious ceremony, or a community gathering.

This chapter considers the manner in which the teleukakay, although no longer a common feature of the Mousgoum homestead, historically took on cultural, social, and political values, constituting part of a larger architectural realm that is a reflection of and a didactic presence in different aspects of Mousgoum life. Relying heavily on local residents' respective memories of the past, oral tales, travelers' accounts, and connections found in the Munjuk language, this discussion is also an attempt to explore what the built environment may have signified in Mousgoum culture before the advent of Islam, Christianity, and European colonialism. For the better part of a century, Islamicized patterns of building and urban design have permeated homesteads and villages throughout Mousgoum country, serving as architectural expressions of cultural change. Nonetheless, plans made by past visitors, stories, dance, and recollections of Mousgoum people allow us to postulate how and what the teleuk may have meant with respect to social practices and cultural identity.

Such an explanation is by no means to suggest that the Mousgoum were an isolated culture—all the available evidence clearly indicates that they were not. It is also not to simply ask, "What is characteristically 'Mousgoum' about Mousgoum architecture?" It is, however, to learn how the teleuk and the family enclosure can teach us more about Mousgoum culture and history more generally. The combination of the little information available about the Mousgoum in tandem with local oral accounts and histories reveal those things that are retrospectively considered to be important in Mousgoum culture.

Progeniture, dance, and beauty were often the major themes that arose when Mousgoum people spoke about the home and cultural meaning. Combined with an understanding of architecture as the making of a site in which the unconscious finds expression, as a blueprint through which various kinds of relationships may be ascertained, as a map that divulges forms of socialization, and as a location that reveals vital information, what emerges through architecture is a view of the ways in which the Mousgoum have made sense of the world. In scrutinizing the Mousgoum built environment, I follow Jean-Paul Bourdier and Trinh T. Minh-ha's suggestion that "architecture" is both a noun and a verb.[2] Thus, it is possible to look at the teleuk in particular and Mousgoum architecture more generally as product and as process; for the act of building presupposes important social, cultural, and religious concerns while also allowing for a richer understanding of the multiple ways in which the Mousgoum have historically defined domestic space.[3]

The Structure of the Homestead

Whether located in the densely populated villages of Musgum and Mala, or in the smaller, less crowded villages of Mourlà or Gaïa, the layout of Mousgoum family enclosures, like those of neighboring cultures such as the Massa and the

FIGURE 7. Mousgoum family enclosure. Photographer: Ernst M. Heims, 1911. Source: Friedrich, *From the Congo to the Niger and the Nile*, 1913.

Toupouri, was defined by a circle.[4] These circular family enclosures were a series of homes, the gaps between which were closed by either a thicket of thorns or an earthen wall five to six feet in height depending on the family's wealth (fig. 7).[5] In each family enclosure stood a house for the family patriarch, one for each of his wives, and one for each of his male sons who are older than ten or fifteen. Families kept animals such as cows, goats, and sheep in the various houses of the homestead as well.

In 1911 von Hagen described a family enclosure in Musgum:

> Several houses that stand around in a circle make a farm. The man of the house occupies his own house, which distinguished from the others by size. Each wife also owns her own house, in which she lives with her young sons and unmarried daughters. Some of these houses are joined with that of the man of the house through a hallway; the latter does not always have its own entrance. The adult, unmarried sons live likewise in their own houses.
>
> Clay granaries stand on posts in the middle of the farm. We see a braided circle made of willow twigs running around the structure. In the rainy season mats are bound onto these, preventing the rain from rinsing away the walls. The whole farm is surrounded by a high clay wall, approximately one meter-high, through which a narrow entrance runs. This is closed at night by thorns.[6]

Von Hagen's description and accompanying image give us some idea about the structure of what may have been a typical Mousgoum family enclosure. A

1952 survey of architecture, entitled *L'habitat au Cameroun*, included the plan of the homestead of Lawane (chief) Atuisingué of Gaïa (fig. 8). This plan, which is by far the best-known rendering of a Mousgoum enclosure in the West, has been published in numerous architectural studies and, in many ways, has come to be regarded as the paradigmatic Mousgoum architectural plan. Compared to von Hagen's description and those of others in the field, the illustrated plan is elaborate, an architectonic display of the wealth and prestige of the lawane. In spite of its size, however, the fundamental layout does not differ very much from von Ha-

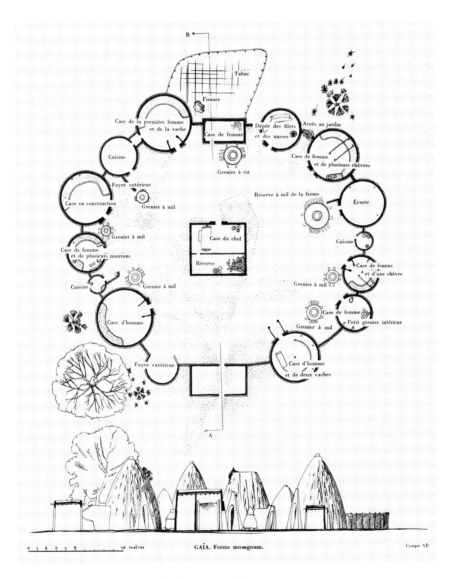

FIGURE 8. Plan of the homestead of Lawane Atuisingué, Gaïa, Cameroon, c. 1952.
Source: *L'Habitat au Cameroun*, c. 1952.

gen's 1912 description. The major difference is the substitution of the rectangular house of the patriarch for the granary in the middle of the court. Descriptions of the "paradigmatic" Mousgoum family compound I acquired in the field were also much in accord with von Hagen's report, including the presence of a large granary in its center. In the 1952 plan, the granary of the family head (labeled *réserve à mil de la ferme*), the largest in the compound, lies to the right of the center house and stands in front of a stable. Behind the compound is a small area for growing tobacco; to the right of the tobacco patch is a garden. While neither von Hagen's description nor the plan indicates cardinal directions, in the past, according to field interviews, the entrances of Mousgoum family enclosures faced south. Although many of the historic images of Mousgoum enclosures suggest that they were all comprised of teleukakay, this was not the case.

Besides von Hagen's report and images, Ernst Heims, a German artist traveling with the German Central African Expedition in 1911, made pencil sketches, watercolors and photographs of Mousgoum homesteads in Musgum. A number of these depict compounds that have rectangular homes and teleukakay (fig. 9).[7] What dictated the type of house a patriarch might build in his enclosure? It would seem as if the choice was not based purely on whether or not one had the required kind of soil for erecting a sturdy dome. The choice seems to have had more to do with the influences on and the volition of the family patriarch. Eco-

FIGURE 9. Mousgoum family enclosure, Pencil sketch by Ernst M. Heims, 1911.
Source: Friedrich, *From the Congo to the Niger and the Nile*, 1913.

FIGURE 10. A Mousgoum teleuk and delemiy, built by Mathala Minsing, Pouss, photographed April 15, 1996.

nomic resources may have been an issue as well, for to have a teleuk in an enclosure, the family head would have to hire a mason who was specially trained to build them. Other houses and granaries were—and continue to be—generally constructed by families themselves.

The Mousgoum make conscious distinctions between different types of houses. Besides the difference in the requirements for building, houses had different names. The teleuk in Munjuk is called a teleuk; other types of houses are called delemiy and feɲiy (fig. 10). When asked about the differences in these terms and the houses, people generally addressed the difference in materials. The distinguishing mark of the teleuk was that it was constructed only of clay. A delemiy and feɲiy refer to houses with straw roofs. Henry Tourneux, in a study of the borrowing of words in Munjuk from other languages as well as borrowings among Munjuk dialects, claims that the word teleuk originally comes from the Munjuk dialect of Pouss and was borrowed by the other three—Bigué-Palam (Cameroon), Kaykay (Cameroon), and Mogroum (Chad). He concludes that "the teleuk is effectively a foreign reality for the people of [these areas]."[8] Tourneux's assertion reflects the fact that not all Mousgoum people built teleukakay.

Besides the types of houses in one's homestead, the placement and size of the buildings were at the discretion of the patriarch. In von Hagen's example, the house of the patriarch is set off by its large size and the presence of a front reception hall. In the lawane's compound, the ruler's house is distinguished by its rectangular shape. Many compounds, including the lawane's, had a large teleuk that was joined to a smaller, closed one. Often this type of structure would serve as the residence of the first wife; the smaller, closed dome would be her kitchen. Von Hagen identifies the one in his example as the house of the family head. It is possible that both claims are correct; conventions varied among villages. In one area, the house of the family head was distinguished by the fact that it was small; in another, the opposite was true.

While many Mousgoum insist that large granaries always occupy the center of the family homestead, the lawane's compound shows the latitude that men had when designing their homes. In this way, the patriarch is a kind of architect, and as architect was able to take control of the land and his family through the manipulation of the built environment. This finds an analogy in Mousgoum conceptions of the relation between the house and the family enclosure. As feminine nouns, *delemiy* and *feŋiy* mean "house" or "room."[9] However, the masculine forms of the two nouns, *dalam* and *feŋ*, mean "compound." In the homestead, the feminine, or diminutive, forms are defined as parts of a larger whole, a whole configured as masculine.

The term *feŋ* also sheds light on the manner in which the Mousgoum conceive of the relationship between the house, family enclosure, and other aspects of their culture. Following the idea that the house (feŋiy) is part of a larger family homestead (feŋ), the compound at the same time is part of a larger village. Hence, *feŋ* designates "compound" and "village." Such chains of relationships highlight the understanding that the enclosure is a family of houses bound together by a wall. Specifically, the enclosure is made up of a set of smaller individual units. Along these same lines, the village is also seen as a family of homesteads.

The compound provides considerable insight into Mousgoum conceptions of the family. Indeed, *feŋ* means "family." Through this link the homestead and the family are tightly bound in a metaphoric association that bespeaks not only the human element in architecture, but also space and place more generally. The head of the household is equated with these potent links as well, for in Mousgoum country he is literally known as the "father of the concession" (*apiŋ-feŋ*).[10] This also implies his ownership of the family compound, since the "father" (*apiŋ*) is also the "proprietor." This notion was expressed by Mme. Djaoro Bara Abourgadaï in her insistence that "the father of the family is in the middle [of the compound] because all the houses belong to him." The use of the word *feŋ* in contexts relating to individuals, families, homesteads, and paradise illustrates the centrality of the built environment in Mousgoum conceptions of both familial and religious realms.

Becoming a Mason

Mousgoum family enclosures are usually built between December and February, the time of year when the weather is relatively cool and dry. Historically, the need to build a home generally occurred when a newly married man was starting a new homestead; when an existing homestead was expanded by the addition of another wife to the family; when a boy became old enough to move into his own house; or when dilapidated houses needed to be replaced. While men alone almost always built houses, both men and women built granaries. Although the construction of delemiy and granaries was relatively easy, that of a teleuk was complicated, requiring the services of a mason. Teleukakay could take anywhere from three to six months to complete.

To build a teleuk, one needed the expertise to erect domes that would not tumble to the ground. While masons were respected, and highly sought, they have no special title or designation. In Munjuk, professions, and at times attributes, are often couched in terms of a person who makes or does something. It is no different for masons. The term for them is simply "man who builds a homestead" (*dif zi rigi dalam*).[11] Moreover, while masons were trained to build teleukakay, their title does not specifically link them to the Mousgoum dome.

Often a father would train his sons in masonry, but this was not always the case. As is true of builders, blacksmiths, and potters in a number of African cultures, there were neither families nor castes of masons in Mousgoum civilization. Afti Doupta, a mason from Mourlà, explained that in a family "one finds all types of people: fishers, farmers, masons, etc. It is all a mix." Doupta, who was trained by his father, compared his masonry skills to those of an engineer who has "created something miraculous."

There was neither a scripted program nor a standard process for training masons. Usually one's training began in informal ways. Gradually the student learned more about building techniques. Math Perleh, also a mason in Mourlà, described his apprenticeship:

> In the homestead . . . when a child sees his father in the process of constructing [a teleuk], he amuses himself by constructing a small teleuk. Another day the child could construct a larger one. At this moment, the father values his child and calls him into his service, and the child begins to put the [the outer designs on the teleuk] and progressively he grows up to build them.

As part of the process, children would also assist their fathers while they worked.

Mme. Abourgadaï, a female mason from Mourlà, was also trained by her father. While almost all the male informants said that only men build teleukakay, there are at least a few instances in which fathers trained their daughters in the profession. Mme. Abourgadaï, the only female mason in Mourlà and Pouss, knew of only one other female mason in the village of Pidi Moungaï, where she was born.[12] Like Doupta and Perleh, Mme. Abourgadaï started to acquire her masonry skills at a young age, only gradually becoming an expert (plate 3). She explained that all the children of a mason would learn something about building; but while some excelled, others would lose interest.

> The first moment consists of looking for the clay. The moment arrives to select the special grass. Then the mix[ing] happens, and one leaves the earth to ferment for at least a week . . . afterwards, one proceeds to build the foundation, the first [ring of the teleuk]. . . . A day later, when the foundation is dry . . . one builds the wall up to a certain level, one [begins] to put the [designs on the wall]. This [process] is the same to the summit, and then one plasters the teleuk.

Golo Agonan also spoke about the learning process.[13] Unlike Mme. Abourgadaï, Doupta, and Perleh, Agonan did not learn his skills from his father; in fact, he did not take up the profession until he was in his sixties. In spite of his

FIGURE 11. Teleuk built by Golo Agonan, Pouss, photographed February 24, 1996.

late start, many Mousgoum regard him as one of the best masons in the region (fig. 11). Beginning his apprenticeship in an unorthodox and clandestine fashion, he recalls:

> Each day I went to the place where teleukakay were being built, and I pretended to see nothing. Then I told the truth. I was there to learn. I saw [the masons'] hand gestures; [I saw] how to attend to the earth. I saw how one mixed the earth, how one put the grass and other materials together, how one allowed the mixture to ferment, how one erected the teleuk, how one put on the feet to construct the teleuk. Then I was well formed. I never missed a visit with the old masons.

Instead of talking about the relationship between apprentice and master builder, all the masons spoke about their training with respect to the actual process of building. For Mme. Abourgadaï, to describe the way one builds a teleuk was to describe how she learned to do it. These masons learned—in their own ways—through looking and imitating the motions of their respective teachers. Their training was experiential: the apprentices learned visually and kinesthetically, points that Agonan made especially clear. The connection of sight and knowledge finds a potent analogy in Munjuk as well, for the word *sidi*, "to see," also means "to know." Fundamentally, the masons' learning experiences and descriptions of their tutelages point to the importance of process, the act of making, in the transmission of knowledge.

Corporeal Architecture: Building the Teleuk

As the process of learning described by the masons focuses on the role of the body-in-action through seeing, assisting, mixing the materials, and actual construction, the teleuk makes constant reference to the human body. From the writings of Vitruvius, the centrality of humanity as expressed through the image of the body has been fundamental in conceptions of architecture. Architectural proportions are routinely defined in terms of the body; architectural parts are routinely metaphors for bodily parts.[14]

Such is also the case in Mousgoum architecture, as key features in the teleuk and other types of houses are named for either parts of the human body or articles of clothing (fig. 12). The doorway of the teleuk is referred to as the "mouth of the place" (*miŋ halay*). Keeping emphasis on the mouth, the hole at the top of the dome is called in turn the "mouth of the teleuk" (*miŋ teleuk*). While openings are frequently equated with the mouth in Mousgoum thought, the window of a nondomed house is often called "eye of the house" (*aray-di delemiy*).[15] The teleuk's outer designs, or scaffolding, are called "feet" (*aziy*). The straw hatch that covers the "mouth of the teleuk" is referred to simply as a "straw hat" (*gidigilik*). The presence of a hat at the top of the teleuk gives the impression that the dome

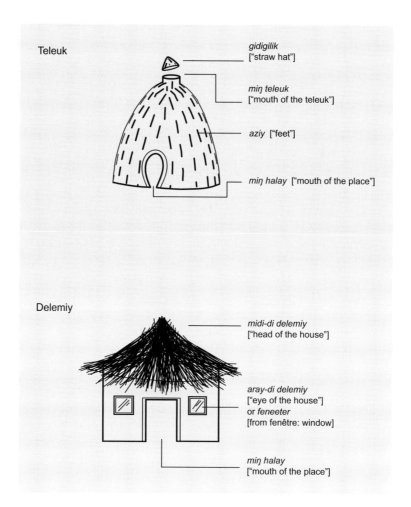

Teleuk

gidigilik
["straw hat"]

miŋ teleuk
["mouth of the teleuk"]

aziy ["feet"]

miŋ halay ["mouth of the place"]

Delemiy

midi-di delemiy
["head of the house"]

aray-di delemiy
["eye of the house"]
or *feneeter*
[from fenêtre: window]

miŋ halay
["mouth of the place"]

FIGURE 12. Diagram showing the parts of Mousgoum houses.

is a human head, and this finds concrete expression in the roof of a nondomed house, the "head of the house" (*midi-di delemiy*). The eyes, mouth, and head of the house give the impression that the structure has a face (*aray*), a part of the body commonly associated with limits and boundaries. *Aray* means "eyes," "face," "sight," "limit," and "boundary." This corporeal house serves as part of the larger construction of the family patriarch, part of the larger homestead, which is, in essence, a portrait of its proprietor. This metonymic figure decodes and naturalizes the spatial world, thus giving it order and coherency.[16] Such a metonymy of place is given explicit voice by the Mousgoum poet Claude Abanga, who in personifying the teleuk calls it his ancestor.[17]

After the patriarch has decided on the placement of homes and granaries in his homestead, the mason becomes the director of the project. Historically, the mason's fee would have been paid in goats and sheep. During the period of construction, it was the responsibility of the wives of the patron to provide meals for the mason. While the mason was constructing teleukakay, members of the patron's family assisted him or her. Once the mason arrived, women gathered the correct kinds of earth, grasses, and animal dung (usually that of cows, goats, or sheep) and brought the water for mixing the clay that would eventually make up the dome. While there were no gender restrictions on the mixing of the clay, it appears that men did it more often than did women. Perleh insisted that the mixture should have the consistency of paste. Once the consistency was attained, as Mme. Abourgadaï stated, the paste was left to ferment for a week or so.

Next, Agonan explained, the mason traced the perimeter of what would eventually become the new teleuk on the ground. After establishing the plan, the mason began constructing the teleuk by building the first ring of the wall. The teleuk's walls are roughly eighteen inches wide; each ring measures between eighteen and twenty inches in height. When Agonon described the height of the rings, he stressed that that it extended from his elbow to the tips of his fingers. The first ring, once dried, was followed by a second. For Agonan, these two rings were the most critical in the construction of the teleuk, and they would in large part determine the success of the dome. He maintained that after the construction of these two rings, it was vital to leave them alone for a number of days before beginning a third. From the third ring onward, it was not necessary to wait as long.

What the masons have detailed in interviews is a version of the coil-pottery technique, a building practice common in the construction of earthen granaries in the West African savannah. The technique, which, according to Labelle Prussin, "maximizes the natural properties of the materials at hand," reaches its optimum, in her opinion, in the "superbly formed, and tapering shells of Mousgoum granaries and housing."[18]

After the construction of the first few rings, the mason begins to build the teleuk's "feet," which function as outer scaffolding and drainage system for the structure. When the height of the wall exceeds comfortable reach, the mason starts to use the "feet" as a ladder, enabling her or him to climb the partially completed house. From this point to the completion of the dome, the mason builds the wall and its "feet" simultaneously. As the wall becomes still higher, the mason begins to taper it. (The height at which this occurs depends on the diameter of the structure.) The tapering of the wall continues until all that remains is the hole, or the "mouth," at the dome's apex.

While the mason builds the teleuk others throw balls of the clay building mixture to him or her. Mme. Abourgadaï claimed that if a man was building a teleuk, a woman threw the balls to him; she also said that in her case, her husband threw them to her. What this suggests is a complementarity of gender in house construction.

The mason's training is perhaps most vital at the point where she or he begins to taper the teleuk's wall, and this has to be accomplished precisely and at a correct angle, otherwise the teleuk will be uneven, or it will simply collapse. On the care with which the mason must mold the dome, Agonan insists:

> The form of the hand [Agonan demonstrates the molding of the wall with his hand as if to reconstruct the existing wall of his teleuk] is in order to submit to the construction [of the dome]. I must be in constant contact with the earth that I am setting. My arms must take the form of a V and I construct everything backwards [he draws his arms towards himself] and the balls of earth are set on the teleuk's wall in order to quickly make an easy advance in construction.

Besides the small hole left at the dome's summit, the mason leaves another, which will later become the teleuk's door, in the dome's side. In order to counteract the negative effects that the holes have on the dome's structural integrity, the mason reinforces the two openings. Prussin has explained this practice as a way for the mason to make up for the reduction in the dome's ability to transmit horizontal and vertical stresses to the ground.[19]

Prussin has written, "Coil-pottery earthen structures depend on communal participation and a collective work-process; specialized skills and tools are not needed."[20] In most West African earthen construction, including that of Mousgoum granaries, she is correct. However, the construction of the teleuk is an exception to her generalization. While its construction is communal to a point, the building's success is almost wholly dependent on the mason's specialized skills.

As in the naming of the various parts of the teleuk and other houses in Mousgoum country, the body takes on central importance in the teleuk's construction. Agonan's focus on the hands and the arms—as opposed to the eye—as being the most important considerations in the successful making of the dome gives primacy to the sense of touch, and touch links the body to the materials used in the building of the teleuk. Instead of controlling the materials, the mason's success is incumbent upon creating a partnership with them. The primacy Agonan gives to touch, the bonding of mason and earth ("I must be in constant contact with the earth") undercuts the primacy of sight in the construction of the teleuk.

The bond, the partnership between the mason and the clay, the importance of touch, and the significance of gesture constitute a language of building that, for Agonan, is articulated through the correct position and movement of the hand, the arm, and the rest of the body. This syntax has a direct effect upon the result of the project, for to successfully create a teleuk, an architectonic body, the mason must speak fluently the language of teleuk construction, the mason must know intimately its grammar, the mason must follow succinctly its rules. Perhaps the most potent example of the articulation of such a language rests in Agonan's body and the way he himself uses it in the construction of the teleuk. As

Agonan is nearly blind and was, at the time he described his career, still a working mason, touch is not only the primary sense through which he understands the process of constructing teleukakay, but also the only sense upon which he can rely to do it correctly.

The Dance of the Homestead

In its connections to the body and the structure of the family, Mousgoum architecture gives physical form to a range of social relationships and hierarchies. As that which translates the invisible into visible form, Mousgoum architecture has much in common with dance. During marriages and funerals, in celebrations of the harvest, and later, in supplication to the Sultanate of Pouss, dance constitutes one of the most important forms of Mousgoum social and cultural expression. In his study on African music, John Miller Chernoff observes that an African dancer, "through the certainty of feet placed squarely on the ground, knees slightly bent, weight moving downward," kinesthetically displays her or his rootedness in and connection with the world.[21]

During his stay with the Mousgoum in 1926, André Gide requested that a group of Mousgoum people do a dance for him. He later described it in detail, reporting:

> It is clear, precise, rhythmical, like their dwellings—like everything I know connected with the Massas [sic]; and varied too. It begins with a strongly accentuated march, the heel of one foot and then the other smartly striking the ground so that the *critala* which the women tie above the calves of their legs are violently shaken. There is no languor. The girls and boys form two separate circles, which revolve in opposite directions . . . .
> . . . A very young girl almost at the same moment left the circle, like a stone shot from a sling, made three leaps backwards, and rolled in the dust like a sack.[22]

It is unclear if this performance was any one particular dance, as it seems to have elements of the *dougate* and *korkoto*, two dances the Mousgoum commonly performed at funerals.[23] The stomping described by Gide is reminiscent of Chernoff's notion in a literal sense, kinesthetically articulating the connectedness of the dancers to the world. Called "vital movement" and "visible form" by Susanne Langer, the gestures, the components of the dance compose the pieces that will give the dance as a whole its evocative force.[24]

The dance also exhibits a multiple play of forces. The first, between the dancers and the ground, comes through the contrast of connectedness, as articulated by the stomping, and the breaking of it, through the leaps and turns of people outside of the circle. The second play of forces is embedded in the play between the two circles of the dance. Differentiated by gender and moving in opposite directions, this play of forces, like that between the dancers and the earth, makes visible the complementary relations between male and female. If this had been the *dougate,* which is danced on the first anniversary of a death, this vocabulary of movement would have also articulated the complementarity between the living and the dead.

In his description, Gide connected dance to the teleuk. While Gide connected nearly everything Mousgoum to the dome, this particular connection warrants a closer examination. The space marked by the circles of the dance is also a boundary. Not unlike the walls of the family enclosure, they define interior and exterior realms. This is not to imply that there is a one-to-one correspondence between the Mousgoum homestead and dance, but to suggest the ways in which the two share fundamental concerns. With respect to gender and the family enclosure, outside of the association of the center of the compound with the head of the family and individual structures with family members, it is difficult to establish whether or not space in the compound was defined or restricted by gender. In Mousgoum funerary practices, the deceased were historically buried in specific places in the family compound. An adult male (married or unmarried) was buried on the right side of the door to his house; a married woman was buried on the left.[25] Such practices suggest that these places had masculine and feminine connotations. Mathala Minsing claims that in a family enclosure, the front (as one looks in from the main entrance) was reserved for men, the back for women and children. Agonan explained that in Massa enclosures the house of the first wife was always set opposite the homestead's main entrance.

While neither Minsing's nor Agonan's words were echoed by others, Françoise Dumas-Champion's research on the Massa in Chad supports the men's statements. She observed that in a homestead of an extended Massa family:

> The traditional arrangement of these residences allows the stranger to identify without error the suite of the head of the family, invariably situated to the left of the [homestead's] entrance—or the house of the "grand wife," the first spouse of the head of the family, situated opposite the entrance . . . . around these two landmarks, the other residences form two half-circles. The suites of the spouses, with their kitchen and granary, occupied the closed half-circle of the enclosure. The other [the opened half-circle] was formed by the houses of the men [fig. 13].[26]

Besides its agreement with Minsing's and Agonan's respective statements, the location of the house of the family patriarch to the left of the main entrance seems to indicate that the associations made between right and male and left and female in this compound are the same as those articulated by Mousgoum burial practices.[27] Given the long-standing contact between the two cultures, the importance of the Massa in Mousgoum tales of origin, and Christian Seignobos's assertion

Disposition traditionnelle des « cases » d'habitation

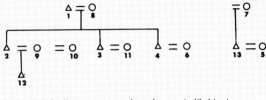

Les numéros du diagramme reportés sur le croquis d'habitation indiquent l'emplacement réservé à chaque individu : sa case d'habitation, son grenier ou sa cuisine.

⬭ case d'habitation

⊙ cuisine

○ grenier

※ auvent

⊥ auvent

FIGURE 13. Plan of a Massa family enclosure. *Case d'habitation* = residence; *cuisine* = kitchen; *grenier* = granary; *auvent* = canopy. Source: Dumas-Champion, *Les Masa du Tchad*, 1983. © Cambridge University Press. Reprinted with the permission of Cambridge University Press.

that the two cultures have common origins, it seems as if the two groups, at some point in time, conceived of social space in a similar fashion.[28]

With respect to space, there are some similarities between the Massa plan and that of the lawane's compound. Although his house is in the middle of the homestead, that of his first wife is situated almost opposite the enclosure's main entrance. In the compound as a whole, the few houses that are occupied by men—other than the lawane himself—are generally located in the front of the circle. As in the Massa enclosure, the door of the house of the family head (number 1 in fig. 13) faces that of the first wife (number 8).

This reciprocity in the semicircles of the enclosure and in the doors between the houses of the head of the family and that of the first wife may also have importance with respect to cardinal direction. "South" and "high" have the same Munjuk word (*amáy*); "north" and "low" do as well (*azemay*). As mentioned earlier, historically Mousgoum family enclosures appear to have faced south. If we conceive of the compound as a vertical plane mapped out horizontally, the open (male) semicircle would be south, the closed (female) semicircle north. In hierarchical terms, to be south is to be in the privileged position.[29]

While the family enclosure may well have been envisioned in such a manner, Minsing insisted that the center of the compound was the domain of the family head. The father of the family, according to Azao Dogo, is "above the whole family" and the person who "gives it order." This finds a literal counterpart in the lawane's compound and is marked by the large granaries in others. In a homestead, the large granary (*vre*) is the property of the head of the family. Placed in the middle of an enclosure, it becomes a representation of the control and power of the family head. He controls the millet within, and he rations this food during the course of the year. The millet used for the beer that once was an important part of Mousgoum ceremonies was taken from this granary as well.[30]

The association of the large granary and the center of the homestead with the father of the house also shows the importance of food in the conception of family hierarchies, underscoring the role of the father as the provider who assures the family's well-being. In highlighting the fruits, or rather the grains, of his labor, the large granary in the center of the compound illustrates Mikhail Bakhtin's observations on the primacy of food and its importance to the human psyche. He writes:

> In the oldest system of images food was related to work. It included work and struggle and was their crown of glory. Work triumphed in food. Human labor's encounter with the world and the struggle against it ended in food, in the swallowing of that which had been wrested from the world. As the last victorious stage of work, the image of food often symbolized the entire labor process. There were no sharp dividing lines; labor and food represented two sides of a unique phenomenon, the struggle of man against the world, ending in his victory.[31]

Certain dances thank the spirits for an abundant harvest in this system, this intricate relationship between food and work. This link, however, is not exclusively associated with men. While the large granary is indeed a metaphor for his work, a small granary (*vray* [f.]), one of which is controlled by each of the patriarch's wives, serves in the same manner, alluding to the importance of her work and place in the family unit. The grains in her own granary are reserved for herself and her children.

In her overview of granaries in West Africa, Prussin has suggested that the inclusion of the granary inside of the family homestead as one moves eastwards across the West African savannah reflects an increased association between the fertility of the soil and of the family. In this movement, Prussin notes that the granary becomes a "formal expression of pregnancy itself."[32] Although the Mousgoum never connected their granaries to pregnancy during my research in the field, connections between the granary, soil, and fertility find expression in Mousgoum sacrifices made to Zigla, the goddess of fertility. In Mousgoum religious practice, when a man and woman had a child who was sick, they offered a black hen and black tobacco to Zigla to rectify their newborn's condition. After this offering, the child's mother made a small granary out of clay and placed it inside her house. She then placed an egg in it. Each evening the child continued to be sick, the father placed it onto the ground next to the granary three times. The child's mother was placed on the ground twice. The family repeated the same gestures at dawn.

In its associations with food and the family patriarch and fertility, the large granary is rife with symbolism alluding to the connections of labor, food, and progeniture—associations further amplified by the position of the large granary in the center of the compound. As is true with the granaries of the Tallensi of northern Ghana and the LoWillisi of northern Côte d'Ivoire, it is possible that the central location of the large granary is an allusion to the complementarity of male and female and the earth and the sky.[33] With respect to fertility, the material well-being of the family and the labor of the family head, the large granary underscores the power of the father, for the two are viewed in Mousgoum country as that which saves the family. Besides this role, the Mousgoum sometimes understand the large granary, according to Mme. Hiri-Hiri Takao, as the "spirit of the family patriarch."

Historic Mousgoum funerary practices further emphasize the charged nature of the homestead's center. In times past, when the family patriarch died, he was buried along with his belongings next to his granary in the middle of the compound.[34] A year later, after the performance of the *dougate,* the compound was destroyed, and the deceased's survivors had to move. When such practices were still in force, upon the death of a Mousgoum adult, the deceased's house would be destroyed: the house died with its resident. When the patriarch died, the whole homestead vanished with his corpse. Once the center dies, the periphery does as well.

Considered as a whole, the houses and wall that make up the family enclosure mark a border that distinguishes the private realm of the home from the public space of the village. Within this private space, the oppositions between male and female, center and periphery, and south and north are psychologically charged, serving to reinforce notions of the power of the family patriarch and the roles of the other members of the family. Similarly, the gendered circles of Gide's dance define a border between the world that exists outside of the dance and the charged, energized world within. The two circles of the dance, like funerary practices and the very form of the family enclosure, make visible the binary, albeit complementary, oppositions between male and female that play an enormously important role in structuring Mousgoum lifeways.

Prussin has observed that shadow and shade introduce motion to architecture, explaining that while forms remain constant, the play of light on their surfaces can create the illusion of movement and change: the change of the sun is contrasted to the static nature of the ground.[35] The raised "feet" of the teleuk set against the smoothness of the wall and other types of houses further amplify the illusion of movement already provided by changing light and shadow. The varying heights of the buildings and the wall also engender the illusion of movement. Day and night, the homestead appears to change, and the bodies that are the teleukakay and other houses "perform." This illusion of movement marks an important kinesthetic event, one that occurs daily. The movements, the poses, the gestures performed by the family enclosure make up an architectonic dance, striking in its metaphoric relation to structures of dance more generally.

The Mousgoum *bawa* dance, performed during marriage celebrations, conveys this idea quite effectively. *Bawa* is not a full-scale public dance, but one enjoyed by women during the preparations for the wedding feast. Although an informal dance, there is still a clear demarcation between center and periphery. In the center a woman using two large sticks beats a mortar; another one, using the bottom of a large bowl as a drum, complements the rhythm of the first. In time with the music, three other women pound millet that lies in the mortar being "played" (fig. 14). While these three women pound the grain, they let their pestles fly into the air, catching them in synch with the music. Women seamlessly switch off in the pounding of the millet. The switch occurs when a woman releases the pestle in the air: at this moment, another woman enters, catches the pestle and continues to pound. Other women, girls, and young boys sing and dance around the pounding of the grain in the center. Like the granaries, *bawa* once again highlights the importance of food.

As Bakhtin recognized, food metaphorically shows triumph through its analogy to human work and its successful completion. For the philosopher, food is inherently triumphal as the act of eating breaks the boundaries between the body and the world, and it is precisely this overstepping of boundaries, marking hu-

FIGURE 14. Mousgoum *bawa* dance, Pouss, photographed April 20, 1996.

man victory over the world, that is an essential part of the banquet scene. This victory, in Bakhtin's paradigm, as representation of life over death transforms the banquet scene into a metaphor of beginnings and conception. It marks a transition and a birth. Bakhtin also compares the banquet to a wedding, calling the wedding feast itself "the potentiality of a new beginning."[36] In the context of *bawa*, food has similar connotations. As the central focus of the wedding celebration, food marks the beginning of a new life for the nuptial couple and the promise of procreation and progeniture. In the center of the *bawa* dance, as with the large granary in the homestead, the center—the center full of food—marks the source of power from which the dance, and, by extension, the newly married couple will emerge.

In the Mousgoum family homestead, the smooth, rectangular "male" house, or the "male" granary, makes a striking contrast to the smaller granaries and "ribbed" teleukakay that dot the enclosure's periphery. Like the dance, the center is the source of power for the whole. The play of light and shadow on the forms, the rich contrasts of the surfaces of the building, like dance, mark the different spaces that socialize and define Mousgoum individuals. In this way, the Mousgoum homestead replicates the forms made visible through dance. Unlike the transient nature of dance, however, the built environment renders the same concerns visible in a more permanent fashion.[37]

The contrast between the immobility of the smooth houses and the constantly changing nature of the ribbed teleuk is critical. In the space where light and shadow combine with the designs of the various houses in the homestead, one can speculate that the family patriarch is coded as stationary, his wives as in motion. With respect to ownership and family hierarchy, the house of the family patriarch is anchored, suggesting an analogy to the partrilocal nature of the Mousgoum. When a woman marries, she moves to the home of her husband (or his family). In the case of a boy who has his own ribbed house, the structure's movement could be seen as an allusion to the point at which he too is changing, and his transformation will culminate in the founding of his own homestead. The complementarity between space and movement also finds analogy with the conjugal union of man and woman. When the two are together, it is the wife who goes to her husband, again coding the patriarch as stationary, his wives as in motion. In all the oppositions between male and female couched as left/right, high/low, south/north, static/mobile, and open/closed, space in the enclosure is gendered in multiple and highly complex ways, suggesting that the many distinctions made in terms of gender in the social realm have direct analogies in architectural practices.

Although neither dance nor architecture seem to be a direct reflection of Mousgoum cosmology, the two have religious overtones. In the *dourmalaye* dance, the community implored the spirits for rain and an abundant harvest. After the harvest, the spirits were thanked through dance for their benefice. During the construction of the homestead, sacrifices were made to the spirits for the protection of the space to be defined, and, by extension, the family who will inhabit it. Protection—mental and physical—is one of the main functions of the family compound, and this is expressed through the materials and through the religious practices that are incorporated in this process. Materially, as the dome could not be easily penetrated or burned, the teleuk was considered to be a container that would save the family in times of war, a notion amplified by the use of a shield for a door. Perleh claimed that the inspiration for the teleuk's form came from that of the termite hill (*baray*) (fig. 15). Common in this region, termite hills are often taller than humans, and they are also known for their near indestructibility.[38] Perleh also insisted that the termite hill served as the home of Math, the bush spirit after whom Perleh himself was named.[39] Another allusion to the importance of the termite hill rests in the naming of children. It is not uncommon for a young Mousgoum girl to be named *Baray*.

FIGURE 15. Termite hill, Maga, Cameroon, photographed April 10, 1996.

Before the construction of the homestead began, the family patriarch con-sulted a diviner, who would tell him the exact sacrifices required for his own sit-uation. In one scenario, a patriarch made sacrifices to each of the spirits during the following days. This particular series of ceremonies, related by Mme. Abour-gadaï, required the use of black tobacco. The family head would hold some of it in each of his hands, throwing it once towards the land of the future homestead. On the morning of the first day, this sacrifice was made to Alaw for the gener-al well-being of the family and home. At dusk the following evening, Math was ritually asked to protect the family from the dangers of the bush and to provide prosperity for their home. To ensure a multitude of children, the patriarch offered a sacrifice to Zigla at the same time the following night. At four o'clock the following morning, a ceremony was held for Bangui for the preservation of sight. Finally, the family head made a sacrifice to Maana the next morning to reap an abundance of fish for the family. After the compound was completed, the family patriarch would go to homestead's center, where he would kill a sheep in sacrifice to Alaw. He then placed the blood of the animal into the earth for Yaye. These two actions were a plea that the home be enshrouded in peace. Abdoulaye Malbourg added that the family head also had to take black tobacco into each hand, enter the new house, and throw the tobacco three times while calling out the names of Alaw, Math, and Maana in order to protect his family from evil.

In the sense that Mousgoum architecture and dance have overtly religious overtones, the two find analogies in the process of constructing the family concession. In keeping with the importance Agonan placed on the body during construction and the series of sacrifices that were incorporated into that process, the resulting enclosures constitute a religiously charged space. Metaphorically, the construction of the homestead is a dance, like the *dourmalaye*, in which the spirits are implored for benefice, and the resulting home becomes a visualization of a dance in a more permanent form.

Beauty and the Home

Salman Mbang Oumar wrote for me a number of stories that his parents had told to him when he was a child. In one of them, a capricious young man refused to marry any girl who did not resemble his mother:

> In a village called Takaye lived a young man who had refused all the proposals of marriage that his parents had made for him. As an excuse he pretended that these young girls were of a feminine quality inferior to his mother: [He pretended] that these young girls did not know how to dress, that they washed their linens poorly, wore their jewels poorly, [and] did not know how to cook. In a word, [they] were not beautiful like his mother.

Complying with the young man's frivolity, his father suggested that the son take a voyage throughout the land of the Mousgoum to find the girl of his dreams. The young man agrees to do so, and after traveling by pirogue throughout Mousgoum country, he fails to find her. Finally, he comes home only to find the perfect woman in his own village. The moral of the tale is fairly straightforward: you do not have to go a great distance to find that which is already under your feet.[40]

Salman's story, in the attention it gives to women who do not look like the young man's mother, explicitly shows a Mousgoum concern with beauty. With

FIGURE 16. Interior of a Mousgoum teleuk, Musgum, Chad. Drawn by D. A. Talbot, 1910. Source: MacLeod, *Chiefs and Cities of Central Africa*, 1912.

respect to women, beauty is defined in the way she washes, in the way she carries herself, in the ways she cooks, and the ways she cleans. Beauty is not something that is genetic, per se; it is rather something that can be learned, something that can be made. And it is the charge of women to do so.

Such is as true in the built environment as it is in other realms of quotidian life. Once the Mousgoum family enclosure has been constructed, women plaster the houses and walls with a layer of clay to protect the buildings from the deterioration caused by winds and summer rains. To plaster a house is to embellish it. It is to give it an outer layer of clothing that will make the home a beautiful one. In the past, the insides of homes were much more elaborately decorated than were their outer walls.

Heims points out the rich ornamentation present inside of one of the Mousgoum homes he visited.[41] Olive MacLeod also describes the prevalence of ornament in a Mousgoum teleuk: "The low doorways were of considerable thickness, and were richly ornamented on the inside by impressions made in the soft mud by fingertips . . . . Elaborate fireplaces stood inside, sometimes attached to high shafts, in which corn for immediate consumption was stored."[42] In an article written for the *New York Times*, she observes that "decorations . . . cover every waterpot, doorway or bedstead."[43] MacLeod went on to describe an elaborate mural she had seen inside a house in Musgum. Drawn by Dory Talbot, who with her husband, the British ethnologist and government administrator P. Amaury Talbot, accompanied MacLeod on her voyage, the images look as if they covered the wall to at least human height (fig. 16). In an example from the lawane's compound, abstract designs have been rendered by the artist to a similar height (fig. 17).

FIGURE 17. Interior of Mousgoum teleuk at the homestead of Lawane Atuisingué, Gaïa, Cameroon, c. 1952. Source: *L'Habitat au Cameroun*, c. 1952.

MacLeod recounts the paintings she saw as a fresco that had been rendered in white chalk and black and red paint.[44] According to this traveler's source, among the animals represented on the mural were a giraffe, an elephant, a black cat, a sheep, and an ostrich. Dory Talbot's drawing also depicts a figure in a hat, a canoe full of people, a woman milking a cow, and a number of men on horses. These figures are all framed by abstract designs, giving the impression of a work done in a series of panels or scenarios. The bottom of Dory Talbot's drawing shows that the base of the wall is rendered in a pattern of triangles and other abstract forms. Such meticulous attention to detail in decoration exists also in the photographs and drawings of the lawane's compound. Elaborate decoration is the way in which the home, like a person, becomes beautiful, and this beauty carries a broad range of significance within Mousgoum culture.

That beauty is not only a physical attribute but also one that has social and metaphysical qualities has been recognized by a number of Africanist scholars, and in much of this work they have generally equated beauty with morality, goodness, and prestige.[45] Sylvia Boone noted how easily people talked about beauty when she was engaged in fieldwork with the Mende. Like many of the people she interviewed, the Mousgoum also thought of themselves as connoisseurs of beauty.[46] As noted in Harris Memel-Fotê's work, beauty for the Mousgoum is physical, metaphysical, and social.[47] The relationship of Mousgoum notions of beauty to goodness, propriety, and cleanliness finds explicit expression through the Munjuk language, where the very words for beauty, *yimí* and *zivi*, also mean "to be good," "to be proper," and "to be clean."[48]

In the Mousgoum built environment, beauty is not so much part of the enclosure as it is a result of the fusion of the homestead and female creativity. I was often told that in the past men did not make beautiful things. In the homestead, the houses were the canvases that could later become beautiful through the feminine hand. Although many Mousgoum today consider the teleuk to be a beautiful building, they far more readily considered plastering and ornament as those things that infused the home with beauty.

Few Mousgoum talked about beauty in the ways that the Mende did in Boone's fieldwork.[49] The focus on beauty for the Mousgoum was based more on actions and practices performed in daily life than it was on the body itself. In the words of Azao Dogo, "the Mousgoum, since the time of their ancestors, washed themselves, they wore beads, [and] the skins they wore were tanned and proper. The first thing was cleanliness. And in order to say that one is someone, the daughter of that someone must eat [and] be proper and then [that person] had honor, glory. They presented to the world that they were so." To have honor, to have glory was to be well situated in the community, and women were the main bearers of such responsibility. To be ugly carried dire social consequences. Salman Mbang Oumar made this point explicitly:

> The Mousgoum love beauty. When the man is not handsome and leaves to search for a girl for marriage, he must first pay the dowry. He also must pay [for his ugliness]. Everyone knows that you . . . are ugly. Everyone says you are bad. So I, as the father of the girl, ask you to give me something—two bulls [in addition to the dowry] . . . . A girl who is ugly has difficulties in having a husband. His father will not buy her ugliness. [It] does not carry much of a dowry.

For women and men, ugliness is not only demeaning, but it is also an indication of one's low stature in the community-at-large. People who are considered ugly, in the minds of many Mousgoum people, are dirty, are morally corrupt, lazy, and prone to activities such as thievery. They are also thought of as being fools. However, ugliness is also avoidable, and Mousgoum people will give explicit instructions on just how to prevent such a demeaning state.

For women, as Dogo and Salman's story of the young man indicates, beauty is a property that lies in one's ability to carry oneself and to dress well. One must fix one's hair and maintain good habits. A woman must be able to cook and take care of a home. Part of her beauty is also derived from her family, in the sense that her family's status is a barometer of the ways in which her own beauty is measured. Conversely, a woman's beauty reflects back onto her family and, if married, that of her husband's family as well. In the social realm, a beautiful woman is respectful, cooperative, docile, and hard working. She also teaches her children to be clean and well mannered. She accommodates guests in her home.

A man attains beauty in the physical realm by dressing and carrying himself well and being clean. Socially and morally, respecting and obeying his parents and being kind to his friends attain this. The handsome man neither fights nor drinks too much alcohol. He becomes handsome through his work and by providing for his family. Although beauty is much more frequently addressed with respect to women, in the case of either gender, beauty consists of a combination of outer ornament and inner discipline. Moreover, the habits that constitute outer beauty are an indication of the quality of the inner soul. As such, outer beauty is the text through which a person can be read.

During conversations about how one becomes beautiful, the family concession was often brought into the discourse. For the home to be beautiful, it must be well covered, and women must look for the right earth and colors, items that will make the compound a pleasing place. As Suzanne Blier observes, for the Batammaliba architectural beauty was based upon the presence of correct proportions that spring from a concern for balance in the built environment. In this context, evenness, straightness, and unity were tropes that found relevance in the architectural and social arenas.[50] To the Mousgoum, however, architectural beauty is based on ornament's ability to articulate order.

There was also a right and a wrong way to build teleukakay, but the criterion against which the house was judged did not fall under the rubric of beauty. Here, the critique was usually lodged against the feet of the house. As is well illustrated in images of the teleuk, there were a number of different ways in which feet were designed on the dome. Some were laid out on the surface of the dome as a series of short, straight modulations; others were laid out as upside-down Vs or wishbones. To a certain extent, the mason decided independently the form that the feet would take, but generally, straight feet were characteristic of teleukakay in the northern part of Mousgoum country; those with upside-down Vs were more common in the south. Malbourg compared these differences to those in language, suggesting, "It is necessary to recognize that the difference [in the design of the feet] resides at the level of cultures. One has the Massa, the Mousgoum, and the people of Bigué, who speak different languages, and in such a case their ways of putting the feet [on the teleuk] must also be different." Thus, the criteria used to judge surface ornament was much more a product of one's origin than it was aesthetically based, and this paradigm showed one's affinity to one's home village more than anything else.

In a Mousgoum context, to insist on decoration and plastering as that which makes the compound beautiful is also to equate it with architecture itself. Outside of the gender differences in building and decoration, once the house was completed, these complementary functions were fused. As in the perception of people and their clothing, one did not separate the homestead from its decoration. Rudolf Arnheim understood ornament as that which supplements form through completion, enrichment, and definition.[51] In this manner, ornament is thought of as additive; it is conceived as nonfundamental to the form to which it is attached. In musical terms, in contrast, Robert Morgan sees ornamentation as the "expansion of a stable structural core," insisting that it has always been an essential part of Western music.[52] While Morgan still separates ornamentation from basic musical structure, he does not see it as an attribute or category that is less compelling than the structure itself, but one that differentiates uses of the same structural core.

For the Mousgoum a similar line of thought is in play. Outside of factors of size and the organization and diversity of houses, the basic structure of a family enclosure does not dramatically change from one compound to another. However, the ways in which the houses are decorated vary widely. It is ornament—not core structure—that truly differentiates one homestead from another. In discussions of wall painting, women consistently asserted the independence of their conceptions and the individuality of their work: this impulse may well have been that of their mothers and grandmothers as well. They also maintained that their work created beauty. The images of MacLeod, Heims, and others, when taken with information in the field, suggest that the diversity of design within Mousgoum family enclosures is striking. Some Mousgoum say that they had never seen the figural murals described by MacLeod and Dory Talbot; others note that their mothers made similar murals in their homes. In this sense, the plethora of ways in which women used ornament to define their enclosures reveals the relative freedom they had (and retain) to use their creativity in the architectural realm.

In Mousgoum terms, plastering and ornament in relief are not an aesthetically insignificant extension of or addition to architectural form, but are inseparable from it. This inseparability makes it quite clear that the homestead is not completed until women have finished their work. This finds relevance in Mme. Abourgadaï's description of her apprenticeship. She explicitly noted that plastering was the last step of the building process and her training. Theo van Doesburg, seeing the possibilities of color in the built environment, insisted on an understanding of it as an integral component of architecture:

> colour serves not only to orientate, by which is meant the visualization of distance, position and direction in reference to space and to the objects which it

contains, but even more to satisfy a need for the visualization of mutual relationships in proportion, scale and direction. It is the arrangement of these relationships that constitutes the aesthetic goal of architecture.[53]

Like light, color also orients space, making allusions to depth, affecting the ways in which the form is viewed over time. In Mousgoum homesteads this facilitates the "dance" and further amplifies the sense of order inherent in the arrangement of the enclosure. Inside the teleuk, color and designs in relief animate the interior walls, and along with the light that streams in through the hole at the summit, highlights different parts of the wall at different times, giving the illusion of movement around the interior of the dome and emphasizing the passage of time. This creates a striking counterpart to the play of light over the feet of the outer dome.

FIGURE 18. Mousgoum granary, Musgum, Chad. Photographer: Ernst M. Heims, 1911.
Source: Friedrich, *From the Congo to the Niger and the Nile*, 1913.

FIGURE 19. Interior of a Mousgoum teleuk. Photographer: Olive MacLeod, 1911.
Source: MacLeod, *Chiefs and Cities of Central Africa*, 1912.

Along with the arrangement of forms, ornament reinforces the importance of the family head. This is particularly evidenced in the elaborately decorated granary photographed by Heims (fig. 18). Moreover, decoration alludes to the importance of food and the necessity of women's work more generally. Inside of a woman's teleuk, her hearth and *hono*, a shelf located above the doorway, are often the places in her home that are the most elaborately decorated (fig. 19). The *hono*, where she keeps her food and cooking utensils, is an intricate series of shelves that are arranged in a number of different ways. In the manner in which these forms are made and decorated, they often fuse with the wall of the teleuk's interior, becoming indistinguishable from it.[54]

As is the case with people, surface decorations are not separate from the bodies of the forms: to decorate is to dress the house. It is the homestead's *toilette*, its adornment. Like Mousgoum women, the body that is the house and the family that is the homestead are made beautiful. This reflects back onto the woman, for in successfully making the compound beautiful, she shows her creativity and her character. This also earns her appreciation and praise from her husband and the community-at-large. In the words of Mme. Arkali Adogoï,

> the obligation reverts to women to make beauty. The man is there only to admire and to praise the beauty of my compound. In Mousgoum country, beauty is a property. [When] one plasters Mousgoum homes, it is for admiration. It is

for attracting the attention of passersby. From that time [on] one will say of a concession that it is the most beautiful in the neighborhood or in the village in order to say that [this] woman is proper.

To make the family concession truly beautiful, it also has to be clean. While ornament was the crux of attaining beauty in the homestead, the compound that was the family had to be swept daily, and well maintained. Besides the obvious attachments to hygiene and healthfulness, decoration and cleanliness constitute windows into the personal qualities of the wives of the compound and the family as a whole.

A beautiful home was—and continues to be—the outer sign of the goodness, morality, and propriety of the family within. Through their creativity and intelligence, women are the ones who express the nature of themselves and their families. In the home, a woman's production of beauty is inseparable from the status of her husband. The house's decoration and cleanliness are a direct reflection on his ability to keep order in the family. Thus, it is not so much the ways in which a man has architecturally arranged his homestead that underscores his control; it is the ways in which his wife or wives have finished the compound that achieve this. Domestic beauty is ultimately an allusion to his inner qualities articulated through the beautiful homestead. On the property of beauty and the home in broad terms, Salman Mbang Oumar put it simply, "When a compound is beautiful, it is good. Really, in Mousgoum country, it is good."

Conclusion

In the metonymic relationship between the house and the body and in the metaphoric relation between the homestead and the family, the Mousgoum have invoked architecture to give form and space to their daily lives. In the family homestead, the arrangement of buildings—the ways in which they are decorated and spatially conceived—have created avenues through which values are articulated and people are socialized. In this context, architecture serves as social reflection and social activator. The Mousgoum have made rich associations that express different aspects of their lives through the built environment. In the connections made between architecture and dance, religion and beauty, the Mousgoum family enclosure is steeped in articulations of social values and relationships. Also, through the arrangement and adornment of the family of houses, the importance of food in conceptions of progeniture and power comes to the fore. With respect to religion, the process of building becomes particularly important, for in it lie the ways in which the worship of spirits is literally built into the home.

The relationship and the complementarity between men and women also play a significant role in aspects of Mousgoum architecture, encompassing conceptions of space and the ways in which the work of women defines men and the work of men defines women. From the consecration of the ground that will become the family enclosure, through the arrangement of houses and granaries, through decoration to the daily sweeping of the compound, understanding of gender difference and the ways in which these forces play off one another is one of the primary ways in which order is established and reinforced in the homestead.

The Mousgoum teleuk is, in the minds of many Mousgoum people and Westerners, an architectural celebration par excellence. In this chapter, the most important issue is how the built environment *as a whole* articulated meaning and social values for Mousgoum people. If one looks at plans and images and closely listens to descriptions of Mousgoum family enclosures, it is evident that as important as the teleuk is on many levels, it was not the *only* important Mousgoum structure. In view of the fact that the middle of the family enclosure is a charged arena, the absence of a teleuk—or even a description of it—as having ever occupied that space requires that the form, *as cultural symbol*, be reevaluated with respect to the past.

Parabolic Paradoxes

How can I come to terms with that which is Other without reducing it to the terms of my own understanding? JOHN FROW, "TOURISM AND THE SEMIOTICS OF NOSTALGIA"

2

The fundamental operations we perform when traveling are almost exactly like those behind the children's program *Sesame Street*'s most famous jingle: "One of these things is not like the others, one of these things doesn't belong." They're not unlike those art history exams some of us, in darkened lecture halls, still give: compare and contrast the two images on the screen. When traveling we constantly ask whether the sites in sight, down to the tiniest, silliest detail, are like or unlike that which we know. Does this person move like I do? Does this store have the same brand breath mints I get at the 7-Eleven near my house? My car dashboard doesn't have that green light. What is that strange plant? My house isn't a dome.

Such negotiation, which is at times, at least in my own experience, quite neurotic, occurs in any person who crosses a boundary. Similar responses and conundrums, as it were, also shape, in large part, the concerns of travelogues and travel writing. While arguably not as shallow as some of my own travel concerns, the things described in the travelogue's pages take on much importance in the rhetoric and traffic in travel, for in its pages those about to travel, or at least curious about the place described, can learn, through the impressions and observations of the text's author, what such a place must be like. They can figure out what to expect should they go there, too. Scholars are not immune to such operations. My own first encounter with the Mousgoum teleuk was in perusing André Gide's *Voyage au Congo: suivi de retour du Tchad,* one of the texts under scrutiny in this discussion. In my own travels in Mousgoum country, I not only sang (if only in my head) songs of *Sesame Street,* and did that standard art historical compare and contrast with the things I saw, but also checked my experiences and responses against, and against the grain of, the travelogues I had read before going there.

Travelogues are strange animals. They record a journey, give insight to a particular place; at times, they serve as blueprints or points of departure to those who come to the same place at a later date. For me, the travelogue is also quite the hybrid form. At times, as is the case with Joseph Conrad's *Heart of Darkness,* a novella that has been routinely interpreted as a travelogue, fact, and fiction, not unlike today's historical novel or filmic docudrama, merge in the genre's pages. At times, as with Gide's and Olive MacLeod's texts, facts are colored by the author's emotional states and concerns not directly related to the experience of travel. In such instances, the travelogue also reads as a journal, a diary of the time away, yielding a text that is more personal, and more complex, than a simple recording of customs and manners as well as flora and fauna.

Be it Heinrich Barth, Conrad, MacLeod, Gide, or some other author, the travelogue, like the scholarly text, is a product of specific historical, social, and cultural circumstances, and in the meeting of European travelers and the teleuk, recorded in these authors' subsequent prose on the house and the Mousgoum, it is possible to think through the ways in which the teleuk in particular and architecture more generally serves as a tool of negotiating the space between the traveler and the place visited. These travelogues articulate and fuel a number of provocative perceptions related to race and gender that were used as ways of separating a civilized European self from a "savage" non-Western other. Throughout most of the pages of these travelogues, such binaries remain quite solidly in place. When our travelers encounter the Mousgoum dome, however, clear distinctions between self and other, between civilized and noncivilized are rendered ambiguous.

That ambiguity is explored here, for it is there where meanings and boundaries are thrown into question, and in this questioning signs become slippery and, perhaps only momentarily, threaten to turn ingrained stereotypes on their heads. But in the case of an individual traveler, the process of putting the strange into one's own language opens up avenues for seeing the tenuous nature of oppositions and, at moments, modernity itself, and this internal struggle is based on the obscuring of self and other, of interiority and anteriority. In a larger sense, this internal tension is also connected to the view that civilization, while constantly evolving forward for the West, was sometimes seen as transitory and fragile, as is exemplified by countless writers who claimed that when placed among the savages, a white man or woman would become just like them.[1]

In their juxtaposition of fragments, their pursuit of the exotic, their focus on the strange and the unconscious, the travelogues under scrutiny here, like travel more generally, are quite surreal, not in the exact sense of a Georges Bataille or a Michel Leiris, but in a more general fashion, a mode in which the pas de deux between the familiar and strange takes on critical importance. Moreover, the presence of Mousgoum architecture in the travelogue—a wonderful montage—and the travelers' respective encounters with it constitute sites/sights that underscore the element of the surreal in the travel experience. As in the surrealist project, the strange and familiar begin to oscillate in a way that threatens to close in on their differences. Like primitivism, these moments of description posit the primal scene as well, throwing identity into question, hence complicating description and momentarily blocking knowledge.[2] Along such lines, this chapter examines how these travelers produce ideas of the Mousgoum, their teleuk and themselves through texts and visual representation.

Heinrich Barth's Probing Architectonics

Heinrich Barth's journey through North, West, and Central Africa was originally conceived by the British government and the Royal Geographic Society as a mission intended to create commercial treaties between Great Britain and African leaders that would abolish the African slave trade and open new trade routes to the continent's interior by way of the Sahara.[3] During the mid-nineteenth century, there was no clear conception of what would later become British imperial policy in Africa, and in the 1850s British government policies were predominantly concerned with abolition of the African slave trade and the establishment of free commerce with the African continent. Africa was rife for exploration, and the possibility of economic gain further fueled European interest in such projects.

Not satisfied with taking part in a purely economic expedition, Barth was unwavering in his insistence that the primary goal of the mission should be exploration—literally mapping parts of the African continent—as well as scientific research and discovery. He also wanted to form alliances of goodwill with African leaders.[4] Certain that he had persuaded the organizers to share his priorities, Barth joined James Richardson, who was trained for the Evangelical ministry and a staunch opponent of the slave trade, and the Prussian astronomer and geographer Adolph Overweg in their journey to Africa.

The three explorers left Tripoli on March 24, 1850; Barth would be the only European to survive the voyage.[5] His monumental *Travels and Discoveries in North and Central Africa* includes every facet of his journey, culminating in over 3,000 pages of text, illustrations, maps, daily meteorological charts, itineraries, and assorted appendices. The volumes must have been reasonably well known, given their simultaneous publication in English and German and their almost immediate translation into French, Dutch, and Danish. While Barth's obsessively detailed text would not enjoy the same popularity as would David Livingstone's *Missionary Travels*, published the same year, Barth's nevertheless received widespread attention in the public sphere.[6]

The popular press regularly highlighted the discomfort, the dangers, the disease, and the constant flirting with disaster inherent in African travel; sporadic dispatches about Barth's expedition appeared in the *London Athenaeum*, *London Times*, and *New York Times*. An almost instinctual attraction to hardship, menace, and death—underscored by the untimely demise of Richardson and Overweg—titillated an early Victorian public that was yearning to receive news of, learn about, and be thrilled by exotic places around the globe. On March 27, 1855,

Augustus Petermann, cartographer for the Royal Geographic Society, reported that a steamboat was being sent up the Benué River to find Barth, who was presumed to be either lost or dead.[7] On April 4, 1855, the *London Times* informed its readers that the tales of Barth's death were unfounded, explaining that the rumor was made up by a petty African ruler. The report continued, "The overthrow of this man was most fortunate, otherwise the fabricated report might have been converted into a stern reality."[8] Gossipy news shorts such as these and the increasing onslaught of published travel narratives further cemented terrifying images of African exploration already circulating in the public imagination. American writer Charles Brigham taps into this perception, insisting, "Of one thing we are always sure, when we take up a narrative of African travel—that it will be a story of pain, disease, and continual bodily prostration."[9]

Besides the popular press, the 1840s and 1850s saw numerous attractions that also tapped into British and American desires for contact—real or imagined—with the exotic and the ancient, which in many minds were one in the same. In 1849 the archaeologist Henry Layard published his popular volume, *Nineveh and Its Remains*; its appearance neatly coincided with the arrival in the British Museum of newly "discovered" Assyrian artifacts from the ancient city. These massive winged genies, ferocious animals, warriors, and kings, like the popular Egyptian exhibits, brought many visitors to the museum. John Dodds describes James Wyld's Great Globe, which stood in Leicester Square from 1851 until 1862 (fig. 20). Sixty-five feet in diameter, the world's continents and ocean floors were modeled in relief in the globe's interior. On its four floors visitors could, at least metaphorically, walk through the world. Panoramas constituted another popular entertainment venue. Attendees could watch wonderful scenes while hearing a reader expatiate about faraway places as disparate as India, the Nile, or even the Ohio River.[10] Be it an exotic locale, the countryside, or nature more generally, such panoramas, while entertaining, helped to reinforce city dwellers' collective conviction of their sophistication, as well as their political and cultural superiority.

In amusements, in the popular press, in travel literature, and in other cultural arenas three important strands come together. The first resided in Victorian society's seemingly insatiable thirst for adventure, that is, a desire to live vicariously through the intrepid, masculine explorer. The second found its expression in the nineteenth century's obsession with positivist, "scientific" knowledge. In her excellent analysis of the production of "Africa" in late Victorian and Edwardian Great Britain, Annie Coombs points to how London's 1890 Stanley and African Exhibition depended upon and exploited the intersection of two Africas: that of the popular imagination and that of scientific, objective discovery.[11] The Africa of the popular imagination no doubt had its roots in the aforementioned popular media and amusements. Coombs rightly locates the genesis of the craving for "Africa" in many different regimes in the Great Exhibition of 1851;

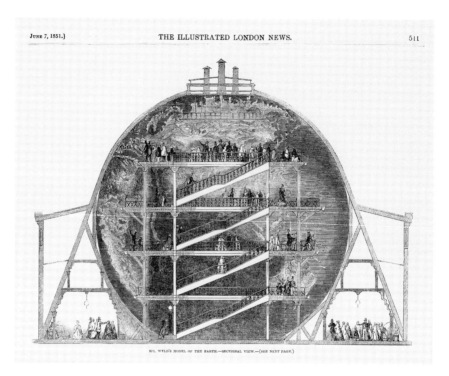

MR. WYLD'S MODEL OF THE EARTH.—SECTIONAL VIEW.—(SEE NEXT PAGE.)

FIGURE 20. James Wyld, *Wyld's Great Globe*, cross-section, Leicester Square, London, 1851. Source: *The Illustrated London News*, June 7, 1851, 511.

Europe's fixation on the Hottentot Venus, a figure captured and frozen in popular engravings, and Britain's widespread concern with the abolition of slavery also contributed to such longings. Saartjie Baartmann, the "Hottentot Venus," had been displayed in Europe in the early nineteenth century. By midcentury, imagery depicting this "aberrant" character proliferated in Victorian popular culture. One therefore cannot discount the role such imagery played in the production of an "Africa" of popular imagination.[12] The third, the one underscored by Barth's interaction with the Mousgoum, is an unconscious attraction to death, a crucial component of the rhetoric related to antiquity and places non-European.

The attraction to death is a staple of nineteenth- and early twentieth-century descriptions of Africa. Europeans routinely articulated such anxieties through descriptions of bodies in pain, the discoloring of the skin, and the broken, hollowed-out image of the traveler-as-survivor. This traveled body was irrevocably marked by the image of "Africa-as-near-death." The inner diseases and hardships made bronze faces grow gray and pale; vigorous souls returned as mere shadows of what they once were as, in Brigham's words, "the airs of the [African] forests breathed upon them."[13] However, death not only reveals itself on the skin or in the countenance of the explorer, but it also rears its head in the distance created by the description and interpretation of customs and manners and scenes abroad. Such passages abound in travel literature, perhaps the most famous being in the oeuvres of Henry Morgan Stanley and Joseph Conrad, and they underscore the explorer's (and the reader's) constant negotiation between the other and the self, between sickness and health, between darkness and light, even between death and life. And in this Dionysian/Apollonian drama, Barth's encounter with the Mousgoum and the teleuk shows how fraught these binaries could be for the explorer.

Barth's perilous, and some would say miraculous, journey added a wealth of knowledge that undoubtedly played a large role in the production of "Africa" in early Victorian England and the codification of scientific and objective data so valuable to the academic and business worlds' construction of the continent. Brigham confirms such a dramatic accomplishment, asserting that Barth's and other travelers' opening up of Africa taps into "twenty centuries of desire."[14] While Brigham refers to the will of Europe to fill the "empty" map of Africa through the gleaning of useful knowledge and the creation of avenues for trade, what is most critical is the equation of African travel with such strong desire.

Dancing with death, dealing with desire, handling hardships, voicing the vicissitudes of daily life are parts of the larger means through which Barth's journals construct a panoramic view of Africa and some of the predominant ways that the explorer, against all odds, becomes a hero. This process, this self-conscious, self-aggrandizing prose, is a staple of what Mary Louise Pratt has called, "sentimental, experiential discourse."[15] Using the travels of Mungo Park as an example, Pratt describes the placement of the European traveler in the center of the expedition's narrative.[16] Within this self-aggrandizing paradigm, Barth recognizes the importance of defining the self as a sentient subject in the wild, and the agent that will bring European civilization to a continent of savagery (2: 167–68).

At the same time, Barth's self-exploration dramatizes the push and pull between an individual and civilization interrogated by Sigmund Freud's *Civilization and Its Discontents*. In discussing his own life, in detailing his motivations for going to Africa, and in highlighting a dichotomy between nature and culture, expressed in his text by the relationship of rivers to commerce (2: 167–68), the explorer negotiates the relationship of his ego to civilization. Freud, analyzing such a relationship, explains that at times one's own actions feel as though they happen outside one's body; at other times, one projects qualities that originate in the ego onto the outside world.[17] For Barth, the latter process is in force; moreover, the relationship between his ego and civilization finds its expression through travel. This resulting projection of the self not only onto the act of travel but also onto people and places constitutes a remarkable play between self and other; in this play, in this movement, the instincts of a child are sublimated, dispersed as it were, among the people, plants, and things in his path.

Such sublimation and projection are important means through which Barth codifies his own civilized state. Besides his self-aggrandizement, his position as a man of reason—articulated through the merger of his training in classics and his travels—marks Barth's ongoing cultural development. This is also an important distinction for, as Freud reminds us, the sublimation of instincts, which the author calls "an especially conspicuous feature of cultural development," is critical, for it opens up the possibility of "higher psychical activities, scientific, artistic or ideological, to play . . . an important role in civilized life." Travel only highlights European perceptions of and often-unstable relations with culture for Freud, who suggests:

> The last but one of these occasions [which occasioned a deep-seated dissatisfaction with and hostility to the existing state of civilization] was when the progress of voyages of discovery led to contact with primitive peoples and races. In consequence of insufficient observation and a mistaken view of their manners and customs, they appeared to Europeans to be leading a simple, happy life with few wants, a life such as was unattainable by their visitors with their superior civilization.[18]

In Barth's travels, such a view of Africans would, in a relative fashion, remind him how much he has evolved. And it is his rendezvous with the Mousgoum and their teleuk that serves as an example and support of how the relationship between Barth and his other in particular, or civilization and nature more generally, is not always a stable one. Barth's encounters with and description of the Mousgoum present a rich example of how architecture and notions of civilization intersect in the travel experience, creating a milieu in which the ingrained perception of the self and its relationship to the outside world are called into question.

As part of his seemingly endless appropriation of "knowledge" on the customs and manners of the people whom he visits and the amassing of botanical, geographic, and meteorological data on a vast area of North, West, and Central Africa, Barth describes architecture in several instances, and many of these passages are not unlike those about the weather, the flora, or the fauna. With respect to the built environment, the traveler is concerned with the materials of construction and, in a manner natural for an archaeologist, what kind of information may be gleaned from it. In the case of "huts," Barth usually describes the level of comfort (or discomfort) afforded for indigenous occupant and European traveler. For example, in Kórom, such dwellings "not only presented an appearance of comfort, but exhibited in a certain degree the industry of its inhabitants" (2: 354).

While comfort is the obvious issue, the ways in which architecture allows Barth to know, interpret, and represent other cultures is a far more critical matter. In this vein, architecture constitutes one avenue through which he can successfully complete one of the chief goals of the voyage, which, in his words, was "to represent the tribes and nations with whom I came in contact, in their historical and ethnographic relation to the rest of mankind, as well as in their physical relation to that tract of country in which they live" (1: xxvii).

The connections Barth makes between architecture and society find a potent analogy in the concerns of late eighteenth- and nineteenth-century art and architectural historians. Antoine-Chrysostome Quatremère de Quincy was perhaps the most articulate in his analysis of the connections between architecture and culture. Long concerned with teasing out the relationship between architecture and the social sphere, Quatremère concluded that architecture and language were the most important constituent and preserving constructs of ancient society.[19] In these paradigms, architecture is not only illustrative of a culture, but, like language, it is also a means to chart evolution and to see relational correspondences among an array of cultures. Demonstrating his adherence to similar principles, Barth explains that in the architecture of the people of Bornú, "The roofs even exhibited traces of various styles, and perhaps a certain gradation in the scale of society" (3: 355). Thus the thatched roof constitutes Barth's barometer, his tool for measuring the level of civilization attained by an African civilization.

But Barth is not so straightforward in describing the Mousgoum teleuk. In 1852, while passing through gloomy, swampy areas of land, the explorer notes, "Already here, besides the huts common to the country, others of a remarkable and peculiar style, became visible, such as I shall describe further on, and as only the most excellent clay soil can enable the natives to build" (2: 412). Barth has set up his reader's expectations, and in the following pages the explorer prolongs his reader's anticipation. Having piqued his reader with the peculiar and the strange, the explorer then leads her or him into the ruins of the residence of Mousgoum chief Kábishmé, which, according to the traveler's sources, had been ransacked the previous year. Barth directs his reader's attention to the physical layout of the enclosure:

> the village itself, and particularly the dwelling of the chief Kábishmé, was calculated to create a great deal of interest, as well on account of the finished and careful execution of the buildings as owing to a certain degree of comfort and homeliness in the whole arrangement . . .
>
> The palace must have afforded a very different spectacle in former times, when it was inhabited, it being at present in such a state of ruin that several features in this arrangement could not be distinctly made out, almost every thing that was liable to take fire having been destroyed, and especially the sheds and inner court-yards, which are so characteristic of the domestic life of these people. At present [the palace] was an empty courtyard of a tolerable round shape, surrounded by huts more or less destroyed, and adorned at the four corners, if we may speak of corners in a building of almost round shape, by buildings of a very peculiar and remarkable character, which at once attracted my attention, as they bore testimony to a degree of order, and even of art, which I had not expected to find among these tribes. (2: 413)

Unlike the roofs of Bornú, Chief Kábishmé's residence becomes a screen through which Barth, textually and pictorially, attempts in an archaeological fashion to imagine the domestic life-ways of the former inhabitants not only of this particular "ruin," but also of Mousgoum people more generally. Despite its decayed state, Barth is able to surmise what characteristics life here shares with neighboring regions. He also is able to tease out the former comforts such a carefully and meticulously appointed dwelling would have provided for its residents.

However, as Barth speculates about the former lives of this place, he also underscores its present state of dilapidation. In doing so, the explorer places emphasis on the past and brings to the surface the always-present specter of death. This tendency to equate architecture with the past appears throughout his volumes, and we can see it in the passage on the Bornú roofs as well. There it is done simply through verb tense and word choice. Those roofs "exhibited traces." The past tense simply implies that the roofs no longer exhibit much of anything. In the end, these traces are things nearly, if not already, extinct.

That barely alive thing carries another meaning as well. A trace is also a small quantity of something. In that sense, these Bornú roofs—these well-nigh dead, inert objects—never really had a full-fledged style, but merely faint glimmers of rationality. Barth's attraction to death appears throughout his work both overtly and under the cover of metaphor. Besides the obvious locales of warfare, slave raids, and the untimely demise of his European colleagues, architecture is another place where death lives. If the built environment is, for Barth, the mirror and sign of civilization, it is also the mirror and sign of its remains, illustrating its final gasps for air. What is left in its wake can never approach the level of what preceded it.

While in North Africa, Barth encountered a number of sepulchers that, in his mind, were built by either the Romans or people who tried to mimic them. These routinely attracted not only his undivided attention, but also revealed the extent of his nostalgia for an imagined civilization that probably never existed in as elevated a state as he had envisioned. Barth, after going into exhaustive detail on the sepulchers' attributes, notes how one stands

> like a solitary beacon of civilization, [rising over a] sea-like level of desolation, which, stretching out to an immense distance south and west, appears not to have appalled the conquerors of the ancient world, who even here have left behind them, in "lithographed proof," a reminiscence of a more elevated order of life than exists at present in these regions. (1: 120)

Such beacons, such traces of a past that was invariably better than the present, show one of the strategies used by Barth in distinguishing himself from the lands and people he encounters on his journey.

The accompanying engravings also attempt to emphasize psychological dis-

FIGURE 21. Sepulcher at Wádí Tagíje.
Drawn by Heinrich Barth; engraved
by John Martin Bernatz, c. 1857. Source:
Barth, *Travels and Discoveries in North
and Central Africa*, 1857.

tance. Sketching the "Roman" sepulcher at Wádí Tagíje, Barth put a lot of energy into delineating the minutiae that he saw on the memorial's façade (fig. 21).
He also paid a lot of attention to the fallen stones to the left of the sepulcher,
which reinforces statements such as the one above. His exactitude in rendering is matched by his text, where he describes every single detail of the structure. Combined with the fallen stones, the background, consisting of a desolate
scene haunted by the setting sun, amplifies the death surrounding the beacon.
Barth's description only drives this point further, for in facing the south and the
west, that is, away from Europe, he anticipates his own movement further and
further away from rationality. And this movement into the twilight is one laced

with death and melancholy. Once the explorer carries on, this illustration of the sepulcher will bear not only the trace of a past civilization but also a vestige of Barth's presence.

By employing architecture, particularly the sepulcher, in such a fashion, Barth underscores the importance of architecture in the production of knowledge in parts unknown. Given his classical training and the high degree of interdisciplinary interchange between architecture and archaeology at the time, the explorer would have been familiar with the work of German architectural theorists. Barth taps into eighteenth- and nineteenth-century discourses surrounding the meanings of the primitive hut in some of his architectural descriptions and also shows his familiarity with architectural writings more generally. He writes, "In examining these structures (huts), one can not but feel surprised at the great similarity that they bear to the huts of the aboriginal inhabitants of Latium, such as they are described by Vitruvius and other authors, and represented occasionally on terra cotta utensils" (1: 114–15). In the course of his training, Barth would undoubtedly have come into contact with the work of Karl Müller, whose popular text *Handbuch der Archäologie der Kunst*, first published in 1830, meticulously outlines his views on the requirements for art and architecture.

Müller's text brings together not only the current thinking of many German academics, but also theoretical debates in art and architecture from Great Britain, France, and Italy, specifically citing the work of luminaries such as Quatremère, Johann Winckelmann, and J. N. L. Durand. Following these scholars, Müller sees art, architecture, and archaeology as inextricably tied to social realities. Representation and architecture, sculpture and visual art were inseparable from a culture's mental sensibilities. Barth takes up similar ideas in his description of presumably Roman sepulchers in North Africa:

> After nearly two hours' march I distinguished something like a high pillar, and, proceeding straight toward it, found it to be one of the richest specimens of this kind of monument bequeathed to us by antiquity, and an indisputable proof that these regions, now so poor, must have then supported a population sufficiently advanced in taste and feeling to admire works of a refined character. (1: 113)

In his description of the sepulcher, Barth experiences a momentary flash of identification with this architectonic heirloom. Barth, like the apparently Roman civilization responsible for building it, is culturally evolved enough to appreciate its refined nature and the richness of its forms. The devolved residents of the area, however, have no such abilities:

> No wonder that the natives of these regions now regard these tall sepulchral monuments, so strange at present in this land of desolation, as pagan idols,

and call them "sanem;" for I myself, when alone in front of the monument in this wide, solitary valley, and under the shadow of the deep, precipitous side of a plateau adjoining the Khaddamiye on the east, felt impressed by it with a certain degree of awe and veneration. (1: 115)

And the perspective used in the illustration only underscores this projected assumption. Here, the structure towers above the depopulated desolation around it. Perspective not only mirrors his text here (this passage is about this particular sepulcher), but also mirrors both the perception he describes among the local residents and his own. Ultimately, Barth asserts here that the indigenous population is without the innate sensibility to make sense of these forms, and that they can understand the edifice only as a god or an object made by one. However, as he emphatically informs his reader that he himself could be induced to worship the sepulcher as well, Barth demonstrates that he can straddle the fence, as it were, for he can understand the awe inspired and the "trace" left by the structure. Through these descriptions and the discourses surrounding art and architecture at large, the level of art, that is, the degree to which it is refined, exists in direct proportion to a given culture's ability not only to make the form, but, more importantly, to appreciate it.[20]

But this accounts for Barth's attraction to death only insofar as it becomes the way that he can describe the difference between these sepulchers and the people who presently live around them. Why is the explorer so attracted to the sepulcher? As one of the more common structures to survive antiquity, they were one of the foci of archaeologists and architectural theorists and would have naturally attracted him. The sepulcher as memorial and tomb was the home of the dead; moreover, this home of the dead constitutes the foundation through which archaeologists and architects could theorize about the nature of the homes of the living. Such a move finds a compelling analogy in the rhetoric surrounding the primitive hut, which, for many architects and philosophers, including Jean-Jacques Rousseau, allegorically represented the lost beginnings of Western civilization. These two paradigms would not have been at all difficult to connect as the hut and the sepulcher were routinely linked to the primordial temple and the edifice that Müller called "the simplest house."[21] Mnemonic traces of the past as well as nostalgia and loss are part and parcel of discussions about the primitive hut and temple, and the attempt to think about or grasp that which was lost in this context commonly results in knots of allegorical substitution and paradoxical formulations.[22]

In a climate where the non-Western and the ancient were often seen as one and the same, the Mousgoum teleukakay threaten to melt into the vast terrain of non-Western decay and death—that place that is always a staple of the encounter between the European explorer and the non-Western tabula rasa. The comfort the houses held has passed, and the dwelling now can be understood only as an architectonic repository containing traces of a more civilized time.

Armed with years of travel throughout the centers of antiquity, and, most importantly, with the gift of a rational, analytical, and empathetic mind, Barth can readily—and sanely—distinguish among a seemingly infinite number of architectural languages, ferreting out their significance in the aesthetic and ethnographic fields. In short, Barth knows the difference between a classical sepulcher trapped in desolation and a primitive dome. But domes are not primitive, and Barth himself is caught off guard, not having expected to find such things in Mousgoum country. And the *Mousgoum teleuk-as-dome* is a threat, a threat that runs the risk of flattening out, negating the difference, predicated on an evolutionary paradigm, between the memorial and the hut, between Europe and Africa, between the explorer and the natives.

Assuming that the Roman sepulcher and the primitive hut are two structures that rest in opposition to one another, their extreme difference would be embedded in and fortified by all the other differences that lie in similar structures. This difference would also mirror the explorer's access to language, through empathy and rationality, and his ability to represent that which he encounters. This is in sharp contrast to the indigenous people who, in their irrevocable instinctual state and their bondage to the land, are constructed as savages—noble and vicious—who, for our explorer, have neither the means nor the desire to even attempt to represent themselves.

As if to acknowledge the impossibility of the teleuk as a primitive structure and to illustrate his intense empathy with the house, Barth describes the dome as having been "calculated to create a great deal of interest" and "carefully executed." Furthermore, they "bore testimony to a degree of order and even of art." Such language directly opens up the possibility that the teleuk was a mirror, one that negated the differences obsessively delineated between civilization and savagery. And these operations occur precisely through Barth's empathetic streak. It is as if in his identification with the Mousgoum teleuk, he understands its tectonic language so thoroughly that it becomes no different from that of the sepulcher; that is, the language spoken and understood by the explorer seems not to need translation. It is as if Barth found his mother tongue in the Mousgoum teleuk.

The dome can be understood as a third component, one that has the ability to create a synthesis between two opposing items in such a manner that their differences are erased. The dome is a notion, an idea, a term that is part of both the sepulcher and the Mousgoum teleuk, and it envelops both of them. So the dome is primitive; yet it is still a dome. The form of the dome strengthens the nexus created between the houses of the dead and those of the living. In the rewriting of antiquity, the dome also represents the birth of cultures and their deaths. The two instances at once recall the complementarity of the discourses of the temple, the sepulcher and the primordial house. Like the dome, the temple traverses the gulf between the places of the living and the dead.

As a dome, the Mousgoum teleuk, like the sepulcher, immediately conjures up not only traces of a former population that was more evolved than its present inhabitants, but also mental potsherds of classical Antiquity and early Christian thought. E. Baldwin Smith, understanding the inextricable link between the dome and Christianity, insists that the architectural form is imbued with associations with ancient sepulchers and memorials to the dead. He also suggests that domes have a very complex history in parts of the ancient world.[23] As an archaeologist who had traveled in the Middle East, Asia Minor, and Northern Africa (including Egypt), Barth would have been intimately familiar with the associations made by Smith. He would also have been familiar with Roman and Hellenic Greek mortuary domes. In the encounter between Barth and the Mousgoum teleuk, the materials did not matter; moreover, the locations and makers made no difference.

Barth's descriptions of the Mousgoum teleuk and the sepulcher reveal how archaeology, architectural theory, and evolutionism meet in an intricate fashion. And in such a vein the explorer's description of the teleuk creates complex and at times paradoxical images. However, the negation of difference vis-à-vis the encounter is fleeting, for once the empathetic streak has run its course, the language that purports to paint a portrait of the teleuk in effect constitutes a self-portrait of the observer himself. The ability of the teleuk's "remarkable" and "peculiar" form to attract the European says little about the structure itself; it says much more about Barth's cultural evolution in particular and that of European civilization more generally. Barth further buttresses his position through the equation of the teleuk with order and art and the verbs used in the past tense. As he did the roofs of the Bornú huts, Barth situates the teleukakay in the past. They do not "bear," but "bore" their degree of order and art. In the past tense the teleukakay, like the sepulcher, are dead forms, signs of an extinct, formerly more evolved existence. Moreover, this past tense carries with it the implication that the teleukakay are objects that could no longer be built, hence robbing the Mousgoum of agency and further relegating them to a permanent past. The reader is left knowing that the European explorer can recognize art, order, and, by extension, civilization wherever he finds it.

However, finding civilization constitutes a projection, an otherworldly manifestation of Western obsessions and desires, and such a feat is accomplished, as Marianna Torgovnick has discussed, through the notion that art and aesthetics are requirements for a society to have culture or political integrity. Torgovnick insists that without such basic requirements, a society devoid of "culture" can then be discovered and developed by those who possess such things.[24] But the Mousgoum dome causes a problem, for *as dome* it can be discovered; however, as one of the paradigmatic and most revered architectural forms, it—like the sepulcher—cannot be developed. For Barth, this is already art, and it is orderly. Hence, it is not only civilized, but it is also a civilized form done well, for the presence of order (and this is not the same as symmetry) implies harmony; it assumes proper proportions; and it articulates a narrative that is pleasant to the explorer.

As part of the language of architectural description, a sense of order immediately recalls the human analogy in architecture. In 1741 John Wood the Elder, echoing others before him, insisted, "Order is that kind of appearance exhibited to the eye by any artificial object or figure, which by the regularity of its composition is pleasing, and answers to the various purposes for which it is made or intended . . . Man is a complete figure and the perfection of order."[25] Finding order is contingent upon finding in architecture not just a human body but a pleasing one. Through his empathy with the dome, Barth finds the body, and it is this body that is paramount in Barth's images of the enclosure.

Along with making detailed sketches of a Mousgoum teleuk and a plan of one that he mistook for a granary (figs. 22, 23), Barth also rendered two illustrations of populated Mousgoum enclosures, which, in the 1857 London edition of his travelogue were engraved in color by John Bernatz, the author of the beautifully engraved 1852 tome *Scenes in Ethiopia*. The first, which stands as the frontispiece to the third volume of the 1857 edition of Barth's text, depicts a Mousgoum chief in what we might assume is his family enclosure (fig. 24). Within the engraving, the chief—in a relaxed pose and leaning against his horse while holding a spear—immediately attracts the viewer's attention. One of his wives, who wears only earrings and a necklace, offers up food to the ruler. Another nude wife in the foreground sits on a calabash. Seemingly exhausted, her left arm supports

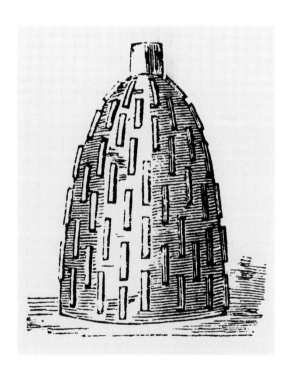

FIGURE 22. Mousgoum teleuk. Drawn by Heinrich Barth; engraved by John Martin Bernatz, c. 1857. Source: Barth, *Travels and Discoveries in North and Central Africa*, 1857.

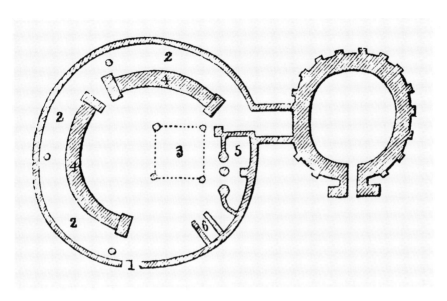

FIGURE 23. Mousgoum teleuk, plan. Drawn by Heinrich Barth; engraved by John Martin Bernatz, c. 1857. Source: Barth, *Travels and Discoveries in North and Central Africa*, 1857.

her head. In the color plate, she also wears a large white lip plug. In the middle ground, another wife pounds millet while two others rest. The engraving's one-point perspective leads the viewer directly to an area between the head of the chief and a teleuk that stands in the background. The viewer is then led to the structures of the enclosure itself and the activity—and its lack—of the wives. In looking at the architecture of the compound, the houses and a canopy work as the framing device that holds the engraving together. Working in tandem with one-point perspective, the buildings organize and control the way in which the viewer understands the image.

The second engraving, which accompanies the description of the Mousgoum ruin, portrays a domestic scene (fig. 25). The women are predominantly nude and busy at various domestic chores—cooking, food preparation, and making a net. The one on the left, like the seated wife in the engraving of the chief, wears large white lip plugs that attract the viewer's attention. Here again, architecture and one-point perspective serve as the framing device for this seemingly intimate and documentary view of private life. The emphasis on architecture is even stronger in this illustration than in the frontispiece: here, perspective and composition lead the viewer straight through the women and children to the dome. The life of the enclosure visually takes on a role that highlights the importance of the architecture.

In these two containers, Barth would seem to have made objective, documentarian representations. Gerald Needham suggests that the reality effect of prints was in large part fueled by the popularization of images of people, places,

FIGURE 24. Mousgoum chief. Drawn by Heinrich Barth; engraved by John Martin Bernatz, c. 1857. Source: Barth, *Travels and Discoveries in North and Central Africa*, 1857.

and things developed during the Enlightenment. Alongside this popularization, guides that taught would-be artists to make pictures of "real" and picturesque subjects were in vogue. Barth's work would have been understood in a similar fashion, constituting an example of how the real could be represented in woodcuts and engravings.[26] Made less than two decades after the invention of photography, Barth's engraving would have been interpreted as factual.

But what is fact? What is documentarian? Barth describes the Mousgoum enclosure as a place of death, as a ruin, yet the two engravings are pregnant with life. The traveler himself gives some insight on this apparent contradiction:

> [The houses] were exactly the same at each of the four corners; but the northeast corner of the yard claimed particular attention, owing to another very remarkable apartment being there joined to the granary, which, as it is best adapted to give a clear idea of the homely comfort of these people, however low the scale of their civilization may be, has been made use of to represent, in the plate opposite, a scene of the domestic life of these people, besides that its ground-plan is given in the accompanying wood-cut. (2: 414)

So the architectural ruin is the trace that allows Barth to envision what life may have been like in this instance. But if art and order are requisites of civilization, this link does not find a visual analogy in the domestic lives of these people. They may have been able to produce something extraordinary, but they are still barely civilized, an idea underscored by an attention given to architecture in the two scenes that is greater than that reserved for humans.

FIGURE 25. Mousgoum family enclosure. Drawn by Heinrich Barth; engraved by John Martin Bernatz, c. 1857. Source: Barth, *Travels and Discoveries in North and Central Africa*, 1857.

However, Barth's imagined domestic scenes are fictions, illustrating a world as he imagined it had been. By fabricating former lives in the ruin, he can articulate his own experience. He can control how his reader will perceive the fictitious inhabitants. These private scenes and the pose of the chief immediately bring back the oppositions and differences between the explorer and the locals. In these scenes, architecture is inscribed with the image of the explorer. Carefully defined, off in the background but ever present, Barth announces his presence through the dome, the detailed form, the one form in the tableaux that can be interpreted as civilized. The image of the Mousgoum chief contained by the architecture further announces the center of the eye/I that is Barth. Moreover, this image sets up images of otherness and peculiarity for the reader, further highlighting the realness of the text in the reader's mind.[27]

But this is not where the story ends. Throughout the encounter between Barth and the Mousgoum, difference pivots around sublimation and desublimation, and in this scenario, in this transcription, there is a playing out of the relationship between the ego and society that relies on the projection of the self onto the other, a playing out that takes place within the shock of difference, the explosion of contradiction, and the attempt to make sense out of the indecipherable. It is in the moment in which Barth comes upon that which he had not expected to find among such tribes, that moment in which the explorer is stopped in his tracks, as it were, that is the location of the near-collapse of nature and history as well as the near-collision of Mousgoum architecture and Barth's body. While the domes are remarkable, their order promotes an empathetic response that gives way to desublimation through the enactment of empathy itself, and this is followed by an almost immediate revulsion and resublimation of those things engendered by Barth's architectonic others. The Mousgoum teleuk constitutes the return of the repressed.

Death pervades the relationship between the ego and civilization for Barth. To turn back to the image of the Mousgoum chief, we know that what is illustrated is dead, as it were. Barth has, in effect, animated a tomb. But the activities that involve the living dead concern the making of food: that which would prolong life, and the wife, who holds a bowl of food up to her breast, emphasizes such activities. In such a scenario, tomb doubles as womb. And in this operation, the analogy between architecture and the body would effectively mark the teleukakay in the scene as representations of the female breast. For Freud, the landscape and the hearth are symbols for the female breast, and the projections of a house can also refer to the holding of well-developed breasts.[28] In this particular scenario, given the connection of the houses to the hearth and to the landscape, the teleukakay represent the breast and the holding of them. This womb/tomb conflates the languages of life and death, showing the constant presence of death in life, and it illustrates what Hal Foster, in the context of the surrealists and the uncanny, has called, "the inertia of life, the dominance of death."[29]

In these doublings, the conflations between nature and history and the bodies of the explorer and the African woman vis-à-vis the transcription of the two in the teleuk is evocative of a primal scene that constantly renders unstable the borders between self and other, nature and culture, life and death. In all the paradoxes that run through the encounter between Barth and the Mousgoum teleuk, meaning threatens to go crazy as the contradictions in the construction of these paradigmatic and ingrained categories come dangerously close to collapse.

Olive MacLeod and the Validation of Experience

By first decades of the twentieth century, Mousgoum architecture had become known throughout Europe, drawing travelers from England, France, and Germany. One such visitor was Olive MacLeod, whose account of her African journey was published in 1912. In the six decades that had passed since Barth's encounter with the Mousgoum, the world had become a vastly different place. European interests in Africa were no longer purely economic or moral, and the African continent had become an indispensable—if only psychologically—part of European imperialism; moreover, by this time most of the earth had been partitioned by a small number of sovereign, "developed" countries (not only European nations but also the United States and Japan), falling under either formal rule or informal political dominance. By 1910, the year MacLeod set out on her journey, Great Britain had amassed a large portion of the African continent, and sub-Saharan Africa was becoming increasingly popular in the public realm.

Curiosity and a thirst for knowledge about Africa during the second half of the nineteenth and early twentieth centuries had grown exponentially, so much so that by 1890, Joseph Thomson, a missionary who had worked in sub-Saharan Africa, insisted:

> One of the most remarkable features of this century has been the phenomenal interest displayed in all things African. One dramatic tale has followed another, and each new tale has seemed more romantic than anything heard before. The popular imagination has been touched by the varied story of the Dark Continent to an unprecedented extent. It has been a story which has appealed in trumpet tones to the philanthropist as well as the mere lover of adventure, to the merchant as well as to the geographer, and to the Christian missionary eager for the spread of Christ's Kingdom as well as to the patriotic politician anxious for his nation's aggrandizement.[30]

Africa had a place in the public imagination in a number of intersecting contexts. Besides highly celebrated expeditions, popular exhibitions, and European colonial aspirations, fiction such as Karl May's boy's novels, Jules Verne's 1863 *Five Weeks in a Balloon*, and perhaps most importantly Conrad's 1902 novella *Heart of Darkness* further emphasized the position of Africa as a place of fantasy and a geographic repository of the strange, exotic, and unknown.

There was other popular nonfiction published through which one could learn about Africa. In 1911, while MacLeod was off in the wilds of Africa, H. H. Johnston, who had held colonial titles all over British Africa, published his book, *The Opening Up of Africa*. Although it was another addition to a long series of books about Africa, Africans, and blacks in the New World, this particular text stands out, for it was part of a series called the Home University Library of Modern Knowledge. The books in this series were produced for easy reading and mass consumption, a fact underscored by the text's almost simultaneous publication in London, Toronto, New York, and India. This pocket-sized volume was, in effect, the greatest hits of Africa and is an excellent example of one of the ways in which the African continent was served up in digestible fashion at the time of MacLeod's trip. After brief chapters dealing with "Prehistoric Africa," as well as Greeks, Romans, and Muslims on the continent, the author gives a schematic overview—one very brief chapter—of the Fula, Songhay, and Bantu peoples. The rest of the book, or more accurately, its final seven chapters (there are fourteen in all) give an account of how Europeans have "opened up" Africa and the benefits that had been and would continue to be reaped from such feats.

These various strands resulted in a rapid increase in travel to sub-Saharan Africa, a factor that in some ways changed popular perceptions of African voyages. While our traveler was in the bush, the British citizen or colonial subject could learn that, in Johnston's words, "since 1885 African discovery has proceeded at a rate so astonishing that there is nothing comparable to it in the history of human civilization." Along with the knowledge gained through travel, the reader would then be awed by the dangers of Africa, but also relieved to find that European ingenuity had resulted in the introduction of new tools to combat disease, wild beasts and vicious natives, some of whom were "separated from [European] culture by fifty thousand years."[31] While danger and inconvenience were still part and parcel of African travel, one reviewer of MacLeod's travelogue, entitled *Chiefs and Cities of Central Africa*, explains that "within the past few years the safety of travel in the interior of Africa has so enormously increased that feats are now possible to a determined woman which a generation ago would have entailed certain and speedy destruction." For this particular reviewer, so many women had recently traveled to sub-Saharan Africa that the phenomenon "[ceased] to astonish."[32] Yet such a claim is belied by the fact that not a single published article about MacLeod's journey fails express surprise that she had gone where no white woman had gone before.

Although her journey was overshadowed by Mary Kingsley's three African voyages during the 1890s, MacLeod wrote an impressive chronicle of her African voyage, a voyage that covered over 3,700 miles in six months. However, what captured the public's attention at the time was not her exploits in Africa but her reason for going in the first place. As a source of lore and fascination, MacLeod's story dovetailed nicely with public fantasy. MacLeod's fiancé, the well-known explorer Boyd Alexander, had made two expeditions through West and Central Africa during the first decade of the twentieth century. However, on his second, in 1910, he was murdered in northern Nigeria. He was buried there. Grief-stricken, MacLeod, who had hesitated to accept Boyd's proposal of marriage until he was about to leave on his fatal African sojourn, decided to set off to Maidugari, Nigeria, to set a cross on her lover's grave. P. Amaury Talbot, a colonial official based in Nigeria and an ethnologist who was with Alexander on part of his first expedition, offered to accompany her. Talbot's wife Dory, also an ethnologist, joined the team as well.

This trip, this romantic drama, was well publicized in the press, which wrote melodramatic headlines such as "Come Bid Me Farewell in My Lonely Grave" and "Sweetheart's Pilgrimage."[33] As in the cases of travelers before her, the media would publish reports that MacLeod was dead only to correct them later. On February 27, 1911, the *London Times* reported that rumors concerning MacLeod's demise at the hands of natives while on her pilgrimage to the interior of Africa, a place "which had never been penetrated by a white woman," were groundless.[34] The paper also noted her safe return to Plymouth, where she was met by her father and sister.[35]

Besides the explosion of interest in and fascination with Africa, the decades between the journeys of Barth and MacLeod were a period in which the West ushered in a new way of seeing the world. Travelogues, once illustrated exclusively by engravings, woodcuts, and lithographs, now used photography as a means to "document" people, places, and things abroad. Alongside this development was a burgeoning marketplace for picture postcards of non-European places, a phenomenon that is crucial to the understanding of the early twentieth-century travelogue. The proliferation of exotic scenes—ethnic and racial types, architecture, animals, and landscape—played an important role in establishing an aesthetic of the faraway that has innate connections to travel photography. And these inexpensive items made exotic imagery more accessible than ever before.[36] Travel photography was championed by the Royal Geographic Society, which, in its book entitled *Hints to Travellers*, advised, "The photographic camera should form an essential part of the traveller's outfit, as it affords the only trustworthy means of obtaining pictorial records of his journey, and it is also helpful in making the survey of a new region, delineating its contours, its geological and botanical features, and ethnographical types of race."[37] These images, the use of photographs in illustrated magazines and newspapers, and the proliferation of photographs in Europe more generally fostered a changed standard in the depiction of the "real." No longer was the woodcut, engraving, or lithograph the visual form of fact (although it could be seen as a form of "reportage") that it had been during the mid-nineteenth century. MacLeod would make good use of photography in her text, combining it with drawings by Dory Talbot to articulate what she saw on her travels in Africa.

MacLeod's travelogue, while full of information about the places where no white woman had ever been, was, by her own admission, a subjective account of her experiences abroad. However, she does not relate the romantic story that propelled her to go to Africa. She instead refers to the dangers of her decision, informing her readers that a shopman in Liverpool gave her "the last touch of sentiment" without which "no expedition is complete." She continues, "the shopman begged me to turn back, even at this eleventh hour, from the dangers of West Africa, where, he assured me, I should almost certainly lose my life."[38] At various points, MacLeod and her companions are faced with potential danger, ranging from the desire of Africans to take the white women to poisonous reptiles threatening to bite them.

If it is true that MacLeod went to Africa with the quixotic notion to place a cross on her lover's grave, then why did she write this particular type of account? One might expect that if she had written anything, it would have been a memoir or journal of the experience. Joan Alexander, who wrote about her ancestor Boyd Alexander, cites a letter MacLeod sent to the deceased explorer's brother Herbert in which she explains, "I am going to try and write an account of my journey . . . I want to write it for two reasons—first that the public may realize it was a sensible journey, for the papers have made it appear that Boyd was engaged to a sentimental ass—secondly to repay father the additional money that the lengthened journey cost."[39] What is so critical here is not so much MacLeod's desire to repay her father for the cost of the trip, but her need to have the British public, which in her mind was all too willing to believe that she was a pathetic fool for love, deem instead that she was a reasonable and sentient human being, and that her journey had intellectual, scientific value. Even though this letter was written after her return to England, her collection of plants and artifacts and her donation of the latter to the British Museum show that the desire to validate her journey was at the forefront of her mind while she was away.

But the relationship between the woman traveler and the need for validation was not only MacLeod's issue; other female travelers shared it. Moreover, these travelers routinely apologized for what they and male readers saw as their "feminine weaknesses." In the preface to her own 1897 travelogue titled *Travels in West Africa*, Mary Kingsley beseeched her readers to "make allowances for [her] love of this sort of country, with its great forests and rivers and its animistic-minded inhabitants."[40] Besides such statements, between sexism and ingrained myths of savage blacks, MacLeod was constantly aware of being a white woman in a place where no white women had ever gone, and for her it was perilous: at times she was trapped by the gaze of Africans; at others, she was convinced that black chiefs wanted to abduct her and Dory Talbot. At still others, she showed deference to her male companions, thankful that they did not throw her sex in her face.

Gender, in large part, structures the ways in which MacLeod perceives the world, and this point vividly emerges not only in her consistent references concerning how others perceive her, but also in the attention she gives to women in her travelogue. In many places, she and Dory Talbot visited African women, trying to learn something about them. Such concerns were rarely deemed either important by or particularly relevant to male travelers. MacLeod's passages on women (like her passages more generally) are at times extraordinarily rich, at other times mundane, and at others neurotic (of course, no more neurotic than those of her male counterparts). While visiting Mousgoum country in late 1910, MacLeod and Dory Talbot visited a number of teleukakay: Dory Talbot made sketches of various items; MacLeod made photographs and wrote descriptions of what she saw.

Once in Musgum, which MacLeod notes is "famous for its beauty," the teleukakay and the Mousgoum become a canvas upon which many of the traveler's perceptions and unconscious fears would be played out. Here, in this lovely village, MacLeod explains, "Tall, picturesque houses tapered upwards, and women and children peeped out from behind them, or gathered in enclosures to gaze at us strangers" (111). Throughout her journey, while MacLeod sees, she is seen seeing. Given that in this particular instance women and children observe MacLeod, was she trapped by what we could call a "native gaze"? Yes and no. MacLeod is under intense scrutiny—as a white person; particularly as a white woman—throughout her travels in Africa, and she is utterly aware of this fact. Staying with the Moundang people in northern Cameroon, she complains, "The

Lamido came first, when Mrs. Talbot and I were still engaged in dodging out of sight of the roof-gazers as we performed our toilettes" (46).

In the case of the toilette, the women, if only phantasmically, are captured by an African male gaze; however, in the case of the Mousgoum women and children, there is no such discomfort. But these two situations underscore MacLeod's difference, highlighting her whiteness and her femininity. Always traveling through areas that had never been penetrated by white women, their being seen further emphasizes their novelty, their white privilege, and their self-importance. That said, this is not the operation that Barth exhibits in his encounters. He is sure of his privilege and of the perception that his is an authorial voice. For MacLeod, however, the highlighting of her own importance is aimed at convincing her reader, as well as herself, that her voice is significant, and that it should be heard.

But this gaze also subtly operates in a similar fashion to that in the panopticon. Joan Copjec, following Michel Foucault, insists that this gaze is intricately related to how the subject is produced in various socially constructed categories of knowledge.[41] In this situation then, for MacLeod, her visibility, her *being there,* defines her subjectivity with respect to Great Britain—produced by the white men of different nationalities—as well as her subjectivity as a white woman in Africa—produced not by the things she sees, but by the ways in which she is seen. But if the panoptic gaze is one of the ways through which MacLeod constructs her own subjectivity, the relationship between the traveler and the Mousgoum exposes the possibility that this construction is perhaps not as solid as it may appear. Within these glances, the boundary between the civilized self and the savage other is called into question, but MacLeod, by putting the spotlight on herself and her actions, allows them not to completely collapse.

Armed with camera, pen, and paper, the white women start to draw, photograph, and describe the Mousgoum. On first sight, MacLeod writes,

> for the first time we saw the 30-feet high conical buildings, with rough-ribbed ornamentation, which we were to find in their perfection at Musgum. They were interspersed with palm-trees, and it seemed as if the aesthetic sense of the people had prompted them to adapt their tall narrow architecture to nature. (105)

While MacLeod's textual description of the teleuk's exterior lacks detail, the visual imagery produced in Musgum provides a striking pictorial account of the house. For MacLeod, these structures are the product of people with, by her own admission, an aesthetic sense, and that sense would imply that they possessed at least a modicum of rational thought. Indeed, it is at least enough for them to consciously adapt their houses to nature and make them beautiful. Like Barth, MacLeod was taken aback by the sophistication of the teleukakay, exclaiming

FIGURE 26. Ruined Mousgoum teleuk. Photographer: Olive MacLeod, 1910.
Source: MacLeod, *Chiefs and Cities of Central Africa*, 1912.

at Musgum, "One hut had become a ruin, but half the shell still stood, and we wondered at the skill that had achieved a perfect dome of thirty feet out of thin mud alone" (112). Like Barth, MacLeod's attraction to and empathy for the house results in her view of the Mousgoum as a people with an aesthetic sense and an appreciation for beauty, attributes that would imply that they are not so distant from the traveler as it would appear on the surface of things. However, while she talks of the pleasant nature of the house, and the aesthetic sense of the people who build and live in them, her published photographs of the structure show the house as a ruined, uninhabitable shell (fig. 26). In this move the distance that threatens to close in between these Africans, people with an aesthetic sense, and MacLeod is reinstated.

But the Mousgoum house photographed by MacLeod is not simply the remains of what had been, it is also a means through which MacLeod, as a woman, strives to be taken seriously. The same reviewer who stressed that it was becoming more and more common for women to travel to Africa insisted in the same paragraph that "it cannot be said that any piece of actual exploration of the first importance has yet been accomplished by a woman." He later concludes that women travelers "must rely for readers upon the intrinsic merit of her observations rather than on her mere sex should she decide to publish an account of her travels." Ultimately, what this one reviewer articulates finds reverberations in pleas by women travelers to the readers of their texts to turn a blind eye to their female subjectivity, and our reviewer, acknowledging such a request, decides not to wield such a weapon at MacLeod's volume. In his opinion readers were "disarmed not only by the preface, but by the unaffected naïveté with which the story is told."[42] Another reviewer found MacLeod's book to be a "beautifully-produced volume [which] is a pleasant and chatty record of a very interesting journey."[43] In her own text, MacLeod describes a meeting with Chief Abbiga, during which he "appeared really interested in Mr. Talbot's projects," but "Mrs. Talbot and I counted for nothing at all" (10).

With respect to Victorian attitudes around women travelers and explorers, these calls for tolerance and pleas to be taken seriously are not surprising. Male travelers routinely were seen as brave, intrepid, and important to the British imperial project; female travelers routinely were seen as pathetic, odd, and of little use to the empire.[44] Under such circumstances, it would stand to reason that a woman traveler might feel the need to find some means to support and validate the intellectual acuity and importance of her own observations. Upon her return to England, MacLeod sent her photographs of the Mousgoum teleuk to Percy Waldram, a well-known structural engineer. Fascinated with the domed building, Waldram made two drawings based on MacLeod's photographs and published them in his book *The Principles of Structural Mechanics*, which appeared in 1912, the same year as MacLeod's travelogue (fig. 27). For Waldram, the teleukakay were amazing on technical grounds:

Very striking evidence of the stability of extremely thin domes when constructed to the same curve as the line of thrusts is also to be found in the mud huts of the Central African natives. The author is indebted to the publishers of Miss Olive Macleod's book, " Across Lake Chad ", * and to that lady, for permission to make use of the illustrations, Figs. 202 and 203, taken by her at Musqum in the German Kameruns. These remarkable

FIG. 202.

examples of traditional structural skill are circular huts about 20 ft. diameter and 30 ft. high, built, without centering, of mud which sets hard in the sun. The shells are so thin as to appear to be almost a structural absurdity : but it should be noted that they are formed to almost perfect parabolic curves, which eliminate all hoop tensions due to the weight of the material. Also they are most ingeniously ribbed on the outside in a manner which

* " Across Lake Chad through British, French, and German Territories ", published by Wm. Blackwood, George Street, Edinburgh.

not only forms a convenient ladder for bare feet, but which also serves to strengthen, as well as to protect, the shell against local injury.

The foregoing theory is, strictly speaking, applicable only to thin shell domes. In thick domes numerous and complicated secondary stresses occur. The dominating fact is that for any given radius, any increase in the thickness beyond which is

FIG. 203.

necessary to carry external loads does not increase the strength at all, the stresses per square inch remain the same.

To go on adding material, whether in a dome or girder, after enough has been provided to do the work, is not only expensive, it is dangerous, because of the added load on the bearings. A segmental or saucer dome supporting its own weight is a most particularly strong form of construction, and the complete hemispherical dome is nearly as strong, unless stone lanterns or heavy

FIGURE 27. Page layout from Percy Waldram, *Principles of Structural Mechanics*, with drawings after MacLeod, 1912.

The author is indebted to the publishers of Miss Olive MacLeod's book, 'Across Lake Chad' . . . and to that lady, for permission to make use of the illustrations . . . taken by her in Musqum [sic] in the German Kameruns. These remarkable examples of traditional structural skill are circular huts about 20 ft. diameter and 30 ft. high, built, without centering, of mud which sets hard in the sun. The shells are so thin as to appear to be almost a structural absurdity: but it should be noted that they are formed to almost perfect parabolic curves, which eliminate all hoop tensions due to the weight of the material. Also they are most ingeniously ribbed on the outside in a manner which not only forms a convenient ladder for bare feet, but which also serves to strengthen, as well as to protect, the shell against local injury.[45]

Waldram's publicly stated admiration for the technical sophistication of the teleuk validates MacLeod's sight. She, a woman traveler, realized how important and unique—on a technical level—the Mousgoum home was, and Waldram confirmed her instincts and observations. Through Waldram's validation, MacLeod thus battles her internalized marginalization as a women traveling in Africa. Through Waldram's validation, MacLeod can demonstrate that a woman traveler is also capable of objectivity in her endeavor. His words therefore allow her to show and to prove her own intellectual prowess to her readers.

To emphasize the importance of her findings and intellectual acuity, MacLeod describes Waldram's response to her photographs in her own text, directly quoting a letter, one steeped in the jargon of engineering, he wrote to her. Waldram writes, "These huts form the most striking example which I have yet discovered of the true theoretical form in thin dome construction, containing minimum thickness with maximum strength. The external ribbing, apparently only ornamental, is also excellently designed to minimize the risk of local injury as distinct from general failure" (112). MacLeod's inclusion of Waldram's letter is her way of showing her readers that she herself is possessed of the rational sense that enables her to make important (and impressive) observations. MacLeod may not be well educated in engineering, but she can recognize extraordinary technological achievements when she sees them.

There is one aspect of Waldram's drawings and descriptions that finds a close analogy with MacLeod's experience in Musgum. The traveler and engineer extol the teleuk, using terms such as "perfect," yet the two have chosen to publish images of a ruined house. For MacLeod, the choice of publishing a ruined teleuk may well have been a way to illustrate the thinness of the structure's wall photographically, further highlighting the dome's curious nature and structural excellence, but for Waldram, who used the same picture as his template, one wonders why he did not simply draft a cross-section of the dome, especially given that the cross-section is a standard form of illustration in his field. Hence, while these are remarkable domes that exhibit an almost perfectly parabolic curve, the drawings, which are placed side by side in his book, give a before-and-after effect; that is, the illustrations project the notion that the domes, as remarkable as they appear to be, are an absurdity (echoing the two texts). The two drawings give an impression of an anomalous, unstable, and perhaps even impossible structure. The appropriation of the ruin suggests the inability of the Westerners to admit that something non-Western could compare in sophistication or skill to that which one might see in Europe or North America. The domes may be "perfect," but they fall down, not only alluding not only to their weakness as structures, but also reestablishing a binary between the Mousgoum and the Europeans that the latter's engagement with the teleuk threatens to extinguish. Moreover, the ruined domes emphasize the permanently underlying specter of death in the African wilds.

MacLeod's photograph of the ruined hut and her other images of architecture in this context flirt with the same paradoxes as Waldram's explanation. The technologically sophisticated yet ruined dome is not really civilized. This notion is amplified by entering the house, where, MacLeod insists, the "ornamentation shows a curious decadence from that found in the neighboring villages" (112). The "perfect" outside, combined with the decadent inside, illustrates uncivilized people who are in even further decline. If the teleukakay are beautiful and technologically sophisticated and display a Mousgoum sense of aesthetics, the Mousgoum people themselves for the traveler can only add to the surprise MacLeod experiences at seeing the domes on the Logone. The contrast between exterior perfection and interior decadence, moreover, implies that for the traveler, the Mousgoum people, at least the residents of this particular village, are not cognizant of the technological (and aesthetic) perfection of the exteriors of their teleukakay.

Besides the striking photograph of the ruined house, MacLeod, like many other Europeans had done, made an ethnographic portrait of a woman wearing lip plugs (fig. 28). This photograph depicts a Mousgoum woman with large plugs, who is framed by portions of two teleukakay. As if to emphasize the two round plugs, the woman, who would by all accounts normally be nude (save for her *cache-sexe*), is covered by a cloth. One of her children stands next to her; a man stands behind. The viewer is focused on the plugs, a factor that is only reinforced by the picture's composition and absence of nudity. Unlike the majority of her male counterparts, MacLeod chose in the staging of her photographs to follow Victorian decorum (even though images of nude African women would not, at this time, have violated such paradigms). Where a male photographer might have been content to make pictures of nude African woman—and the vast proliferation of such images by men attests to such contentment—MacLeod dressed her subjects. Such a choice foregrounds the way that gender structured the traveler's encounters with Mousgoum people.

FIGURE 28. Mousgoum woman with lip plugs. Photographer: Olive MacLeod, 1910. Source: MacLeod, *Chiefs and Cities of Central Africa*, 1912.

MacLeod writes at length about lip plugs, and she was simultaneously drawn to and repelled by the sight of them. She is perversely fascinated by them. She neurotically explains:

[Dixon] Denham, in his journey of 1822–24, saw a Musgu woman in Bornu, and commented on the plug she wore in her lip, the size of a shilling, to make room for which her front teeth had been taken out. Since then the barbarism has increased, and women now wear plugs nearly three inches in diameter.

As little girls, between eight and ten, the outer skin of their lips is slit open, and light metal disks, approximately circular, with rounded groove encircling the rim,—like the rim of a bicycle wheel,—are inserted between it and the flesh. This is done both in the upper and lower lips, and often in the lobe of the ear as well. Their size is gradually increased, and the women learn to use them as a sort of sounding board, over which they clutter their tongues in terrible shrill wails that curdle the blood. Pronunciation is so distorted that their own people often find it hard to understand what is said, and, most disgustingly of all, a steady stream of saliva dribbles from the unclosed mouths.

We hardened our hearts, and in the interests of science offered to buy some spare disks, and immediately one woman after another took these grisly objects from her lips, leaving visible a gaping fissure and a loosely hanging half-wheel of skin.

We could bear no more, and turned to go with our eau-de-Cologne bedrenched handkerchiefs held tightly to our noses, so that they might conceal an expression of disgust we did not care to show. (115–16)

MacLeod also photographed the interior of a teleuk, focusing on the doorway and the *hono* (network of shelving) above it (see fig. 19). Two Mousgoum people stand to the left of the opening. As a reflection of the body, the attention to the teleuk, its interior doorway and the mouths and lip plates of Mousgoum woman point to a subconscious relationship between architecture and the female body for MacLeod. Through this connection, the binary oppositions she would like to keep in place threaten to collapse.

There is another link that binds the teleuk to the female body for MacLeod, and it is one that is far more complex than merely being the equation of the house and the female breast. What we see in MacLeod's long excursus on the lip plugs is a woman who is bordering on an obsession with them, and it is this obsession—based in the deformation of the body and thinly masked by the plugs' importance to "science"—that leads her into a discussion of her disgust with the practice and its results: not only the body's deformation, but also, and as importantly, the blockage of language. Given MacLeod's concern with her own voice, that is, her fear that she will not be taken seriously as a female traveler, her attention to Mousgoum lip plugs and the literal blockage of language for those who wear them constitutes a transference of her own anxiety as a woman who feels silenced by men both European and African. Her attention marks a significant moment, one in which the Mousgoum woman, whose lip plugs rob her of clear speech, stands as a metaphor for MacLeod's own state: a woman who sees her male peers and a British public that thinks her a fool as elements that would silence her.

Just as important, however, is what she perhaps sees as the worst consequence of all—steadily dribbling streams of saliva, which in tandem with the plugs and skin and fissures, further makes the mutilated female mouth disgusting. The attention to the mouths of Mousgoum women and the concurrent issues it raises constitute a wonderful example of what I would like to call the ethnographic *informe*. These deformed faces, dribbling saliva, missing teeth, and nearly decimated language, signal in MacLeod's text the uncanny, the return of the repressed. The metaphors of the body also suggest the fleeting nature of rationality, the tenuous nature of identity that is always an integral part of the primal scene. To think of this as the ethnographic *informe* involves the acknowledgment of an unconscious attraction to bodily deformation and decomposition on the part of MacLeod that is not unlike the explicit, obsessive attention given to the same issues by Georges Bataille and the surrealists. Although decorporealization and human decomposition haunt MacLeod (and countless other travelers and novelists), they titillated the surrealists and served as "ethnographic data" for them.

The mouth as well as saliva, orifice as well as bodily fluid are potent data in surrealist paradigms. In the surrealist journal *Documents*, both the mouth and saliva become objects that are to be analyzed, demystified, and remystified. Marcel Griaule's saliva was not unlike Plato's pharmakon; more than merely the product of a gland, it could either help or hurt. He goes as far as to insist that saliva, which to the anthropologist is "balsam or dirt," constitutes "the soul in motion."[46] For Michel Leiris, saliva is the water of the mouth, and, not unlike MacLeod's response to the drooling of Mousgoum women, he finds that it is repugnant, repellent. However, the revolting ejaculation of saliva also has erotic overtones; hence, not unlike a car wreck, it is also strangely and unconsciously attractive. In its unstable nature, in its lack of structure, Leiris insists that saliva is the symbol of the *informe*.[47] It cannot be quantified. It has no opposition. It resists definition. And in its formlessness, saliva, or spit, represents the return of the repressed. In Africa, in the travel account, spit can wreak havoc, it can disintegrate the boundary between nature and culture, between civilization and savagery, between self and other.[48]

Bataille offered a definition of the mouth in 1930 accompanied by Boiffard's photograph of a mouth that stretches itself open. The caption beneath reads, "Heinous terror and suffering make the mouth the organ of agonizing cries" (fig. 29). In the definition itself, Bataille explains that the terror signified by the mouth is ever present in the Western mind, but unlike in "primitive" cultures, this violent signification is repressed, lurking beneath the surface. The mouth also calls up the possibility that the repressed can be desublimated and, for Bataille, this violent threat refers to other operations and objects commonly linked to the state of the *informe*, most notably constipation and feces.[49] Again, this further doubling underscores the organ's primacy and its position as a metaphor of female genitalia and the anus, ultimately signifying the uncanny in its manifestation through the return of the repressed.

The dribbling streams of saliva that emanate from the mouths of these Mousgoum women, however, are no balsam for MacLeod. They are emblematic of the dirt and putrefaction that surround the beautiful village of Musgum. They are also metaphors for the decadence of the teleuk's interior. On the heels of her lip plug horror, MacLeod complains:

> It was fortunate we still had a bottle of eau-de-Cologne, and we carried it with us, for, besides being the loveliest, Musgum is also the dirtiest city one can imagine. It has never occurred to its inhabitants to use the river as a drain, and the stench that everywhere permeates the air is unutterably nauseating. In spite of our precautions, we were all more or less actively the worse for our visit. (116)

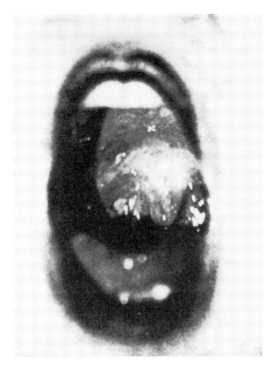

FIGURE 29. Jacques-André Boiffard, photograph.
Published in *Documents* 2, no. 5 (1930).

This dirt, dirt that cannot be seen but only smelled, also undermines the perfection of the teleuk, for beauty coexists with dirt, hence thwarting the traveler's minimal expectations of civilization, which, as Freud explains, are cleanliness, beauty, and order.[50] The teleukakay are beautiful, but like everyone and everything in the village they are dirty, and they are again compromised structures. As such, the Mousgoum can be cast by the traveler as people without the minimal expectations of civilization.

The way in which the structure becomes further compromised is through analogy to the female mouth as vessel of filth. That is to say that the lip plates of the women are the issue that propels the traveler to register her discomfort not only with the women themselves, but the teleuk as well. However, unlike the women, hygiene places the teleuk into an abyss where the boundary between civilization and nature becomes unstable. Along similar lines, Mary Douglas asserts that dirt is order's offending other.[51] The perfection of the teleuk and its beauty would suggest that they are well ordered, if surprising, structures. They are even more surprising in this place of disorder, a metaphor for those who cannot sublimate their instinctual natures. But ultimately, in the encounter between MacLeod and the teleuk, the traveler can come to voice, she can construct herself as a rational and serious traveler, she can show the reader her expertise—via Waldram's validation—, and she can project her fear of the disorderly within the orderly, here encased in a layer of dirt that is unseeable, but highly noxious.

André Gide and the Impossibility of Forgetfulness

André Gide and his protégé Marc Allégret left France for Africa in July 1925, just seven years after World War I and during the period commonly understood as the apex of European colonization in Africa. Although traveling in a semiofficial capacity for the French Colonial Ministry, the author claimed that he and his companion were traveling "for pleasure."[52] Gide was fulfilling a desire he had harbored for over thirty years—to make the journey to the Congo (4). It was during this journey that Gide wrote what has become the most famous and most often quoted passage on the Mousgoum teleuk:

> I am astonished that the few rare travellers who have spoken of this country and of its villages and huts have only thought fit to mention their "strangeness." The [Mousgoum] hut, it is true, resembles no other; but it is not only strange, it is *beautiful*; and it is not its strangeness so much as its beauty that moves me. A beauty so perfect, so accomplished, that it seems natural. No ornament, no superfluity. The pure curve of its line, which is uninterrupted from base to summit, seems to have been arrived at mathematically, by ineluctable necessity; one instinctively realizes how exactly the resistance of the materials must have been calculated. A little farther north or south and the clay would have been too much mixed with sand to allow of this easy spring, terminating in the circular opening that alone gives light to the inside of the hut, in the manner of Agrippa's Pantheon. On the outside a number of regular flutings give life and accent to these geometrical forms and afford a foothold by which the summit of the hut (often twenty to twenty-five feet high) can be reached; they enabled it to be built without the aid of scaffolding; this hut is made by hand like a vase; it is the work, not of a mason, but of a potter. Its colour is the very colour of the earth—a pinkish-grey clay, like the clay of which the old walls of Biskra are made. (emphasis in original) (217–18)

Gide's beautifully written passage, one of the most outstanding in his *Voyage au Congo: suivi de retour du Tchad*, is also beautifully complex in its language and significance. His description of the Mousgoum teleuk also invites a host of questions that lay at the heart of this inquiry: What role does the teleuk in particular and architecture more generally play in Gide's voyage? How are race and gender implicated in Gide's notions of Mousgoum architecture? How are such notions articulated in the traveler's experience with the teleuk? How does this journey affect how we understand the aesthetics of the teleuk? What role does the teleuk

PLATE 1. Model of a Mousgoum teleuk, Expo 2005, Aichi Prefecture, Japan, September 14, 2005.

PLATE 2. Palace of Lamido Mbang Yaya Oumar, Pouss, built c. 1911, photographed April 21, 1996.

PLATE 3. Teleuk built by Mme. Djaoro Bara Abourgadaï, Mourlà, Cameroon, photographed
February 25, 1996.

PLATE 4. International Exposition. Source: *L'Illustration*, no. 4616, August 22, 1931.

PLATE 5. Teleuk built by Apaïdi Toulouk, Mourlà, Cameroon, 1995.

PLATE 6. Mme. Mal Idrissa, wall mural, Pouss, 1995.

PLATE 7. Mousgoum fantasia, Pouss, photographed April 26, 1996.

PLATE 8. Mousgoum Cultural and Tourist Center, Pouss, 1995.

PLATE 9. Mme. Daniel Mainiazanga, wall mural, detail, Pouss, 1995.

play in the construction of modernism and modernity in 1920s France, and what does this journey have to do with it?

As was the case at the times of Barth and MacLeod's journeys to Africa, in many Western minds, to make a similar voyage during the 1920s was still to do something dangerous, something extraordinary. (Many hold similar views even today.) While French Africa was well established as part of the French colonial dominion, the region—particularly French Equatorial Africa—continued to be constructed as a place that was shrouded in darkness, full of peril. Gide echoes such views in *Voyage au Congo*. One of the book's many reviewers wrote:

> Not by the wildest stretch of the imagination is it possible for the average man to think of himself as embarking on such an expedition. Tropical Africa, wild beasts and at best half-wild blacks, poisonous reptiles, sickness-breeding flies—the picture is so repellent in its details that the thought of the vast majestic beauty of the jungle, the romance of the idea of setting foot where few white feet have trod, are not sufficiently powerful to lure the curious.[53]

The combination of peril and beauty, of danger and exoticism was what lured Gide to Africa. He was fascinated by the strange, the exotic. As he writes in his 1927 *Journal of the Counterfeiters*, "I am not drawn toward what resembles me, but towards what differs from me."[54] *Voyage au Congo*—part travelogue, part journal, and part documentation of colonial abuses in the areas he visited—chronicles one of the author's numerous elongated immersions into difference.

Like many nineteenth- and early twentieth-century travelogues *Voyage au Congo* was enormously popular with mass audiences. Between 1927 and 1929, at least three editions had been printed in France; moreover, the book was available on both sides of the Atlantic. There were also excerpts from the book and photographic essays of the journey in periodicals throughout Western Europe. Within these articles, the Mousgoum teleuk was often the featured exotic tidbit.[55] The widespread exposure given to the teleuk—commodified as the product of Gide and Allégret's "cottage industry"—would have undoubtedly cemented it in the Western psyche as an icon of the exotic and the strange.

What does it mean to consider Gide's relationship to the exotic and the strange? What is it that Gide hoped to find through immersing himself in that which was "not himself"? At the beginning of his journey he wrote, "Everything here seems to promise happiness, ease, forgetfulness" (6). Gide would spend over a year looking for the fulfillment of such a promise. Forgetting himself, however, was not only the traveler's wish in Africa; it was also his wish in writing. In his *Journal of the Counterfeiters*, Gide exclaims, "I have written nothing better or with more facility than Lafcadio's monologues, or Alissa's journal . . . . In this sort of thing I forget who I am, if indeed I have ever known. I become the other person." For Gide, to forget himself, to push himself towards self-oblivion is the means through which he can actually experience that around him. He can write without putting words in the mouths of his characters. He can suspend himself, becoming a vessel for the words of his characters. He can get out of his own way. To write oneself to the point of self-oblivion, to have a conversation with another person, and to travel to places faraway are just three ways in which he could efface himself, eradicate his own subjectivity. On this issue, Gide writes:

> In life as well [as in writing] the thoughts and emotions of others dwell in me; my heart beats only through sympathy. This is what makes any discussion so difficult for me. I immediately abandon *my* point of view. I get away from myself—and so be it.
>
>   This is the key to my character and my work. The critic who fails to grasp this will botch the job—and this too: I am not drawn towards that what resembles me, but towards that what differs from me. (emphasis in original)[56]

What Gide calls "forgetting," "self-oblivion," "becoming the other person," and "getting away from himself" are the qualities of people thought of as chameleons. Like the small lizards, such people are changeable, readily adapting to their surroundings. They pick up attributes of the people and things around them.

In his search for the strange and exotic, Gide is an example of what Tzvetan Todorov calls the "impressionist" traveler. This figure, which has time to travel, usually is interested not only in the flora and fauna of the faraway, but also in the human beings. Often, the impressionist traveler will bring back both cliché photographs and written sketches of a local setting or individual. Perhaps this traveler would write a journal of impressions of the place. However broad this tourist's interests may be, she or he remains the sole subject of the experience. Asking why this traveler sets out, Todorov, using Pierre Loti and Charles Baudelaire as his examples, explains, "Sometimes, like Loti, because he no longer succeeds in *feeling* life at home, and the foreign framework allows him to rediscover his taste for life . . . . On other occasions . . . he hopes to find a framework that matches the experience he is already living, the being he has already encountered" (emphasis in original).[57]

In the forgetting that is achieved only through writing, discussions with other people and traveling to exotic locales, Gide can also ponder the larger questions that concern him: life, death, culture, art. Gide, during one of a number of sojourns to North Africa, insisted, "You must have tasted, have *relished* the desert, to understand what is meant by: culture" (emphasis in original).[58] The insistence on going away illustrates nicely Todorov's proposition, for Gide needs to experience the faraway to encounter what is meant by culture. However, Gide's insistence on going away also exposes a paradox. Gide needs to travel to forget, and forgetting involves *not* engaging in questions of one's own life (or one's own larger existence); yet his forgetfulness enables him to do precisely that.

Gide overtly inscribes himself in the pages of *Voyage au Congo* to a degree that is far greater than that of the authors of nineteenth-century travelogues. The reader has Gide's diary—this book serves as his journals for much of 1925 and 1926—and the reader is thereby privy to his desires, his goals, the texts he read, and the perils and inconveniences of travel in the region. Gide, like MacLeod, is also frankly subjective, and emphasizes his position as an outsider. He writes, "I realize that it is impossible to get into contact with anything real; not that things here are factitious, but civilization interposes its film, so that everything is veiled and softened" (16). As an outsider he also highlights the impossibility of a complete integration with his surroundings. Looking through the veil, one that cannot be removed, Gide can never grasp the whole. Gide can never see Africa clearly. Gide can never fully know or understand what is on the other side.

Even if Gide cannot translate, see clearly, or really "know" Africa, he can record his mediated impressions of it. From the oblique lens of the civilized traveler, the traveler's own requirements for culture constitute the tools utilized to gauge, describe, and even empathize with the people, places, and things behind the veil. In *Voyage au Congo*, architecture, as it does for Barth and MacLeod, articulates the degree to which Africans had climbed the great ladder of civilization. Gide writes:

> We passed quantities of insignificant little villages—if one can give this name to a group of wretched huts, whose inhabitants sit beside a miserable fire, or on the threshold of their doors . . . The huts remind one of the rough sheds our charcoal burners make in the woods. A trifle less and they would be like animals' dens. And [the inhabitants] absence of welcome when we arrive, of smiles and greetings when we pass, does not seem to mark hostility so much as profound apathy, the benumbed dullness of stupidity. When one goes up to them, they stir hardly more than the animals of the Galapagos. (146–47)

In a far more subtle fashion than Barth, Gide taps into evolutionary, specifically Darwinian paradigms surrounding the development of civilization, and, like Barth's gradations, the huts are tools through which Gide can define the inhabitants. The residents of these houses, little better than animals' dens, are just as wretched and sordid. To drive this point home, Gide ungenerously compares them to the animals of the Galápagos, a place routinely associated with isolated and static biological forms, a place that in evolutionary terms was frozen in time.[59] The built environment is thus the introduction to and metaphor for those who live within it.

Gide's readers understood well the connections Gide made between architecture and those who built it. The aforementioned reviewer of *Voyage au Congo* reported, "Apparently the African Tribes differ quite as markedly from one another as the various tribes of American Indians have been reported to differ; with one the huts would be squalid and ill-shaped, with another, if not exactly clean would, at least, possess symmetry."[60] For Gide, as for his reviewer, symmetry in architecture was a way to measure how far a culture had risen on the great scale of Civilization. In such rhetoric, a house that was symmetrical denoted a people who had "risen" to a nominal level on the great scale. Those that were squalid and ill shaped denoted barbarians. Architecture, for the reader and for Gide, was a window into a people's customs and manners.

Conversely, Gide invokes the nature of a people as a window into their architectural practices. Thrilled at his arrival in Fort Archambault, the traveler exclaims, "We are on the other side of hell. At Fort Archambault, on the marches of Islam, barbarism is behind one, and one enters into contact with another civilization, another culture. . . . In the regions we have just been through, there are nothing but down-trodden races. . . . Here are to be found real homes" (157). Reiterating his view of Islam as "rudimentary," Gide knows that he can at least expect a built environment that illustrates Islam's higher place on the great scale of Civilization than those heretofore seen on his journey. Ultimately, Gide and his readers followed a well-rehearsed equation between architecture and culture: people are where they live.

Gide's apocalyptic, melodramatic descent into the wilds of Africa and ascent from its "heart of darkness" finds its inspiration in the metaphoric descent into and ascent from hell represented by Marlow's journey to the Belgian Congo and back in Joseph Conrad's novella *Heart of Darkness*. Marlow plunges into hell, the darkness that is the Belgian Congo. After seeing how the "savagery" therein has claimed Kurtz, the man whom Marlow obsessively seeks, Marlow returns to the light of civilization, living on as the voice that can utter the unspeakable horrors of Central Africa.

Conrad's readers interpreted his novella as fact; indeed, many understood it as another true and titillating narrative of travel in Africa. Gide knew Conrad's oeuvre quite well, having taken some supervisory duties for French translations of Conrad to be published by the Librairie N.R.F.[61] He also translated Conrad's novel *Typhoon*, which appeared in 1918, into French.[62] Most importantly, Gide modeled his own journey after Marlow's. Gide, like many other readers, was thoroughly convinced that *Heart of Darkness* was factual, and wrote in his own travelogue that Conrad's novella "still remains profoundly true and I shall often have occasion to quote it" (11). Moreover, he dedicated *Voyage au Congo* to Conrad. Underscoring the truth-value of the tale for Gide rests in what he calls Conrad's "cruelly exact" description of the region traversed by the Belgian-built railway (11). Gide's use of Conrad is also his intense attempt to attach his journey to the glamorized yet dangerous expeditions of the nineteenth century, where explorers either met their deaths or came back as heroes. Within these myths of Africa and the genealogy Gide constructs in his travelogue, the author's rhetorical move is quite effective. It allows his reader to conjure up a series of representations of Africa—disease, moral decay, insanity, and so on—that had already been put in place by a centuries-long history of representing Africa in the

West, a history, ingrained in the West through museums, books, journalism, film, fine arts, and popular imagery, that reached its crescendo with the publication of *Heart of Darkness*. Together, these diverse venues reified and reinforced myths about Africa.

Yet it is not only exactitude that Gide finds so compelling in Conrad's oeuvre. Although Gide's travelogue is at times excessive in its description of the mundane, Conrad's economical writing style falls nicely into Gide's requirements for art. Gide writes:

> The quality of temperance is an essential one in art, and enormity is repugnant to it. A description is none the more moving because ten is put instead of one. Conrad has been blamed in *Typhoon* for having shirked the climax of the storm. He seems to me on the contrary, to have done admirably in cutting short his story just on the threshold of the horrible and in giving the reader's imagination full play, after having led him to a degree of dreadfulness that seemed unsurpassable. (14)

Temperance may be an essential quality in art, but it is not the only one that raises Conrad's oeuvre in Gide's mind. About twenty years before the above passage, Gide insisted, using the Greeks and Christians as examples, that the horror of death was the thing that generated art.[63] Temperance in description, combined with the specter and threat of death—the leitmotifs of *Heart of Darkness*—makes the novella particularly relevant for Gide. It validates his own concerns; it gives him a way to articulate his own experience. However, the ability of *Heart of Darkness* to work as a model for Gide points to the paradoxical nature of translating Africa, for Conrad's novella is peppered with adjectives that point to Marlow's inability to translate the continent. At one moment, something is "unspeakable," at another "inconceivable," at another "inscrutable." Gide begins where Conrad ends. He may see through a veil, but Gide's Africa is anything but indescribable.

Besides articulating the degree to which a culture had ascended the great scale of Civilization for Gide in his quasi-Marlowesque trek, architecture also measures—along with vegetation, animals, and insects—the degree of strangeness, exoticism, and beauty he encounters. "Before lunch in the baking sun, we went to see another village . . . a village so strange and beautiful that we had found in it the very reason of our journey and its very core" (42). In this respect, the built environment—the barometer of strangeness, the measure of civilization—works in tandem with the author's desire to find forgetfulness, to plunge into the seas of self-oblivion. Although Gide's unbreakable tie to civilization makes complete self-abnegation impossible, within the author's attempt to do so is embedded a complex milieu in which Gide at once identifies with and distances himself from his African surroundings. These processes are best revealed through Gide's description of the Mousgoum teleuk, and the passage is worth reiterating:

I am astonished that the few rare travellers who have spoken of this country and of its villages and huts have only thought fit to mention their "strangeness." The [Mousgoum] hut, it is true, resembles no other; but it is not only strange, it is *beautiful*; and it is not its strangeness so much as its beauty that moves me. A beauty so perfect, so accomplished, that it seems natural. No ornament, no superfluity. The pure curve of its line, which is uninterrupted from base to summit, seems to have been arrived at mathematically, by ineluctable necessity; one instinctively realizes how exactly the resistance of the materials must have been calculated. A little farther north or south and the clay would have been too much mixed with sand to allow of this easy spring, terminating in the circular opening that alone gives light to the inside of the hut, in the manner of Agrippa's Pantheon. On the outside a number of regular flutings give life and accent to these geometrical forms and afford a foothold by which the summit of the hut (often twenty to twenty-five feet high) can be reached; they enabled it to be built without the aid of scaffolding; this hut is made by hand like a vase; it is the work, not of a mason, but of a potter. Its colour is the very colour of the earth—a pinkish-grey clay, like the clay of which the old walls of Biskra are made (author's italics). (217–18)

Although Gide consistently notices and describes the built environment in his text, none of his passages compares to that of the Mousgoum teleuk. Incredibly rich and complex, the author's enthusiasm for the structure underscores his attraction to difference. It iterates the exotic experience par excellence. At first glance, we might think that Gide has achieved self-oblivion, that he has forgotten himself. As the author reminds us, "I often use ["strange" and "beautiful"] together in this notebook, for when the scenery ceases to be *strange*, it at once recalls some European landscape, and this recollection is almost always to its disadvantage" (emphasis in original) (76–77). Thus the conditions for beauty would seem to be embedded in strangeness, the unlike, that which is unattached to memory or lived experience. Moreover, having found beauty in such a fashion to a large extent fulfills his expectations of coming to Africa, which, for Gide, can be satisfied only by leaving "the beaten track," entering "profoundly, intimately, into the heart of the country" (61).

While the Mousgoum teleuk is strange and beautiful, it is the structure's beauty, more than its strangeness, that moves Gide. And it is this split between the two adjectives, a split that exists nowhere else in the text, that begins to uncover what Todorov calls the "constitutive paradox" of exoticism. Todorov asserts, "Knowledge is incompatible with exoticism, but a lack of knowledge is in turn irreconcilable with praise of others; yet praise without knowledge is precisely what exoticism aspires to be."[64] As Gide's passage flirts with the paradoxical relationship between exoticism and knowledge, it also threatens to collapse exoticism through knowledge. Once strangeness is separated from beauty, Gide *is* reminded of Europe, and this time, it *is not* to the disadvantage of the thing described. The author's painstaking attempt to describe his impressions of the teleuk leaves a complex set of linkages, combining the language of modernist architecture, the sumptuous materiality of the structure and his own perceptions of art. The dome is exotic, yet it is not.

Through language that could describe equally well the goals and products of Purism, De Stijl, or the Bauhaus, Gide rhetorically links the Mousgoum dome with European modernist architecture. Like modernist architecture, the beauty of the dome is described through its technological sophistication. For Le Corbusier, the dome was one of the noblest and richest architectural elements. It is also the product of the mathematician, whose work, in the words of Le Corbusier, "remains none the less one of the highest activities of the human spirit."[65] Describing the Mousgoum dome in such terms suggests the impossibility of self-oblivion and Africa as a place of absolute difference for Gide. Moreover, the passage creates a space in which Gide can identify with the structure, thus throwing any binary opposition between the traveler and Africa into question. Gide further emphasizes this liminal space by comparing the light that streams into the teleuk's interior with the light that shines into the interior of the Pantheon, which also has a hole in the top of its dome. This classical connection and the modernist prose, which seem to lift the veil that separates the traveler from his foreign surroundings, make the dome knowable, translatable, like the West.

Furthermore, artists and thinkers followed Gide's lead, connecting the teleuk to both classical and modernist architecture. Ozenfant, in his 1928 manifesto *Foundations of Modern Art*, took pains to characterize the successes and failures of modern architecture. In Ozenfant's (and Le Corbusier's) paradigm, the ancient Greeks held the pinnacle of great architecture, one to which modernist architecture should ascribe. Just below the Greeks appeared the Romans. For Ozenfant, modernist architecture had achieved the status of the best of Roman architecture. Just after comparing modern innovation with Roman achievement, he exclaims, "We have our Romans and our Negroes too. What we are waiting for are our Greeks!"[66] While his passage is striking in its suggestion that Africa had any architecture at all (many did not believe this to be the case), it is extraordinary in the place it accords African buildings on the evolutionary ladder of architectural achievement and development.

Ozenfant, who described Gide as one of the most influential people on the arts of the early twentieth century, knew his work well. He was also quite familiar with *Voyage au Congo* and Allégret's photographs of the journey. (Ozenfant published a photograph of Gide and Allégret in Africa in the pages of *Foundations of Modern Art*.) Moreover, Ozenfant peppered his own text with Allégret's photographs of Africa, and he used one of the traveler's images of Mousgoum teleukakay—Ozenfant's symbol of "Negro architecture"—to accompany the above passage (fig. 30). Gide's description of the teleuk also colored Ozenfant's view of the building and African architecture more generally. Gide's comparison of the teleuk to the Pantheon found new life in Ozenfant's text. "Negro architecture," or the Mousgoum teleuk, separated from its African milieu, was thoroughly impressive, and it offered a standard against which he could measure the success of modern architecture. Furthermore, for Ozenfant, there was no binary opposition between modern art and architecture and that of other places and times. In his words, "Masterpieces are always modern."[67]

Alongside the comparison between the Mousgoum and Roman domes, Gide also links the house and death in a fashion that immediately recalls Barth's nexus of the teleuk, the dome, the sepulcher, and death. Once inside the Pantheonesque temple/home, Gide exclaims:

> Here, in the dim twilight of an Etruscan tomb, the family spend the hottest hours of the day; at night the cattle come in to join them—oxen, goats and hens; each animal has its own allotted corner, and everything is in its proper place; everything is clean, exact, ordered. There is no communication with the outside as soon as the door is shut. One's home is one's castle. (218)

Like Barth's Mousgoum enclosure, the place of life and of nurturing also constitutes the place of death. Time has stopped. Time has also been split into two, for while a family is in its house, the notion of the teleuk as an Etruscan tomb implies that at the same time, this family has been placed into the past, suspended between life and death. They are alive and dead. If modernist prose lifts the veil, the specter of death and metaphors made between the teleuk and classical Antiquity replaces it. To be in the house is to be dead and to be in the past. Inside the teleuk, family remains fixed in a frozen past and an inert space.

Allégret's pictures, perhaps more overtly than Gide's text, also partake of the tension between the living and the dead, between the present of the European and the ethnographic past of the Mousgoum. Allégret's photographs of the teleuk appear to meditate upon architecture as pure form. Daniel Durosay, Allégret's biographer, points out, however, that there was an inherent contradiction in Allégret's photographs, embedded in their aspirations to be at once natural and objets d'art.[68] This contradiction, one that can never be resolved, finds an analogy in Gide's *The Counterfeiters*, where Edouard hopes that his novel both represents reality and becomes art.[69]

In one of Allégret's photographs of Mousgoum teleukakay, the very one used by Ozenfant, the photographer's utilization of a bird's-eye view captures the houses, which recede into the distance. Architecture is here aestheticized, operating as compositional elements, pieces that will contribute to the harmonious structure of the whole. The aestheticization of the houses is further highlighted by the absence of doors. These domes without entrances do not quite read as houses. Instead the teleukakay oscillate between being regarded by a viewer as the landscape or as the compositional parts of an abstract photograph. Without

FIGURE 30. Village of Musgum, Chad. Photographer: Marc Allégret, 1926.
Source: *Cahiers d'Art*, no. 7/8, 1927. Reprinted with the permission of CNRS Editions.

doors the buildings also lack scale. In either vein the exotic/erotic undertones of the photograph conflates the non-Western and gender.

The domed photographic landscape exists as a tableau in which the photographer enacts a primal scene, one that momentarily calls identity into question. Faced with the feminine and feminized landscape, Allégret's photograph suggests the possibility that nature and the instinctual could herald the death of the rational. These threats to the masculine body are the consequences of the breakdown of binary oppositions suggested by Allégret's photograph. What Allégret presents is a labyrinthine landscape, a maze with neither entrance nor egress. In this trap, in this labyrinth that is feminized by the connotations of landscape and the teleuk as female breast, the self becomes lost in the houses that recede towards the horizon. In her essay on Alberto Giacometti, entitled "No More Play," Rosalind Krauss discusses the impact of the "primitive" on surrealist artists and writers in the late 1920s and early 1930s. One of the underlying premises in her text is the degree to which the primitive by this time had become ingrained in

FIGURE 31. Mousgoum family enclosure, Mala, Chad. Photographer: Marc Allégret, 1926. Source: Allégret, *Carnets du Congo*, Paris: CNRS Editions, 1993. Reprinted with the permission of CNRS Editions.

the language of modern art.[70] Primitivism, embedded as ethnographic data, was a tool that could help the surrealists transgress the boundaries of art through problematizing form. And in the space between the document and the objet d'art, Allégret's photographs perform a similar operation.

By the time Gide and Allégret traveled to Africa, Europeans had been deflowering virgin lands for centuries, and such excursions posited a non-Western body as the site of many projections routinely used to affirm or transgress the boundaries of art, assist in the theorization of the *informe*, and simultaneously validate or resist Western imperial policies and practices. The Africa that became the backdrop for Gide's diary and Allégret's objets d'art was Europe's source of food and part of Europe's source of inspiration. In Allégret's photographs of the Mousgoum teleukakay, Africa becomes the mammary glands that give the photographer essential nourishment for creation.

Some of Allégret's photographs rely on clichés of naked African women as proto-pornographic canvases and the fetishization of their skin as sexual object for their evocative force as either reportage or objets d'art. But if we consider the pictures of the teleukakay in tandem with the nudes, we can see how architecture also exists as a site, beyond its characterization as landscape, where the body simultaneously attracts and repels the photographer. Allégret made a photograph of a Mousgoum family enclosure in which a granary takes center stage (fig. 31).[71] Two teleukakay bring the viewer from the foreground of the photograph to this structure. A rectangular house stands behind the granary, setting it off. There are four people in the photo: a man next to the door of the rectangular house, a woman who crouches next to him and two children who are next to large fish nets.

Structurally, the viewer almost misses the people in the photograph. Its strongest elements are the granary, and the open, black doorways of the three houses. Allégret also made a photograph of six seminude Mousgoum women who stand inside of a family enclosure (fig. 32). The photographer draws the viewer not only to the women's breasts but also to their lip plugs. Behind five of them stands a clay wall; behind the farthest woman on the right, a void or corridor that whisks the viewer to and past the doorway of an unadorned house. Here, Allégret, like those before him, taps into a perverse fascination with depicting Mousgoum women.

Like MacLeod and countless other visitors to Africa, Allégret felt both a fascination and a repulsion with the lip plugs that they (and other African peoples) wore. Furthermore, almost all the existing photographs and drawings represent-

FIGURE 32. Mousgoum women in a family enclosure, Mala, Chad. Photographer: Marc Allégret, 1926. Source: Allégret, *Carnets du Congo*, Paris: CNRS Editions, 1993. Reprinted with the permission of CNRS Editions.

ing the Mousgoum depict the teleuk, the Mousgoum woman with lip plugs, or both: both have achieved iconic status in the economy of African images. On February 16, 1926, he writes, among other comments on the subject, "Saw two old Massa women, totally nude, with large drooling disks in their lips and in the mouth a small pipe. Lamentable sight." He adds, on the same day, "The gracefulness of the Massa. Their physical beauty, the bodies of men and women; and the heads of men. Perhaps one will get used to deformed faces."[72]

Gide also has a strong reaction to Mousgoum women and their lip plugs. "There is not one [woman] who has not her lips frightfully distended by metal disks. . . . I must add that the wearing of these plates causes a continual flow of saliva" (221).

Thinking about Allégret's portrait of the six Mousgoum women in the family enclosure in terms of not only the bodily metaphors above but also against the two travelers' texts reveals a number of issues that destabilize both image and text, linking them to the discomfort and terror of the uncanny. The two travelers stressed that Mousgoum women were always nude except for the rows of beads around their waists; yet in Allégret's photo, their midsections, covered by tattered rags, reminiscent of MacLeod's dressing of her subjects, imply that the photograph was staged. The effect of the veiling of genitalia in the photograph places more emphasis on the women's lip disks and mouths, further supporting an unconscious link to the above metaphors. However, the door at the right of the photo also attracts our attention, becoming a link to the women, their mouths and their breasts, and their genitalia.

The architectural equation of openings and orifices is a connection not lost on Allégret, who himself calls the hole at the top of the teleuk a "*goulot*," which translates as "gullet." It is also slang for mouth.[73] In the photograph of the women, the metaphor between the top of the teleuk and the *goulot* is given visual expression in the pairing of the women's mouths (with their adornment) and the door of the house. Ultimately, the mouth and the door constitute the doubling of life and death and threaten to trap the travelers in the entropy of the other. Although it is embedded much further into the fabric of the composition, these doublings are also present in Allégret's photographs of the family enclosure and his bird's-eye landscape.

The family enclosure is rife with pairings between architecture and the body. This tableau rehearses the collapse between reality and the imaginary in its coupling of the teleuk and the granary. The granary, that place where food is stored, becomes the womb of the enclosure. Included around the womb are breasts (the teleuk and the smaller structures to the right) as well as genitalia (embedded in the two doors to the left and the door to the right of the granary). In this sense, the tableau becomes a metaphor of the female body; one that has been penetrated by the traveler. This is a body that can conceive and feed its young. This is a body that can also give way to the death that is lurking in the travelers' perception of the non-Western other. This is the body and civilization on the brink of decay.

In the labyrinth, the teleuk pushed up closest to the foreground has a gaping hole in its top. To enter the labyrinth, one must pass over or by the *goulot*, and in this terrifying, potentially deadly space lays the specter of death. For falling into the mouth that is the top of the house as opposed to entering through the door is tantamount to being ingested by the necropolis, and once cannibalized, the body will decompose, becoming physically and mentally transformed into the state of the *informe*. As a metaphor of the mouth and as vagina, such terror can also be linked to both saliva and the symbolic vagina dentata. Literally a vagina with teeth, Freud brought this term into the Western lexicon as a means to think through his theories regarding castration anxiety. To fall into this abyss would signal not only the loss of the masculine body, but it would also herald, perhaps even more importantly, in dissolving the binary between the travelers and the Mousgoum, a threat to their masculine power.

The unaccountable beauty of the domes fascinates Gide. He comes close to being seduced by the perfection of their form, the flawlessness of their curves. In its exoticism, the Mousgoum teleuk, like a siren, calls the voyagers into the necropolis, and in operations that at once threaten identity and exoticism, Gide and Allégret find themselves, as it were. If the domes are truly beautiful Gide sees them as dirty, paradoxically noting that good hygiene would diminish "the purity of these prime numbers" (218–19). Similar to MacLeod's predicament, the appeal to good hygiene saves the soul, and the splitting of good hygiene and beauty allow the threat of binary collapse to be repressed once more.

But it is not only dirt and scary orifices that distance the travelers from that structure that, like the best of Western architecture, was arrived at through the perfect combination of mathematical and geometric details. For the Western architect of the 1920s, the utilization of carefully planned curves, unadorned simplicity, and geometric perfection would underscore his mastery of the discipline and attest to his genius. For Gide, the Mousgoum ability to achieve such balance and perfection in the built environment is merely a habit, a practice that has remained the same for centuries. In one passage, the Mousgoum are not architects, they are potters who work on a grand scale. In another, the "perfection of the forms makes [Gide] think of the work of certain insects or of a fruit—a fir-cone or a pineapple" (216). In these analogies, Mousgoum agency has to be qualified: it is reduced at best to a craft that has withstood centuries of inertia and at worst to the work of insects or Mother Nature herself. Hence, the technological sophistication that implies intelligence, rationality, and civilization among Westerners becomes an impossibility in the Westerner's characterization of the Mousgoum. At times, particularly when describing his servant Adoum, Gide entertained the possibility that Africans did possess a minimal capacity for abstract reasoning; however, reading Lucien Lévy-Bruhl's *La mentalité primitive* upon his return to France, he concluded that his own observations were inaccurate (272). Embedded in binary oppositions between culture and nature as well as art and craft, Gide's inability to acknowledge Mousgoum agency aids in the reinstatement of oppositions and the repression of the uncanny.

Furthermore, the description of the dome as an unchanging product of nature, combined with its connection to tombs and death, reinforces the placement of the Mousgoum into a permanent past. Gide makes several allusions connecting the Mousgoum dome and his own ideas of nature—the color of the ground, the habit of building, the characterization of the dome's perfect curves as a shell, and the old buildings of Biskra, an Algerian city visited by the author at the beginning of the twentieth century. These become yet another way of distancing the self from the other; it allows the Mousgoum teleuk to be a mirror insofar as its reflection is the product not of the Mousgoum, not of reality, not of objective fact, but of personal projection, a narcissistic process that in the end constitutes Gide's desire to protect himself from the suffering inflicted upon him by his own civilized condition. As fraught and complex as Gide's encounter was with the Mousgoum and the teleuk, the author never really lost himself. He could never really find forgetfulness. Neither he nor Allégret could ever really have left the beaten track.

Conclusion

The ways in which travel and exploration, going away and coming home allow the Westerner to enter that place where the boundaries between the real and the imaginary, culture and nature, and interiority and anteriority can crumble, expose how the Mousgoum and their teleuk in particular and Africa more generally were a blank canvas, a tabula rasa, that, in its virginal state, laid out before the traveler, enabled the projection of personal fantasy and desire, which constitute an integral part of the travel experience. Freud, in his analysis of civilization and Western expectations of it, perhaps best articulated what these travelers imply. The perceived absence of any one of beauty, cleanliness, or order as demonstrated in the experiences of Barth, MacLeod, Gide, and Allégret threatens to snowball into something uncontrollable. From that point of horror, the categories they engaged could topple over, erasing hierarchies as well as psychological and formal artistic boundaries.

The conflations that resulted from these encounters find expression in the encounters between the Western traveler and the Mousgoum. The teleuk was feminized, used as a screen for projection and transference. For the form of the dome, its tectonic statement, its technological sophistication, and the teleuk's architectonic representation as the body of the mother revealed the contradictions inherent in the binary oppositions that were a fundamental component of these travelers' respective cultural lenses. The teleuk could not be comfortably distanced, it could not be fully translated, and it could not be fully integrated into Western terms. Ultimately, the travelers' transcription into the terms of architecture in their respective encounters with the Mousgoum teleuk announced the ability of the structure to be recast as an architectonic repository of longing and of "new" experiences that actually matched those that they had already undergone. Perhaps in the empathetic meeting between the European traveler and the Mousgoum teleuk, in the house that was at once womb and tomb, those who went away found their primordial homes.

A Pineapple in Paris

Oh! Great Angel, what do you want from me? All my humiliation?
Do you not see the dance of the masters? Their cries of victory?
Their conceit? Their lack of concern at the zenith of their glory?

They are the ones who, first, baptized me barbaric,
They are the ones who, early, called me an avatar,
They are the ones who designated me the son-in-lay of savagery,
They are the ones who denied my humanity and my brotherhood . . .

BASKOUDA J. B. SHELLEY, *Kirdi est mon nom*

3

By May 6, 1931, the opening date of the International Colonial Exposition, the French colonies were well ingrained in the imaginary of the *métropole* (plate 4). In many ways, France expressed its perceptions of and fantasies about sub-Saharan Africa through the body of Josephine Baker, and during much of the 1920s and 1930s the African American entertainer's visage was ubiquitous in Paris and its environs (fig. 33). The implicit association of the body of Baker with the colonies became explicit in 1931 when the entertainer was named "Queen of the Colonies" in the exposition.[1] In response the journalist Jacques Mauny mused, "It would not be surprising if a painting representing the apotheosis of Miss Josephine Baker, the popular colored star of the Folies Bergère, were to be substituted for Puvis de Chavanne's celebrated mural at the Pantheon: 'Sainte Genevieve, Patronne de Paris, Watching Over the Sleeping City.'"[2] Besides the overt conflation of Baker and France's colonies, ever-popular travelogues, exotic fiction, adventure writing, and colonial postcards of the nineteenth and early twentieth centuries further asserted the predominance of the colonial in the French psyche (fig. 34). By 1931 the colonial was not simply a sideshow in French life, and it had not been for some time. As early as the fin de siècle, Gaston Donnet noted, "We collect colonies as connoisseurs collect bric-à-brac or tapestry . . . the progress of exploration on the Nile, or the Tchad, or Niger is followed as eagerly as the difficult course of a steeplechase. It would not be surprising if we took to betting on it."[3]

The curious could find a stunning array of things colonial in a wide range of French sources including *L'Europe nouvelle*, *La grand review*, geographic journals, and the biweekly periodical *La quinzaine coloniale*, which appeared from 1897

FIGURE 33. Paul Colin, poster for *La Revue Nègre*, 1925. © 2005 Artists Rights Society (ARS), New York/ADAGP, Paris. Photograph courtesy of Snark/Art Resource, New York.

to about 1935. Perhaps most notably, the 1929 work *Le domaine coloniale français* provided four copiously illustrated volumes of geographic and ethnographic information on the colonies, describing in great detail French administration in each. Whenever information about French Equatorial Africa appeared images of the Mousgoum teleuk and/or Mousgoum women provided visual evidence of the colony's exoticism and strangeness (figs. 35, 36). Combined with the proliferation of André Gide's descriptions and Marc Allégret's images of the house in the European popular press and publications on modern art and architecture in the late 1920s, the image of the teleuk was entrenched in the French imagination well before the opening of the exposition. The exposition's French Equatorial Africa

11. Cases-obus du village de Bangadgi sur le Logone (Région de Bongor)

FIGURE 34. Postcard of Mousgoum domed houses, Bangadgi, Chad, c. 1910.
Courtesy Yale University Library.

FIGURE 35. Mousgoum women. Coll. Ag. Econ. A. E. F.

FIGURE 36. Mousgoum domed houses, Chad. Coll. Ag. Econ. A. E. F.

Pavilion, designed by Léon Fichet, epitomized the entrance of the Mousgoum te-leuk into the lexicon of French "primitive" icons (fig. 37).

As posters for the exposition attest, one could visit Paris's Bois de Vincennes from May to November of 1931 and take a "tour of the world in a day" (fig. 38). The 1931 International Colonial Exposition eclipsed in scale and grandeur the Colonial Expositions of 1906 and 1922 in Marseilles and the 1924 British Empire Exposition at Wembley. Inarguably the largest display of imperialism to date, the 1931 exposition was intended, according to the French government, to "make each colony feel that is part of France."[4] The 1931 exposition was also a means for France to show its successful evolution of colonial ideology and, particularly in the cases of Algeria and Morocco, the creative ways that the French used colonial administration. If one could indeed tour the world in a day, that tour was to have been an educational one.

France's far-flung empire was highlighted in different pavilions, the creation of which had its genesis in the expositions and dioramas of the nineteenth centu-ry, each designed to show the unique character of France's colonies.[5] Two of the larger colonial reconstructions at the exposition were inspired by the fourteenth-

FIGURE 37. French Equatorial Africa Pavilion. Architect: Léon Fichet. International Colonial Exposition, Paris, 1931. Source: *L'Illustration*, no. 4616, August 22, 1931.

century Great Mosque of Djenne (rebuilt with the aid of the French in 1909), representing French West Africa, and the twelfth-century Temple of Angkor Wat, representing French Indochina (figs. 39, 40). By 1931, France ruled colonies in Africa, Asia, and the Caribbean; close to one-third of the earth's population was under French domination. Such a feat inspired the 1922 observation, "As a matter of fact, there are only a few hours of the day when some part of the French colonial domain is not in the full glare of sunlight."[6]

This discussion focuses on the manner in which the architecture of the French Equatorial Africa Pavilion was used as a form of propaganda in the service of France's imperial project. In such a framework, the invention of French Equatorial Africa through the appropriation of objects such as the Mousgoum teleuk constitutes not only a depiction of an exotic locale but also an active self-portrait of France. The fabrication of what Toni Morrison has in another context so aptly called "an Africanist persona" in the Colonial Exposition articulates French imperial power, an assertion of French nationalism that invokes the definition and exploitation of the colonized to reinforce the empire's self-image.[7] In this milieu the French Equatorial Africa Pavilion merged architectural primitivism, the objects and peoples of the region, and didactic information to transform the French colony into a necessary part of France.

FIGURE 38. Poster, International Colonial Exposition, Paris, 1931. Research Library, The Getty Research Institute, Los Angeles.

FIGURE 39. French West Africa Pavilion. Architects: Germaine Olivier and Jacques-Georges Lambert. International Colonial Exposition, Paris, 1931. Source: *L'Illustration*, no. 4608, May 23, 1931.

The fabrication of an "Africa" in the French Equatorial Pavilion, how the staging of the colony uses not only architecture as its material but also time as a constitutive element of identity allows us to rethink notions of culture, seeing it not only as something steeped in similarity, space, or racial/ethnic identities, but one also predicated on time, difference, and the obscuring—at least psychologically—of geographic boundaries. I do not mean to claim that the Colonial Exposition is a precursor to what would today signal ideas of the global village—although one can make a compelling case for the fairs as being the inspiration for present-day Las Vegas—but that, like a culture of exploration or travel, the Colonial Exhibition depends on the suspension of disbelief and a suspension of place for its success.

Auberlet, Sculpt.

Blanche, Archi.

35 TEMPLE D'ANGKOR-VAT

FIGURE 40. Temple of Angkor Wat, Indochina Pavilion. Architects: Charles and Gabriel Blanche. International Colonial Exposition, Paris, 1931. Research Library, The Getty Research Institute, Los Angeles.

French Colonial Administration and Sub-Saharan Africa

The exposition opened in the midst of what Jean Suret-Canale has called the "Golden Age of Colonialism," which for him spanned the period between the two world wars.[8] Before 1880, European interests in Africa were predominantly commercial and within this milieu, Europeans had already wielded considerable influence on different parts of the continent. However, by the late nineteenth century, economic factors, combined with burgeoning European nationalism, fueled the scramble for Africa. By 1884, Great Britain, France, Belgium, Portugal, Germany, and Italy were racing about the African continent in order to satisfy these diverse yet interrelated needs.

The Berlin Conference of 1884–85, attended by Germany, France, Great Britain, and Portugal, did not literally partition the continent, but created policies for the annexation of African lands by European powers. These policies, set forth in the Berlin Act of February 26, 1885, required that a European nation claiming territory in Africa notify the other signatory powers of such an action in order to legitimate their annexation. These annexations were then to be followed by effective occupation in order to be legitimate. Treaties between African rulers and European nations were to be considered as valid titles to sovereignty. Finally, any imperial power had the privilege to extend its coastal holdings into the interior, within certain limits, as a means of extending its sphere of influence. The Berlin Act also passed resolutions ensuring the free navigation of the Niger and Benué Rivers.[9] By the end of the First World War, Liberia and Ethiopia were the only fully independent nations remaining on the African continent. France's highly successful subjugation of sub-Saharan Africa was completed by 1920. By this time Great Britain was France's only formidable rival on the African continent.

France, unlike Great Britain, used direct administration in ruling its colonies. The Second Empire's senatus consultum of May 3, 1854, laid down the principles for colonial administration. Article 18 of the document ordered that "[the colonies] shall be administered by decree of the Emperor until a statute be passed in respect of them by a *senatus-consult*." Suret-Canale emphasized that such a statute was never issued. Moreover, this form of administration went unchanged until the application of the 1946 French constitution. He saw a negligible difference in the ways the colonies were administered under the Third Republic, maintaining, "The Third Republic kept religiously to this decree, and the despotism of the authoritarian Empire continued in colonial affairs under the republic."[10]

The direct administration of French colonial rule was embodied in two policies: assimilation and association. One of assimilation's earliest and most influential supporters was Louis Faidherbe. A captain in the French naval infantry, he had assumed leadership of Senegal in 1854. According to Patrick Manning, Faidherbe's devotion to the principles of assimilation was threefold. First, the officer was faithful to the liberal beliefs of revolutionary France prevalent in the public imagination and carried out in the wake of the 1848 revolution. His support of an assimilationist vision for the French Empire, inextricably tied to the tenets of the revolution, assisted in convincing the French National Assembly to grant French citizenship to the inhabitants of the French colonies, including St.-Louis. Second, his ideology was deeply influenced by his military service during the conquest of Algeria in the 1830s. During this time he became rabidly anti-Muslim, which may, in part, account for his espousal of assimilation (it could be utilized as a tool to combat Islamic rule and conversion). Third, Faidherbe was devoted to the principles of the Second French Empire and Napoleon III's campaign for proficient colonial administration, which, nationalist in tone, set its sights on the colonization of Indochina, Mexico, and Africa.[11] Although the Mousgoum were first colonized by the Germans at around the turn of the twentieth century and would not come under French rule until 1916, these nineteenth-century events would play a part in the relationship between France and the Mousgoum sultanates.

Assimilation, in its simplest form, was the gallicization of France's colonized. That is to say that assimilation, in theory, was designed to raise, through French goodwill and benefice, the black, brown, and yellow colonized to the "civilized

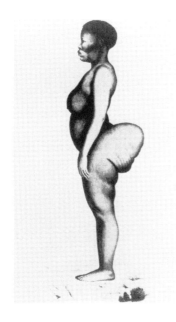

FIGURE 41. "The Hottentot Venus." Source: Georges Cuvier, "Extraits d'observations fait sur le cadavre d'une femme connue à Paris et à Londres sous le nom de Vénus Hottentote," 1817.

condition" of the French themselves. As if illustrating the possibility of colonies becoming overseas copies of the French provinces, the Senegalese communes of Gorée and St.-Louis received municipal status in 1872, Ruisque in 1880, and Dakar in 1889. As communes of full mandate, these entities were given the right to elect a general council and to send a deputy to the French Parliament, privileges previously enjoyed by only the Antilles and Réunion. The people under these mandates were granted French citizenship in 1916, a bestowal tied to military conscription during World War I.[12]

The granting of municipal status to a small number of areas and of citizenship to a tiny portion of the colonized held out the possibility that the newer residents of the French Empire would participate in and benefit from the same democratic processes, processes those in France proper enjoyed. In reality, however, assimilation and the citizenship granted under it did not produce a larger body of French nationals, but rather a caste of French "subjects," upon whom, unlike "citizens," the government could inflict prison, fines, and corporal punishment by a simple ruling. Assimilation, in practice, required the military routing of indigenous peoples.

Within the context of Darwinian theories surrounding physical (and by extension, social) evolution, assimilation as a policy was rife with contradictions. This antithesis found its visual articulation in the Hottentot Venus, thought to occupy the absolute lowest rung on the food chain of humanity (fig. 41). Furthermore, William Cohen has suggested that even Faidherbe, one of assimilation's strongest supporters, was an adherent of the structures of scientific racism, citing the former governor-general's views that "Africans were weak-willed and lacking in initiative."[13] According to Faidherbe, this lack of will was caused by "the relatively weak volume of their brains."[14] Given the former governor-general's support of assimilation, his views on blacks would seem quite incompatible with, or even contradictory to, his support of this policy. The physical proof of black inferiority—weak brain volume—would seem to indicate that there was no possibility of gallicization for people such as the Mousgoum, who were perceived—and could be "read"—as the binary opposite of the French citizen.

Tzvetan Todorov focuses on the contradiction entrenched in assimilation, writing, "Colonialism thus makes use of contradictory or incompatible ideologies in order to justify a policy that remains consistent in its overall outline."[15] According to Todorov, assimilation was upheld by universalists and was intended to "make over the indigenous 'races' in the image of France, out of a belief that France is the perfect embodiment of universal values."[16] What then becomes paramount for the universalists is the primacy of French culture. The contradictory nature of the assimilationist paradigm does not obscure beliefs in French superiority, and arguments supporting assimilation routinely emphasized the superiority of French culture over those of the colonized. In the final analysis, such incongruities point to an important catch-22 in the relations between France and its colonized peoples; in order to assert its cultural primacy, France needed to believe that the cultures of those within its colonial domain were weaker and less civilized than its own.

By the end of World War I, the French government had declared that assimilation is demagoguery and decided that it could not work for the colonies. It was thus replaced by association. Henri Labouret writes:

> The policy of association is based on respect for customs, manners, and religions; everywhere it substitutes mutual aid for the exploitation of native energies and for the usurpation of their property and their lands. It stimulates their intellectual development. In other respects it is realistic and wise, preserving with resolute firmness all the rights and necessities of domination. It does not intend to create equality, which at present is too often impossible.[17]

Labouret waved away assimilation (as well as its demagoguery) in the above passage by underscoring the ability of French direct administration under association to substitute mutual aid for exploitation. In contrast to assimilation, association did not assert the possibility of the gallicization of the colonized. Association's rhetoric instead suggested that the colonized could choose between, or negotiate, indigenous lifeways and French culture. Also, in focusing on the intellectual development rather than on the gallicization of the indigenous "races," France could mediate the contradictions between assimilation and scientific racism through cultural relativism. Such a mediation further buttressed French perceptions of their own cultural and racial superiority.

What then might have constituted association? As Manning has noted, for Pierre Savorgnan de Brazza, association meant the creation of a community of shared interest between Africans and Europeans.[18] Thus, association could re-affirm difference and deflect complaints about the militaristic requirements of assimilation, hence making the colonial project more palatable to the French public. By this time, the Mousgoum had become part of the French Empire, and colonial officials created an alliance with Mbang Mati of Pouss, whom they considered to be a loyal subject to the colonial administration.[19]

Maréchal Lyautey, the governor-general of the Morocco protectorate from 1912 to 1915, most successfully utilized association in his administration of the region. Through association, he advocated the separation and hierarchical organization (based on evolutionary models) of the colonizer and colonized. Lyautey believed that these ideological beliefs could be cemented through architecture and urban planning and advocated programs capable of satisfying his political agenda and vision for the colony. These programs were highly successful. Lyautey became a hero of French colonialism and the driving force behind the 1931 International Colonial Exposition.[20]

Labouret's assertion that association "does not intend to create equality, which at present is too often impossible," further nullified the pretenses to full French citizenship proposed under assimilation. This impossibility, fueled by centuries of French racism, is based on the perception that black Africans were still too primitive to become French. André Gide touches upon similar issues in his *Voyage au Congo: suivi du retour du Tchad*.

> The people of these primitive races, as I am more and more persuaded, have not our method of reasoning; and this is why they so often seem to us stupid. Their acts are not governed by the logic which from our earliest infancy has become essential to us—and from which, by the very structure of our language, we cannot escape.[21]

Filtered though Lucien Lévy-Bruhl's *La mentalité primitive*, Gide entertains the possibility that Africans are not intellectually inept, but they just cannot think in the same ways as Europeans. While Gide's views of Africans are more sympathetic than those of many of his contemporaries, they nonetheless point to the notion that peoples such as the Mousgoum could not be regarded in the same light as Europeans. Instead of pointing to black brutality and overt barbarism, Gide depicts Africans as children and noble savages. On Adoum, one of his African assistants (and one it is said he had a physical attraction for), Gide "sees nothing in him that is not childlike, noble, pure and honest."[22] *Le domaine colonial français* stresses similar ideas far less subtly than does Gide:

> One counts in the vicinity of 120,000 Massas [the Mousgoum are included here]. They live in the valley of the Logone, the Mayo-Kebbi, the region

surrounding Bongor and Mousseille country. They are the most primitive race, where men and women go completely nude, but robust, healthy, and industrious.[23]

As bedfellows, the noble savage, the childlike primitive, and beasts—especially in the nude—were all signposts of black inferiority and thus of white superiority. And as *Le domaine colonial français* made clear, this inferiority could be read on the nude black body. Reading the body as a means of placing peoples on the great scale of humanity was perhaps most clearly illustrated in the anthropologist Georges Papillault's guidelines for the fair's anthropological exhibits.

SCIENTIFIC LAWS

1. The diverse human races who populate our globe show, in their morphological constitution, *evolutionary characteristics* that are actually fixed at very different levels.
2. In a very general fashion, their aptitude and intellectual and moral effort are in strict correlation with the progress of their organic evolution.
3. The hybrid products of cross-breeding, descended from the meeting between two races having attained some very different levels of evolution, present, often at the beginning, some already considerable variations; but in their general effect, their evolutionary characters and their aptitude possess an intermediary value to the two races that have produced them. The hybridization has therefore resulted in elevating a less evolved population and debasing a more evolved one.
4. The differences of the level in the morphological and functional evolution of the human races are occasionally sufficiently marked in order to create an irreducible opposition to all temptation of assimilation and unification in the moral conceptions and social particularities for [the races] and in the practical organizations that spring from them.

APPLICATION TO THE NATIVES OF THE GREAT FRENCH COLONIES

1. North Africa, Syria, etc., are populated by *white races* of a very evolved condition. Their progressive assimilation to French civilization is possible and desirable.
2. The negroids of Africa and of the Pacific can be, in a certain measure, educated, not assimilated.
3. The indigenous Malagasy are half-breed negroids. They can be educated, not assimilated.
4. The indigenous Indochinese are half-breed veddoids and negroids. They can be educated, not assimilated.
5. Among these last three groups, a slow assimilation can be done by a cross breeding more and more frequent with the French (emphasis in original).[24]

This passage illustrates the same impulses as those that resulted in the replacement of assimilation by association, giving an excellent example of the ways that scientific racism could be digested and transformed in order to satisfy the French need to maintain their own cultural superiority, a need that found social, political, and legal expression. In its understated fear of miscegenation, these guidelines also articulate another reason for the collapse of assimilation. Cross-breeding would raise the great unwashed by making them genetically French, but it would also make the "pure" French into a "weaker race." These same ideas, as Patricia Morton so clearly elucidates, became an integral part of the ideological program of the 1931 International Colonial Exposition.[25]

Military suppression, as pointed out earlier, was necessary in bringing Africans under French rule and ensuring that French culture would eventually permeate its colonized under assimilation. Association, on the other hand, still stipulated the necessity of European domination over Africa, yet it purported to achieve this in the spirit of peace and mutual cooperation. However, under association, military incursions in Francophone Africa continued. They were not rare. By the time association became the policy of French colonial rule, sub-Saharan Africa, with the exception of French Equatorial Africa, had already been militarily suppressed. The completion of the military conquest of French Equatorial Africa in 1920 came with the advent of association and could be considered as either a vestige of assimilation or as an event that exposed the purely rhetorical foundation of "peace and mutual cooperation." Furthermore, under both policies, forced labor and exploitation of the colonized thrived. In certain respects, this made life in the sultanate of Pouss almost unbearable for some, as the lamido *and* the colonial government reserved the right to enact forced labor. Under the hand of either the Mousgoum leader or the French colonizers, this was nothing but a thinly veiled form of slavery.

Although association stressed respect for the customs and manners of the colonized, many African social, political, and cultural institutions had already undergone massive transformation before association became the accepted policy of French colonial administration. Salman Mbang Oumar maintained in an interview that when Europeans arrived in Cameroon, the manners and customs of the Douala and Beti cultures were the blueprint against which all other cultures in Francophone Cameroon were judged. Those civilizations that had not changed would begin to do so shortly after coming under French rule. Following the example of the British, the French sometimes retained already extant chiefdoms; sometimes they created them where none had previously existed. In Salman's mind, to treat the Mousgoum like the Douala or the Beti, two cultures who lived hundreds of miles to the south and with whom they had no commonalties, was one of the ways in which the Germans and the French were able to disrupt Mousgoum cultural practices. Within these massive changes, a sovereign maintained some control over his subjects, but for all intents and purposes, his power was reduced to the service of the empire; he became a puppet ruler, often performing degrading or purely ceremonial duties. Suret-Canale emphasizes:

> In view of the meagre advantages involved [in being an indigenous canton chief], the duties were many and onerous: collection of taxes, requisitioning labour, compulsory crop cultivation and provision of military recruits. He had to give accommodation and food, on a royal scale and free of charge, to emissaries or representatives of the administration on tour. He had to entertain the agents or representatives of the chief town of the circle who had been sent to deliver the orders of the commander; to pay an educated secretary, and to maintain an armed body of law-enforcement agents. . . .[26]

In this disruption of indigenous African political structures, social and cultural transformation followed. For the Mousgoum, French domination left the sultanate of Pouss intact but stripped Mbang Mati, with the exception of dictating forced labor, of any real authority over his dominion.

To meet the demands put upon them by the French, indigenous chiefs would often become petty despots, and the Mousgoum did not escape this fate. M. Robin, a colonial administrator who served in a neighboring region, reported that to avoid abuse by the lamido of Pouss, Mousgoum people were leaving the sultanate for points north and east.[27] Official reports alleged that Mbang Évélé Oumar, who, succeeding his father, became the lamido of Pouss in 1931, illegally inflated taxes on people, animals, and granaries in his sultanate. It was also contended that the sultan illegally took bulls, cows, and wives from some of his subjects.[28] According to a 1932 report, he "had taken with force" from Azao a daughter named Mouti. Azao had betrothed Mouti to Sultan Youssouf of Logone-Birni, a sultanate to the north. When Azao went to Yagoua, the capitol of the subdivision, to lodge a complaint against Évélé's actions, he was immediately imprisoned.[29]

Patcha Alouakou, who served as minister of defense under Mbang Évélé Oumar and Mbang Mati, was renowned for his despotism as well. As the right arm of Évélé Oumar, he carried out the ruler's demands on the Mousgoum population.[30] Not simply the messenger of the lamido, Patcha Alouakou was considered to be extremely powerful and was feared in his own right. Azao Dogo remarked during a 1996 field interview that Patcha Alouakou was instrumental in taking taxes, often in the form of livestock. Dogo commented, "There was also forced labor [during the 1930s]. The work did not pay, and it was difficult. As they loved life, people preferred to go elsewhere." Echoing Dogo and official documents, Dana Goodhue points out that Patcha Alouakou was extremely brutal, often fighting "with the Mousgoum [village] of Begué [Bigué]," pillaging "their cows, crops and daughters in the name of tax collection." She continues, "It is also told that on occasion [he] would kill a man upon entering a village for the sole purpose of instilling fear. Once installed in the town he would secretly slaughter a sheep and roast it, reveling in the illusion that he was eating human flesh."[31] One could argue that

Mbang Évélé Oumar's despotism could have been due, at least in part, to the demands placed on him by the French. (I would not, however, attempt to make the same case for Patcha Alouakou.) In the sphere of material culture, this migration affected how the Mousgoum lived at the time. It is perhaps needless to say, but such brutality would not come to light in the Bois de Vincennes.

Cultural change and diffusion were the results not only of the actions of despotic African rulers such as Mbang Évélé Oumar but also of the French policy for the sublimation of Africa. William Ponty, governor-general of French West Africa from 1908 to 1915, underscored this practice before the council of government of French West Africa, insisting, "We must destroy all hegemony of one race over another, or one ethnic group over another; fight the influence of the local aristocracies so as to make sure of the sympathies of the communities; suppress all great municipalities which nearly always act as a barrier between us and the mass of people under our administration."[32] As Suret-Canale asserts, "'Divide and rule' was the golden rule of the colonial administration as it had been that of the conquerors: to play upon the tribal conflicts and social contradictions."[33] People fleeing despotic rulers and forced labor, new chiefdoms where none had previously existed, and changes in extant ones constituted only a few of the byproducts of this French colonial strategy. To further exercise colonial control, traditional chiefdoms were divided into subdivisions, subdivisions were divided into cantons, cantons were divided into villages.

Ideologically, however, the French deployed assimilation and association to rationalize and legitimate imperialism in the national and international spheres and to dilute oppositional arguments about forced labor and taxation in the colonies and attempts by the French to destroy indigenous civilizations. Although the French couched the two policies in fictions that told of the responsibility of Europeans to raise the great unwashed, association was in the final analysis a far more effective strategy, for it suggested that economic exchange could flourish between France and its colonies without exploitation. The two policies validated the goals of colonization to an anxious *métropole*, and in its role in normalizing the French imperialist project, association could ideologically refute any possible opposition to the treatment of the colonized at the hand of despotic colonial administrators. Whereas the Third Republic first tried to convince its citizens that assimilation would gallicize the savages and then that association would retain the "purity" of indigenous cultures while simultaneously "raising" them to a certain level of civilization, the two policies suppressed and ignored indigenous African practices, replacing them with French structures and educational systems that were qualitatively but a pale shadow of those in France. Ironically, just at the time the French appropriated the teleuk for the French Equatorial Africa Pavilion, the government initiated sweeping changes in Mousgoum culture that anticipated what would later become the near extinction of the house. Many older Mousgoum people routinely noted that the teleuk had begun to disappear in the 1930s as a result of Mousgoum people fleeing persecution from Mbang Évéle Oumar, Patcha Alouakou, and French forced labor. Politically, such changes also underscore the real fact that association—at least in the case of the Mousgoum—neither respected Mousgoum cultural values nor gave the colonized any real choices between different lifeways.

Strange Fruit: The French Equatorial Africa Pavilion

During this "Golden Age," French colonial propaganda was highly effective for many in the West. Norman Harris, writing in 1926 about the European conquest of Africa, stresses:

> A magnificent colonial empire has been . . . won for France. The lion's share of West Africa, the western Sudan, and the Sahara, together with a large portion of the Congo region have passed under her control. To these Morocco, Algeria, and Tunis are now joined, so that her protection extends over an area almost as great as the United States excluding Alaska. From the earlier experience of France in Algeria and the Far East, it was inferred that the efforts of the Republic to establish a successful administration in these regions would more than likely end in failure. But the world has been happily disappointed. The twenty-five years of progressive and enlightened government prior to the war demonstrated that the French deserve a place in the front rank of the world's greatest colonizers.[34]

Harris was convinced about the arrival of France on the world imperialist stage; many saw the 1931 International Colonial Exposition as the three-dimensional representation of such a feat, and these "happy disappointments" were most prominently displayed in the colonial pavilions (fig. 42). As the art critic Paul Fierens writes, "The Colonial Exposition is a résumé of the history of humanity and the demonstration of a civilizing effort of which France may be proud."[35] It is precisely this résumé that was the impetus for Jean Boudon's assertion that "the formation of the French Colonial Empire has been one of the great deeds of our history and even the history of the world. Its development must be one of the essential preoccupations of our politics."[36]

Moreover, the exposition was immensely popular. Its opening ceremonies were broadcast via shortwave radio throughout Europe and North America.[37] By the beginning of June 1931, a mere three weeks after it had opened, more than 3.5 million tickets had been sold.[38] Unlike most world's fairs, the 1931 International Colonial Exposition was also a financial success. By the exposition's close roughly 33.5 million visitors—almost twelve times the population of Paris at the time—had passed through its gates.[39] L'Illustration had devoted space in at least four issues to the event as well. The exposition's reproductions of colonial landmarks sit at the intersection of Western colonialism, Western history, memory,

34 PAVILLON DE L'AFRIQUE EQUATORIALE FRANÇAISE

L. A. Fichet, Arch

FIGURE 42. French Equatorial Africa Pavilion. Architect: Léon Fichet. International Colonial Exposition, Paris, 1931. Postcard: personal collection.

and fantasy. All these were embedded within ideological processes that, in large part, helped to normalize and maintain a false consciousness with respect to the French civilizing mission.

The 1931 exposition was the first in which French Equatorial Africa—a region that once included modern-day Congo, Gabon, Central African Republic, and Chad—was represented by its own pavilion. This complex, organized by a decree of July 26, 1927, covered a triangular area of 5,600 square meters and was bordered by the comparatively immense French West Africa Pavilion to the south, the Pavilion of the Overseas Forces to the southeast, the North African pavilions to the east, and Asian pavilions to the north. Although the domed Pavilion of the Governor General was the complex's centerpiece, it also included an annex, an indigenous village (with restaurant), indigenous vegetation, and exhibits of companies that had economic interests in the colony.[40] Within this complex, the organizers of the exposition ostensibly attempted to "illustrate" various characteristics of the colony; the attempt shows how, in the end, France invoked the colonies to reproduce itself.

The circular Pavilion of the Governor General (henceforth referred to as the main pavilion) was flanked by two guard houses. The bottom third of the main pavilion was covered by a series of geometric motifs in "very pure colors": black, white, and red ocher.⁴¹ At regular intervals, the outer wall was studded by simply sculpted, unadorned columns designed to support the structure's roof. The top of the main pavilion took the form of a twenty-meter-high white teleuk, which was internally supported by sculpted columns whose sense of depth was augmented by paint. The structure was twenty-seven meters in diameter. Its interior space, extending from the inner circumference of the dome, served as an exhibition space where the viewing public could learn about French Equatorial Africa through seeing colonial bric-a-brac (figs. 43–45). In short, the complex was designed accommodate three interrelated themes. First, the pavilion was to evoke the history of the region before colonization. Second, it was to document French exploration and conquest of the region. Third, it was to illustrate the positive, productive results of the civilizing mission.⁴² The rest of the complex supplemented the main pavilion's goals.

In describing the complex, Marcel Olivier creates a textual tour of sorts, attempting to bring to light the things of the pavilion within the context of the exposition. On the main pavilion, he writes:

> From the principal entrance, between two information bureaus with dioramas, one found, to the right, the gallery of indigenous art, weapons, fetishes, masks, musical instruments, etc., which gave a precise idea of Congolese folklore, almost unknown by the general public.
>
> The musical instruments permitted the evocation of the strange ceremonies that had illuminated, in the heart of obscure forests or in the middle of the savannah . . . the magnificent equatorial moonlight: dances of initiation, of marriage, of war, of rejoicing, of death, etc., The fetishes showed the religious aspect of the life of these people: household gods of the Batékés or the Babembès, Baktota mortuary masks, which surmounted the caskets of bones, "Kébé-Kébés," in the two faces of the Kougous and their swords of war, ornate like those of the Arab armies, fetishes with nails, sexual or not, of the Loangos; all these objects, of an occasionally great artistic interest, reconstituted the beliefs in different spirits, benevolent or more often hostile, and the complicated cult that made them.
>
> In a second section, the retrospective of the period of exploration and exploitation recalled that the African Center was, without doubt, one of the lands whose mystery remained whole for the longest time: reconstitution of the Congolese era, evocation of French colonial history, of the rivers from the Congo to the Sahara, from the Atlantic to the Egyptian Sudan: Savorgnan de Brazza went back up the Ogooué in 1879, descended the Alima and founded a modest post on the north bank of the Congo which came to carry his name and became the capitol of an empire five times the size of France; then, in the equatorial region, the resistance by the tribes stirred up by the religious exhortations of ambitious sorcerers who found in the hostility of nature herself their principal support was disseminated; finally, further north, the combat

116 [CHAPTER THREE

FIGURE 43. *(above left)* Interior view, French Equatorial Africa Pavilion. Architect: Léon Fichet. International Colonial Exposition, Paris, 1931. Source: Olivier, *Exposition coloniale internationale de Paris, Rapport general*, vol. 5, pt. 2, Paris: 1932–34.

FIGURE 44. *(above right)* Interior view, French Equatorial Africa Pavilion. Architect: Léon Fichet. International Colonial Exposition, Paris, 1931. Source: Olivier, *Exposition coloniale internationale de Paris, Rapport general*, vol. 5, pt. 2, Paris: 1932-34.

FIGURE 45. *(below)* Interior view, French Equatorial Africa Pavilion. Architect: Léon Fichet. International Colonial Exposition, Paris, 1931. Research Library, The Getty Research Institute, Los Angeles.

against the black Muslims and fantastic groups under the authority of cruel and despotic sultans, of whom the most famous, Rabeh, succumbed only after desperate battles.

All these sources of resistance controlled, French Equatorial Africa was opened to improvements, and it is the results obtained in this domain that were presented in the third and last section of the Exposition, in placing under the eyes of the visitors the work accomplished in the course of the last ten years: construction of the Congo-Ocean railroad, development of the network of routes, organization of education, battle against disease.

This Exposition would have been incomplete if it had been limited to showing the visitor the role of administration: close to the official pavilion were installed stands where diverse traders exhibited their efforts and the results obtained: nine companies having interests in French Equatorial Africa had solicited the privilege of a site on the grounds of the general government.[43]

FIGURE 46. Restaurant, French Equatorial Africa Pavilion. Architect: Léon Fichet. International Colonial Exposition, Paris, 1931. Source: Olivier, *Exposition coloniale internationale de Paris, Rapport general*, vol. 5, pt. 2, Paris: 1932–34.

FIGURE 47. Pylons at the entrance to the indigenous village. French Equatorial Africa Pavilion. Sculptor: Bouarel. International Colonial Exposition, Paris, 1931. Source: Olivier, *Exposition coloniale internationale de Paris, Rapport general*, vol. 5, pt. 2, Paris: 1932–34.

Behind the main pavilion stood gardens and buildings that housed individual stands, and an indigenous village and restaurant. Far simpler in composition than the main pavilion, these were quite unspectacular and far more rustic in character (fig. 46). The French artist Bouarel created three sculpted and painted pylons, each topped with a replica of a Fang *bieri* figure, which marked the entrance to the indigenous village (fig. 47). The goal of the village, for Olivier, was the evocation of an indigenous street where the visitor could see French colonial subjects in their natural habitats. It also served as the actual habitats for Africans—twenty-two men, thirteen women, and two children—imported from the colony for the exposition (fig. 48). Here, the indigenous plants brought to Vincennes mingled with "natives," and small houses decorated in the same general motif as the main pavilion served to supplement its facets.

Springing from a desire to see behind the mask of the newest and one of the least known colonies in the French Empire, the planners envisioned that the pa-

FIGURE 48. Women from French Equatorial Africa at the Bois de Vincennes. International Colonial Exposition, Paris, 1931. Source: Trillat, *L'Exposition coloniale de France*, 1931.

vilion and its annexes—through statistics, painting, photography, and architecture—would work in a didactic fashion and show the region's precolonial history and (more importantly) its submission to the French conquest. It would also show the results of French economic, hygienic, social, and moral improvement of the territory and the indigenous life of the area.[44]

In creating the pavilion and indigenous village Fichet had access to a wide range of sources, from the architecture of previous fairs and photographs of the colonies to anthropological exhibits. With respect to the dome itself, Fichet undoubtedly would have seen references for it in a number of venues as there were many photographs and engravings of the teleuk in the popular media by the late 1920s.

From the beginning of the twentieth century, the Mousgoum and their teleukakay had appeared in postcards, travelers' photographs, drawings, paintings, and engravings; the teleuk was the subject of short descriptive passages in colonial ethnographic studies and periodicals. It was also the logo for a colonial rice company (fig. 49). In the Colonial Exposition at Marseilles in 1922, the teleuk was part of the ornamental program of the tower that served as the entrance to the West Africa Pavilion as well. In the 1925 Exposition of Decorative Arts in Paris, a dome that was a hybrid of the summits of the mosques of the

Djenne region and the Mousgoum teleuk formed the apex of the fair's French West Africa Pavilion (fig. 50).

In 1927, Fichet could have seen Marc Allégret's photographs of the Mousgoum and their teleukakay, which had been widely published, and viewed the scenes shot by the Logone River in the 1927 film *Voyage au Congo*. Furthermore, Gide's text was controversial due to its castigation of French colonial practices in Central Africa and, as a result, it was very popular in France, Great Britain, and the United States. In reviews of Gide's text and in written accounts of the Paris Exposition, authors routinely commented on the teleuk's renown and its prevalence in travel literature. The travelogues of both Barth and Adolph Friedrich, the duke of Mecklenburg, had been translated into French shortly after their respective 1865 and 1913 publications. There were also photographs of the teleuk in the Musée de l'Homme dating from 1912, and Allégret's photographs of the Mousgoum dome also appeared in Ozenfant's 1928 *Foundations of Modern Art*.

Fichet seems to have had no choice other than to use the teleuk as the highlight of the main pavilion. The reports of an international congress on urbanism in the French colonies and in tropical countries more generally noted that local architecture in French Equatorial Africa "does not exist."[45] One of the participants in the conference stressed that there was no architecture in the region that architects or planners could adapt for use in the colony. He then stepped back, noting that the region's "only remarkable [architectural] type is the [teleuk], of the middle Logone . . . It is the type that inspired the pavilion of French Equatorial Africa at the Colonial Exposition."[46]

FIGURE 49. Logo for the Logone Rice Company, Maroua, Cameroon. Photographer: David Joselit, July 27, 1994.

However, in planning the pavilion's design, Fichet likely did what many of his predecessors had already done. To gain access to the colonies, in whatever fashion or for whatever purpose, European planners, architects, artists, and writers enjoyed access to a vast array of objects that had traveled from the colonies themselves, expositions, images, books, periodicals, fiction, travel literature, scholarship in anthropology, ethnography, and archaeology, and other media that planted various intertwined ideas of the colonies—many of which had existed for at least a century and a half before the opening of the Colonial Exposition in the European imagination. Most stunning about all of this is how *easy* it was to gain access to ideas about places non-Western by the 1920s. It is these stereotypes about the colonies that form the basis for the descriptive and representational strategies of the exposition. Labelle Prussin, discussing visual sources related to West Africa, describes the outright plagiarism that often occurred in the popular literature about the continent.[47] Stock images would repeatedly appear in literature on Africa, thus reinforcing myths of the continent. With respect to the teleuk, Barth's 1857 engraving of a Mousgoum chief standing in front of the structure was reproduced, combined with an Arab chief on horseback (fig. 51). This image appeared as a color lithograph in a late nineteenth-century text on Africa.

Paris — Exposition Internationale des Arts Décoratifs, 1925

PAVILLON DE L'AFRIQUE FRANCAISE (Germain Olivier, Arch.)

FIGURE 50. French West Africa Pavilion. Architect: Germaine Olivier. International Exposition of Decorative Arts, Paris, 1925. Research Library, The Getty Research Institute, Los Angeles.

FIGURE 51. "Afrique Centrale." Lithograph after Barth, late nineteenth century. Personal collection.

This sort of collage and plagiarism can also be seen as a fundamental part of the modus operandi of the appropriation of forms and ideas for the Colonial Exposition. Perhaps the only thing more stunning than the easy accessibility of things and ideas colonial at this time is the complete lack of originality in the way Europeans understood, interpreted, and used them.

What is readily apparent in Fichet's pavilion is that it is nothing new. It is yet another replay of primitivism. The spectacle of the colonial book, the appeal of the exotic, Paris's Negro vogue—a staple of 1920s entertainment in the grande ville—has borne fruit in the 1931 Colonial Exposition. What the pavilion in particular, and world's fair architecture more generally, makes vivid is the primitivism of the colonial book and the colonial periodical. *Le domaine colonial français*

FIGURE 52. "Dance and Music of the Hottentots." After an eighteenth-century engraving made by Cochin. Source: *Le Domaine Colonial Français*, 1929.

is perhaps one of the best examples of how the collage of text, prints, and images works to inscribe the glory of French imperialism onto the colonies while simultaneously placing disparate elements within the grand narrative. In the section on French Equatorial Africa, text on the economics, flora, and fauna of the region is peppered with images of the land and people of the region. Many of the photographs are the same as those appearing in earlier volumes on the colonies. However, there are also two prints of the South African Hottentot Venus included in the section, showing the ability of the French to create fictions while purporting to show facts (figs. 52, 53). This porous, unstable line between fact and fiction, enacted through the amassing of science and ethnography, and its ultimate nullification through collage are extremely similar to the structure of the colonial pavilions. And in their reception, the pavilions' use of collage—like the book—can contain fiction and fact in the name of imperial power. Here, the knowledge on the colonies served the pedagogical, social, and ideological roles of the empire. It is all quite conservative; the book's didactic narratives have been played out spatially.

Although Lyautey wanted to separate the exposition from Paris's Negro vogue, although the leader wanted an exposition that would educate rather than entertain, although he envisioned an idealized space that would leave the messiness of avant-garde and popular primitivism outside the borders of Vincennes, visitors regarded and understood these scenes within the same discursive networks. They gained much of the same kinds of pleasure from this as they might from seeing Baker in the *Revue négre*. They were titillated and shocked as they would have been by seeing a surrealist work. While the drives behind these various manifestations of the primitive are not precisely the same (although they are all to some degree narcissistic), they all explore white anxiety, white fatigue with bourgeois existence, and white curiosity with the nonwhite world. When contrasted with the use of the primitive by the surrealists or even Picasso two decades earlier, the primitive truly becomes tantamount to a blank canvas.

FIGURE 53. "The Hottentot Venus." After a nineteenth-century British lithograph. Source: *Le Domaine Français*, 1929.

Pierre Courthion, writing about the architecture of the Colonial Exposition, identified three discernible types of architecture—and three discernible types of viewers—at Vincennes. The first, "original creations more or less independent of context," was sure to satisfy the artists. The second, "stylized interpretations of certain homes and buildings in the creation of a characteristic ensemble," was for the pleasure of the dilettantes. The third, "copies and exact reproductions of indigenous houses and palaces," was for the admiration of ethnographers. He observes:

> The artist will ask to be transported by the pleasing combinations of lines, of beautiful arrangements, a daring confrontation of volumes; the dilettante will rejoice in seeing the walls and the columns supporting the buildings augmented by bas-reliefs and sculptures "in the oriental taste"; finally, the ethnographer will have joy in contemplating an entirely picturesque folklore.[48]

For Courthion, the buildings in the first class were the Cité des Informations, the Musée Permanent des Colonies, the Metropolitan Section, and the Pavilion of the Catholic Missions (figs. 54–57).[49] Many of the colonial pavilions, including those of French Equatorial Africa, French West Africa, Cameroon and Togo, Belgian Congo, French Oceania, and Madagascar, occupied the second class (figs. 37, 39, 58–61). Among the third Courthion included the colonial pavilions of Indochina, French Somalia, and Morocco (he did not categorize all the pavilions in the exposition) and those of Italy and the United States (figs. 40, 62–65).[50]

These categories also correspond in hierarchical order to Courthion's general likes and dislikes. He mostly approves of the first class, finding most of the buildings to be well proportioned and original. He gives mixed reviews to the second; he is impressed by the Cameroon and Togo Pavilion, but the French Equatorial Africa Pavilion draws his ire, "French Equatorial Africa is less successfully represented by a hut in the form of a shell, inspired by those of the Logone and composed . . . of a dome in the form of a pineapple, too large for the proportions of the rest of the building."[51] If he dislikes this pavilion, his utter disdain is reserved for the third class of buildings. This class, he quips, "is the dead part of the exposition; it is that which one can know in traveling, in reading a book, in going to the cinema, it is that which can be had for a pile of money."[52] For Courthion, the mimetic copying of indigenous buildings is neither desirable nor particularly interesting. Even within the context of the Colonial Exposition, the critic is looking for originality in form and the harmonious proportions of architecture, and he echoes the planners' general aesthetic guidelines. However, in the end, Courthion is not especially moved by the overall decorative effect of the exposition, musing, "In general the decoration is poor, these are still those graffiti of which the [1925] Exposition des Arts décoratifs has spread the vogue, and when the motif takes a break, we then see the appearance of the pineapple of which our

CITE DES INFORMATIONS

Bourgon et Chevalier, Archs.

FIGURE 54. *(above)* Cité des Informations. Architects: Jean Bourgon and Fernand Camille Chevalier. International Colonial Exposition, Paris, 1931. Research Library, The Getty Research Institute, Los Angeles.

FIGURE 55. *(below)* Musée Permanent des Colonies. Architects: Léon Jaussely and Albert Laprade. International Colonial Exposition, Paris, 1931. Research Library, The Getty Research Institute, Los Angeles.

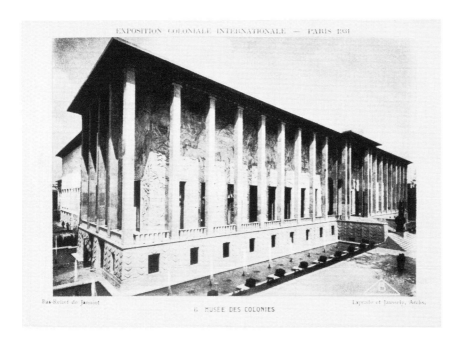

Bas-Relief de Janniot

Laprade et Jaussely, Archs.

MUSÉE DES COLONIES

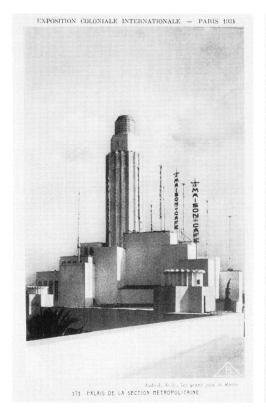

FIGURE 56. *(left)* Metropolitan Section. Chief architect: M. Duhayon. International Colonial Exposition, Paris, 1931. Research Library, The Getty Research Institute, Los Angeles.

FIGURE 57. *(right)* Pavilion of the Catholic Missions. Architect: Paul Tournon. International Colonial Exposition, Paris, 1931. Research Library, The Getty Research Institute, Los Angeles.

artists are talking and about which the exposition is perhaps a little too boastful."[53] Although Courthion's categories constitute an illuminating firsthand account of the architecture of the Colonial Exposition, they are by no means stable, for the viewer can project onto the structures a range of possible meanings. The reproduction of Angkor Wat, which was "dead" to Courthion, was quite alive to Yvanhoé Rambosson, who asserts:

> One cannot without emotion go through these places that appear to be impregnated with a magic ambiance, and in which, to the tiniest detail, is entirely living harmony. The most extraordinary [quality] is that the most characteristic elements of two periods of our history of art seem to merge in an intimate fashion. In effect, junctions are made between the temple of Angkor and our Gothic cathedrals; at the same time it would be easy to find in the ornamentation of its walls the equivalent of many of the motifs of our Renaissance.[54]

109 CAMEROUN-TOGO — GRAND PALAIS

L. H. Boileau & Carriere Archs.

FIGURE 58. *(above)* Cameroon and Togo Pavilion. Architect: Louis-Hippolyte Boileau. International Colonial Exposition, Paris, 1931. Research Library, The Getty Research Institute, Los Angeles.

FIGURE 59. *(below)* Belgian Congo Pavilion. Architect: Henry LaCoste. International Colonial Exposition, Paris, 1931. Research Library, The Getty Research Institute, Los Angeles.

EXPOSITION COLONIALE INTERNATIONALE — PARIS 1931

218 PAVILLON DES ETABLISSEMENTS FRANÇAIS DE L'OCEANIE   MM. Billecocq, Archs

FIGURE 60. *(above)* French Oceania Pavilion. Architect: Ernest Billecocq. International Colonial Exposition, Paris, 1931. Research Library, The Getty Research Institute, Los Angeles.

EXPOSITION COLONIALE INTERNATIONALE — PARIS 1931

Gabriel Veissière, Archs
41 MADAGASCAR — FAÇADE PRINCIPALE

Exposition Coloniale Intern.ᵉ Paris 1931

2047. CÔTE FRANÇAISE DES SOMALIS
Ch. Wulffleff arch.ᵉ D.P.L.G.

PAVILLON DU MAROC

A. Laprade et Fournez, Archs

FIGURE 61. *(opposite, bottom left)* Madagascar Pavilion. Architect: Gabriel Veissière. International Colonial Exposition, Paris, 1931. Research Library, The Getty Research Institute, Los Angeles.

FIGURE 62. *(opposite, bottom right)* Pavilion of French Somalia. Architect: Charles A. Wulfleff. International Colonial Exposition, Paris, 1931. Research Library, The Getty Research Institute, Los Angeles.

FIGURE 63. *(above)* Morocco Pavilion. Architects: Robert Fournez and Albert Laprade. International Colonial Exposition, Paris, 1931. Research Library, The Getty Research Institute, Los Angeles.

FIGURE 64. *(below)* Italian Pavilion. Architect: Armando Brasini. International Colonial Exposition, Paris, 1931. Research Library, The Getty Research Institute, Los Angeles.

PALAIS PRINCIPAL DE L'ITALIE

Brasini, Arch

Jacques Greber, Arch. des Jardins   Charles K. Bryant, Arch. des Bâtiments
112 SECTION DES ETATS-UNIS — REPRODUCTION DE MOUNT VERNON - MAISON DE GEORGE WASHINGTON

FIGURE 65. United States Pavilion. Architect: Charles K. Bryant. International Colonial Exposition, Paris, 1931. Research Library, The Getty Research Institute, Los Angeles.

On Courthion's second category, some writers interpreted the appropriation and recontexualization of indigenous buildings as having had no effect on the original "style" of the referents. In some respects, the intervention of the European architect was actually seen as an improvement of "colonial style." Rambosson cites M. Alphonse Séché, who "very justly pointed out, in *Marseilles-Matin*, there is a small moment that the [pavilions] of West Africa, of Equatorial Africa, of Madagascar or of the Belgian Congo were not the strict reproductions of indigenous buildings, but realizations much more vast, conceived in the spirit of the country, *but imagined by the minds of the white man*" (emphasis in original).[55]

No matter the category remarked upon, critics did not fail to project the metropolitan self onto the appropriated forms of the colonized. And in this context, the colonial pavilions—like the things of the colonies more generally—are blank canvases, and they routinely allow narcissistic explorations of a European self. French narcissism in the Colonial Exposition is fabulously striking: Angkor Wat can be a lesson in the history of French art; a French reproduction of a "characteristic" colonial form can be more real than its non-Western referent.

Olivier performed a similar operation in addressing the interior of the main pavilion. For Olivier, Fichet's translation of forms "directly inspired" from the region speak much more about the French self. This is evident in Olivier's description, where he retells the history of the French domination of the colonies and the crushed resistance of indigenous cultures.[56] This becomes even more apparent in his physical description of the main pavilion. Olivier notes that Fichet "had conceived a dome twenty meters in height, which produced a central hall crowned with a cupola; it was almost a hall of honor."[57]

But it is the honor of France, particularly with the advent of the Great Depression, that is glorified here. Georges Hardy understood this, insisting, "Without neglecting the picturesque, without depriving the visitors of a delicious impression of disorientation, the colonizing nations have wanted to display something, and that something is all in their honor."[58] Although Hardy seems to discount the aesthetics of the Colonial Exposition, the desire and ability to successfully display "honor" is dependent upon them, and Olivier's connection of the pavilion to a hall of honor, like the French art history lesson and the perception that the French have the ability to make forms that are more "real" than their antecedents, transforms the exotic into the universal. And in this allegorical process, the original is erased. In this sense, architecture and decoration make up a "reality effect" that has no precedent and needs no antecedent. Roland Barthes has stressed that in the making of myth, "the Other becomes a pure object, a spectacle, a clown. Relegated to the confines of humanity, he no longer threatens the security of the home."[59] It is this ideological and social function that then allows the translation of the other into narratives of the self. In France's self-projection, one predicated on the appropriation of the colonized, the allegorical replacement of meaning has managed to domesticate the colonies and their imagined threat to the *métropole*. While there may have been anxieties in France around miscegenation and the hybrid, as Morton explores in detail, notions of hybridity, could, like those things purely colonial, say *anything*. And at the exposition the hybrid stories tell visitors about French ingenuity and France's triumph over one-third of the earth's population at that time.

Olivier placed emphasis on the teleuk on two occasions in his description of the main pavilion, revealing that through architectural appropriation, the exotic dome had been translated into a portrait of the self. Like Gide's attraction to the morphological qualities of the teleuk, Fichet's choice to employ it as the summit of the French Equatorial Africa Pavilion can be linked to the significance of and reverence for the architectural form of the dome in its ability to signify political power, formal purity, and religious associations in the Western psyche. Olivier himself described Fichet's augmentation of the dome with rose-colored cathedral glass, further highlighting some of these connections.[60] Le Corbusier stressed the nobility of the dome. With respect to Michelangelo's St. Peter's Church in Rome, he asserted, "the real aim of the building was the dome."[61] This is no small detail, for in his reverence for the dome, Le Corbusier is able to connect modernist architecture with the best of the High Renaissance and to those structures regarded as the greatest achievements of ancient Roman architecture: the Pantheon and Hadrian's Villa, both built in the second century CE. Le Corbusier's manifesto also reinscribes a Western genealogy of architecture that extends from classical antiquity through the Renaissance to the first half of the twentieth century. Within this genealogy, what is paramount is the emphasis given to the correct proportion of space with respect to the fundamental forms of architecture and their relationship to the Western body. With respect to the main pavilion, Fichet's appropriation of the teleuk is also reminiscent of Gide's comparison of the hole in the top of the teleuk to that in the top of the Pantheon.[62] Through such connections, the teleuk has been universalized, incorporated into the rhetoric of Western imperialism that was constituted, in large part, by the departicularization of the exotic.

In the design of the French Equatorial Africa Pavilion, Fichet did attempt to create an architectural unity out of a set of seemingly disparate parts. In his use of the teleuk as its summit, he attempts to connect the structure to the same genealogy of space and Western architecture as Le Corbusier and his contemporaries. He also ties architecture to a similar genealogy as a reader could find in books on the French colonial conquest. In these mountains of words, France's successful amassing of colonies is consistently and unselfconsciously compared to that of Rome.[63]

What is the significance of the dome's nobility? For Le Corbusier, it lies in its purity and, within its purity, its ability to evoke a human response. Although secularized in his text, the dome's religious significance is still paramount. Christian Norberg-Schulz has written, "The Pantheon unifies a celestial dome and a longitudinal, extended axis into a meaningful whole. It unifies cosmic order and living history, and makes man experience himself as a god-inspired explorer and conqueror, as a maker of history according to divine plan."[64] In Judeo-Christian and Islamic thought one can find connections between the dome and heaven or paradise. For Norberg-Schulz, the Pantheon epitomizes the integration of "the sacred space of the vertical in the organization of interior space."[65] It is clear that the verticality of the Pantheon's domed rotunda and spatial integration is an architectural articulation of a human relationship to the divine, connecting the realms of heaven and earth. The analogy between the dome and heaven is made even clearer with respect to the main banquet hall of Nero's Golden House. Suetonius wrote, "The main banquet hall was circular and constantly revolved day and night, like the heavens."[66] Citing this passage, Oleg Grabar has asserted that this rotating dome of heaven signified a "spectacular implication of the ultimate achievement for a creator of visual forms, patron, or architect: the capture, taming and mastery of time."[67] What is critical in Grabar's interpretation is the connection of religion and issues of architectural mastery. Implicating time in his text, he treats the dome as the ultimate architectural articulation of a human ability to control the elements. For Grabar, the dome signifies as well the construction of heaven as "most potent image of power on earth."[68] The architectural capturing, taming, and controlling of time also implies the ability to represent time and those things associated with it. (In this instance, in the realm of heaven and earth, this can be *anything*.) In the end, the Mousgoum teleuk is no longer a domed house, but simply a dome, a cupola, and what it underscored is a French ability to literally control time, to capture it, to spatialize it, to mold it to suit French needs.

In the general reports on the exposition, the planners, under the direction of Lyautey, give a retrospective overview of its aesthetic goals:

> The exquisite visions of colonial exoticism, with their unforeseen harmonies, that could have appeared to the adventurers of another time under the tropics or in the countries of islands, as well as to the devotees of ruins and the wilderness, as well as to the romantic dreamers, had to preserve, in their multiple evocations, all their seduction and all their prestige.
>
> That is why the pavilions of the French and foreign colonies were to be integral or properly authentic reproductions, in their principal appearance, of monuments of a characteristic exoticism, to be stylizations in excellent taste, capable of offering vibrant compositions to the gaze and to the sentiment.
>
> It all at once became advisable to be faithful to reality, in presenting, for example, souks, a minaret, the huts of an indigenous village, and to join to it, elegance in the magic of the daily and nightly settings, that which could surrount the artist or the contemplative passerby in dreams and mystery.
>
> However, the instructive plan of the numerous particular exhibits contained in the Exposition and this character of pedagogical eloquence must not have become neglected for the initiated as well as for the masses.
>
> The decorative architecture of the interiors equally comprising museums and counters, documentary dioramas capable of reproducing in turn the atmosphere of a historic scene with its important people, types, of an equatorial forest, of a port or of agricultural cultivation and tools, of commodities, of graphics, was supposed to inspire more or less a local color. But, at the same time, it was supposed to respond to the problem of logically explaining the manners of the inhabitants, of classing the products of a region and to establish, with exact inventories and precise summaries, the victorious evolution of the civilizing idea across the world.
>
> Although the program was similar, the methods of arrangement and presentation could only be different. It was advisable to respect the grand principle of destination appropriation that is supposed to reign in all of the domains of applied art. In this regard, the autonomy and personal initiative for each of the projects, in the necessary shared general conception, was the most favorable in the specific value of the expressions, as well as in the interest, in the appearance, [and] in the attraction of the spectacles.[69]

This passage illustrates the connection between the aesthetic program for the exposition and ingrained myths of the colonies. Through this program, the colonies are not in the present, but have been displaced, residing in a crumbled, primordial past reinforced by Lyautey's exoticism. In this sense, Lyautey's "vision of colonial exoticism," laced with the romanticism of the *philosophes*, illustrates the primitive not as an object, but as what Johannes Fabian has called "a category of Western thought."[70] Within this *temporal* category, the colonized are not thought of as primitive, per se, but in the terms of the primitive, as a projection to a distant past on a scale of evolutionary time.[71] The architectural program of the Colonial Exposition bears the burden of spatially illustrating distance based on this scale. This distance, a mirror of those described in Papillault's scientific laws, became the major trope of justifying the imperial project. In this context, anthropology's connection to political and colonial agendas has been extended to the architectural realm. Through authentic stylization—a faith in the reproduction of a "reality" that has already been reshaped by the lens of ingrained Western myths—the mystery and romantic dreams of France *d'outre-mer*, always a part of colonial "reality," were reinscribed at Vincennes.

Man and god, dome and proportion, the vertical as religious and thus powerful constitutes the historical baggage that Fichet encountered when designing the French Equatorial Africa Pavilion in the Colonial Exposition. Even in the modern world of the twentieth century, the dome still had strong religious associations; it remained a staple of religious architecture and was ingrained in the vocabulary of political architecture as well. One need only consider monuments of Neo-Classicism, the use of architecture in history painting, and structures of the Industrial Revolution to see how the dome's religious overtones were invoked and brought into the articulation of Western political ideology. Important as well are the issues of European control that come into play through the successful integration of architectural elements. In this sense the relationship between the dome and man's ability to control space and time is echoed in the descriptions of the architect's ability to control and re-create the colonial at the exposition. This control became a means of articulating the category of "the primitive" and depicting evolutionary time through the built environment. Furthermore, it is this universalization that is seen as a goal of the aesthetics of the main pavilion itself. In describing the general ideas for the site, Olivier emphasizes simplicity of line and form and the universality of visual expression.

> The circumference of the pavilion was directly inspired by the huts of the rivers of the Congo; its pointed roof, supported by a peristyle and sculpted columns, lends itself to a harmonious mural decoration, made of simple geometric lines enriched by lively colors and purely ornamental drawings of an evident stylization. The diamonds, squares, bands, segments, and rose shapes were combined, were blended, and their amalgamation was so ingenious that the eye discerned only with difficulty the point of departure and termination of each arrangement. It is curious to think that these drawings, not without analogy to Pompeiian or Etruscan motifs, have been a key to art under all latitudes.[72]

As a means of explaining the aesthetics of the main pavilion, Olivier moves from the particular to the universal. Here, direct inspiration combined with the genius of the Western architect allows a universal expression that transcends time and place: an expression that is at once both ancient and modern, both colonial and metropolitan. Olivier conflates Western history, visual production, and time in such a way that the colonial has been integrated, assimilated into the *métropole* via the architect's spatialization and racialization of time.

Carol Duncan, following the groundbreaking work of anthropologist Victor Turner, interprets the museum as a ritualized space in which "visitors bring with them the willingness and ability to shift into a certain state of receptivity."[73] Within the French Equatorial Africa complex, visitors also became receptive to the objects on display and the architectural ambiance of the structures. Given the multiple associations of the building with respect to the taming of the exotic and the glory of French colonial achievement, the visitor could confront and resolve without difficulty the dichotomies that were in place. Examining the American Museum of Natural History, Donna Haraway notes that "this structure is one of North America's spaces for joining the duality of self and community."[74] The Colonial Exposition can be seen in the same light, for within its pavilions, didactic messages defined the scope of citizenship for the visitors who passed through its gates, binding the individual to the state.

The conflation of the ancient and the modern, the illusion of distant countries and distant pasts allowed for multiple levels of signification that could take effect as one walked through the complex. The movement from the main pavilion to the village could be interpreted as metaphor of traveling from the *métropole* to the colonies. While the interior of the main pavilion is evocative of a faraway place, these designs and sculpted columns are far more reminiscent of the beaux-arts architecture that became the rage in the aftermath of the 1925 International Exposition of Decorative Arts in Paris. Moreover, the primitivized beaux-arts interior of the French Equatorial Africa Pavilion is actually the inside of an ethnographic museum replete with cases containing information on different aspects of the "culture" of the colony. This is a striking difference from the interior of the 1922 French West Africa Pavilion in Marseilles, in which the architects sought to create an atmosphere infused with the same exoticism that inspired the outside of the structure (fig. 66).

The large hall of the West Africa Pavilion at Marseilles was supported by squat columns, which here can be read as the connections the architects may have interpreted as existing between French West Africa, particularly the Soudan (present-day Mali) and Egypt. However, in an attempt to make the interior seem more "African," the architects punctuated these columns with poles—a characteristic quality of the architecture of Mali's Djenne region. To further add emphasis to the "Africanness" of the interior, supports were constructed stretching from the lintels above the columns to the ceiling.

FIGURE 66. Interior of the French West Africa Pavilion. Architect: Germaine Olivier. National Colonial Exposition, Marseilles, 1922.

If we think about the 1922 interior with respect to the connections between architecture and the human body, specifically the Western body, what Germaine Olivier, the architect of the pavilion, strove to achieve was a means through which architecture explicitly articulated the difference between the *métropole* and the colonies. From Vitruvius to Le Corbusier, the most successful architecture has been that which most harmoniously reflects the "perfection" of the human body. As Johann Winckelmann stressed in the mid-eighteenth century, the perfect body was that of the Greeks. In architectural writing at that time as well, much energy was expended on theorizing the beginnings of architecture and within this rhetoric, most claimed that while Egypt had building, per se, true architecture began with the Greeks. Much of this work was based on the relationship of the Greek built environment to Winckelmann's perfect body, and one of the ways in which it was expressed through architecture was in the utilization of the column. For Western architects, columns that were slim, refined, and tall illustrated the correct or, we could say, the preferable, pleasing humanistic form. From the Greeks to the present, this slim column has been a staple of Western architectural vocabulary. Proportion was also Courthion's main criterion in evaluating the architecture of the Colonial Exposition.

What about these bulky, "incorrect" columns of the 1922 West Africa Pavilion? Columns such as these were incorporated into buildings on both sides of the

Atlantic, often embellished with "Egyptian" vegetation, and these forms showed an architect's familiarity and/or connection to Egypt. But for the West, the nineteenth- and early twentieth-century attachment to Egypt was not what one could call an attempt to construct an architectural genealogy such as we have seen with Le Corbusier, but rather a means to exoticize the built environment, positing Egypt as part of the curious collection of Western imperialism. The architects have enhanced the exoticism of the 1922 columns by their squat quality, a quality that signals an unfamiliar, strange, and imperfect, even incongruous relationship between architecture and the Western body. In this strangeness, architecture creates the necessary exoticism for displaying France's colonies in 1922. But what is also important here is to understand how this "incorrect" proportion signifies a displacement of Egypt from the genealogies of Western architecture as well. The connection of Egypt to the Soudan takes Egypt from the position of being the antecedent for Greek "genius" and connects it to the French African colonies, a quality that is only reinforced by the ways that these columns—unlike Western orders—seem to give in to gravity, the way they drive the viewer earthward. Given the insistence on metaphors made between the body and buildings, this truncated, deformed order would have been the anathema of *any* Greek column.[75]

For the 1922 pavilion, this connection aids in reinforcing the perceived stasis of West Africa as well. That is to say that this connection helps architecture cast the colonies, through the invocation of ancient Egypt, as ancient entities themselves. These weighty, fleshy columns transform the pavilion's interior into an architectonic equivalent of the Hottentot Venus. This caryatid *sans* head allows this pavilion to stand as the architectural absolute other of the metropolitan buildings in the exposition.

In contrast to 1922's explicit use of "exotic" forms to emphasize the otherness of French West Africa, the interior of the 1931 French Equatorial Africa Pavilion articulates similar things far more subtly, and this subtlety conveys a different message. Upon entering Fichet's pavilion, the dome and the slim, "correct" columns are much more in line with what was familiar in Western architectural vocabulary. The proportions here are similar to those put forth in the West over the past two thousand or so years. But while the columns are correct, they had been exoticized (as had the interior walls) with abstract designs presumed to have been informed by the things of the region. The same thing can be said of the dome itself. Like the squat columns of 1922, a dome with no drum, as was constructed in the 1925 French West Africa Pavilion (see fig. 50), directly conjured up architectonic ideas of otherness. While the dome exudes an exotic tone, Fichet, through the gift of a drum as the form's anchor, has "Europeanized" the Mousgoum teleuk by more fully assimilating it into the language of Western architecture.

The simultaneity of this normalization and exoticism falls squarely in line with the 1931 exposition's goals. The mixture of the familiar and the unfamiliar articulated France's desire to show the colony as having become a fully integrated part of the larger empire. The difference between 1922 and 1931 also suggested the further integration of these places *d'outre-mer* as an ongoing process weaving the empire together, but this integration also points out the contradictory nature of colonial representation. Here, the attempt to represent Papillault's laws and the policy of association flirts ambiguously with the abandoned principles of assimilation. In architecture, this attempt, this articulation of the integration of the colonies and the *métropole* is confused, for the pavilion itself, despite Papillault's laws, seems to signal the possibility that Africans could be assimilated or gallicized. Morton sees such ambiguity expressed in much of the architecture of the exhibition. Understanding these moments as failures in Lyautey's larger architectural plans, Morton, following Homi Bhabha and Frantz Fanon, explores the fair in terms of colonial ambivalence as well as the failure to enact a strict separation between colonizer and colonized. In my mind, such fissures reinforce the relationship between colonial bric-a-brac within and without the fair's boundaries, and this constitutes a failure on the part of Lyautey to keep the fair free from outside contamination.

Returning to the movement from the main pavilion to the indigenous village, the contrast between the modernity of the main pavilion and the primitiveness of the indigenous village, emphasized by the imported vegetation and Bouarel's sculptural group, could have made the metropolitan viewer feel as if she/he had made a metaphoric journey. As P. J. Philip, a reporter for the *New York Times*, writes:

> Those who know the curious civilization on the Island of Madagascar or the white courtyards and buildings of Morocco, the mud huts of Central Africa or the queer mud houses of Timbuctoo, declare that the replicas and their surroundings are so well constructed that momentarily, at least, it is easily possible to believe that one has been transported back to the original scenes.[76]

Olivier notes that the amalgamation of the designs of pavilion were so ingenious that the eye could not discern the beginning and the end of each drawing; the same difficulty would have plagued the visitor throughout his or her visit to the French Equatorial Africa Pavilion. Similarly blurring the lines among parts of French Equatorial Africa, Olivier tells us that the exposition "did not offer to the public a special presentation of each of the four colonies of the group. The Congolese block forms a single entity at the heart of the black continent; it is shown as such at Vincennes, representing the Gabon, the Middle Congo, Oubangui-Chari, and Chad."[77] Like the teleuk and the other "purely" African elements of the pavilion, the complex did not intend to give particulars, and this "whole at the heart of the black continent" allows a symbolic impulse that focused on the glory of French achievement.

In effect, the visitor walked through a diorama that was not quite dead, but certainly not alive. Reinforced by a "universal" shell, the inhabitants no longer have a distinctive cultural identity. They are timeless. And this is not because of time's absence, it is rather because it is all time: past, present, and future. They have a colonial history, one free of forced labor and other forms of exploitation, Judeo-Christian history, and French metropolitan history. The pavilions are containers that are full, yet sit empty. French Equatorial Africa's hundreds of cultures have been reduced to one, and this "whole" has been constructed as having neither its own history (precolonial or otherwise) nor a possibility of coming into civilization. Here, the noble savages represented the West's originary state, a time before writing and, ultimately, that simpler time before rational thought. As the museum produced citizens (under Duncan's analysis), here, in its projection of the self and domestication of the other through universalization, the exposition could produce a French citizenry through an engagement with the architecture, objects, and people of the French Equatorial Africa Pavilion.[78] Citizenship within this process was based, in part, on the experience of travel and tourism. This point is further emphasized by the publication of travel guides to the various colonies in tandem with the Colonial Exposition.[79] People did perceive of what they saw as real, but this realness was as much about the civilizing mission as it was about the metaphoric transportation to faraway places and times. Here too, that voyage ties the viewer to the fantasy of going away, becoming a tourist. And tied to the civilizing mission, as well as the trope of the traveler, this "going away" constitutes part of the intersection between modernity and colonialism. In this fantasy, the visitor can become the official, the consumer, and a metaphoric explorer, thus tying her or him to the honor and moral righteousness of France's colonial project.

This metaphoric journey, a trip through boundaries that are rather porous, brings up notions surrounding authenticity, and authenticity is inextricably part and parcel of the representation of time and space. The authentic is always a part of the past, and the realization of the pavilions ensured pastness while simultaneously buttressing Western agency. In discussing the Cameroon and Togo Pavilion (see fig. 58), Lyautey writes:

> The project was far from being a copy of the indigenous model. It originated by equivalence and, all remaining in a relative truth, that is to say in applying to the important buildings the principle of the indigenous huts, it was kept with much of the taste . . . in the picturesque excess of a black village of the exhibition.
>
> The diversely envisioned buildings . . . ought to present the same fundamental characteristics: a roof a thatch in steep slopes almost vertical, resting on a cob-wall, of straw mats or raffia palm, of the colonnades of primitive character, made from tree trunks rough-hewn and enveloping most of the buildings.[80]

While the planners allude to capturing the essential qualities of the colonies in the exposition, like the general aesthetic program, there is no attempt to create a mimetic copy of them. With respect to equivalence, success does not require a mimetic loyalty to indigenous buildings (which on many levels would have been impossible and nonproductive), and we have seen that such a notion was not considered to be fertile ground for inspiration. However, Courthion did find some merit to the reinterpretation of indigenous structures, although these did not always bear the correct fruits. What is at stake—especially in enabling the many metaphors signified by the pavilions—is the capability to produce a simulation of the colonies.

If the issues of time and the colonies are considered within the rubric of the "authentic," then it is possible to think about the manner in which the latter functions with respect to the aesthetic goals of the Colonial Exposition. Christopher Steiner has noted that in the quest for African art, the authentic always reflects Western taste and taxonomic categories through its reference to the non-Western other.[81] Reviewing the definitions of authenticity as they have been articulated by art historians and anthropologists concerned with African art, the focus is usually on how the term is attached to issues of value and commerce. Within this milieu, value is placed on the mythical original object that exists free of non-African influence. In the exposition, there is also this desire for an "original," but with a twist. Here, the authentic refers to the reproduction that could ostensibly *be* the original. However, in representing the presence of the colonizer on the lands of the colonized, authentic stylization as mimetic faith or the reproduction of "reality" is an oxymoron, a paradox of sorts. In the end the "authentic," like the original, is not understood as being part of the present, but as a part of the past. Perhaps best illustrated by the importation of carvers for the indigenous village, the authentic is distanced (fig. 67). Susan Stewart has noted that "the labor was the labor of the hand, and the product, in its uniqueness, was a stay against repetition and inauthenticity."[82]

James Clifford has stressed that "authenticity in culture or art exists just prior to the present, but not so distant or eroded to make collection or salvage impossible."[83] The disconnection, this place of the colonial in the past, allows the projections that commonly take place in the encounter between the West and the rest. The distance, insists Stewart, allows the exotic to offer "an authenticity of experience tied up with notions of the primitive as child and the primitive as an earlier and purer stage of contemporary civilization."[84] As a result, the pavilions, like the souvenir, characterize an intense anteriority, occupying a space outside of present existence that is marked by its fixity in a never-to-be-reconciled evolutionary past. The difference between the almost pastoral role taken on by "the labor of the hand" lends an aura (in the sense of Walter Benjamin) to the way in which we interpret the scene as well. Not only as a stay against repetition, the display of the carvers in the indigenous village serves to remind the overwrought

FIGURE 67. African carvers, French Equatorial Africa
Pavilion. International Colonial Exposition, Paris,
1931. Source: Olivier, *Exposition coloniale internationale
de Paris, Rapport general*, vol. 5, pt. 2, Paris: 1932–34.

Westerner of precapitalist systems of exchange in a fashion similar to the display
of artifacts in museums. John Frow describes this perception in such terms. "The
charm of displays of preindustrial implements and artifacts in old houses and
museums thus resides in their proclamation of the immediacy of use value: they
are rough, differentiated, lacking the homogeneity of the commodity."[85] However, it is this distinctiveness, the lack of homogeneity, and the construction of
the "authentic" that become means to legitimize the commodification of the colonies—and its residents—at the exposition.

The drive to appropriate and reproduce the ambiance of the colonies and
France's role within them is also emblematic of what Craig Owens has called the
allegorical impulse. Owens asserted that "allegorical imagery is appropriated imagery; the allegorist does not invent images but confiscates them. He lays claim
to the culturally significant, poses as its interpreter."[86] This interpretation, this
translation enabled the French to superimpose a new meaning onto the forms appropriated for the pavilions, and in this process, the original meaning has been
lost. The appropriated objects bear the symbolic weight of the new producers.
Owens also stressed that allegory functions in the abyss between past and present, and that a strong belief in the remoteness of the past and a desire to connect
it with the present are allegory's two predominant impulses.[87] Functioning in
that space of cultural and temporal distance, allegory allows the pavilions to hold

out the possibility of uniting a French past with a French present. Hence, the displaced colonies, represented by a decorative "faith" in stylization have yet another deed to fulfill. Already placed *en abyme*, as it were, the structures must then be able to convey the history, function, commodities, and imagined lifeways of the "natives." That is to say, the colonies must simultaneously depict France's "Garden of Eden"[88] (further emphasized by showing the labor of the inhabitants) and its modern "bread basket," hence strategically coding the colonies as part of a growing, functioning nexus of economic, social, artistic and political interchange.

Yet this aesthetic program, which negotiates (and attempts to reconcile) seemingly disparate stances with respect to the colonies, is flexible enough to allow individual taste within a unified whole. Olivier stressed that during the process of designing the French Equatorial Africa Pavilion, Fichet studied the buildings of each region and "strove to conventionalize the elements to create an ensemble corresponding to the program that was imposed on him."[89] In admitting such flexibility, it is evident that the overall aesthetic plan was not concerned with a slavish mimeticism with respect to creating the colonial pavilions. Moreover, in tandem with the complex burdens placed upon architecture in this program, it was impossible to (re)create the colonies in the *métropole*. Nonetheless, it was certainly possible, in fact desirable, to create an *effect* of the colonies.

What immediately becomes clear is the complexity of the aesthetic program for the Colonial Exposition. Like the policies of assimilation and association, the design of the colonial pavilions has contradictory goals and serves conflicting needs. The pavilions were supposed to preserve the ideas of exoticism while simultaneously articulating the economic value of the colonies; they were supposed to be authentic stylizations while simultaneously expressing architects' personal expressions within a general aesthetic paradigm; they were supposed to be representations of the other while simultaneously serving as blank canvases for the projection of metropolitan fantasy; they were supposed to be repositories replete with educational information squarely placing them in the modern world while simultaneously symbolizing the quintessential idyllic garden of a Western past. Like the civilizing mission itself, with its images of the colonies and policies of colonial administration, the colonial pavilions presented tableaux that used contradictions to codify French cultural and political superiority. They were able to negotiate fear and desire, identity and disavowal. This is, however, inherent in the imperialist production of knowledge and appreciation of material culture. On the one hand, material culture can be appreciated within Western norms of aesthetic criteria while the producers are trapped in racialized discourses that work to ensure their inferiority.[90] That is to say, the appropriation of the teleuk is indicative of the manner in which the French were able to edit and isolate the indigenous forms in such a way that contradictions between these indigenous forms and the anthropological laws of science were buried, left unaddressed, and disconnected from material culture.

Architecture was an explicit, necessary means by which the French sought to show the colonies as parts of the French Empire, but in such a way that "indigenous cultures" were "respected," that is, untainted by French civilization: a tenuous, uncomfortable mix of assimilation and association. And the lesson for the French was to show their genius in colonization, as well as the ways in which the white man's burden actually "helped" the colonized. At the same time, the focus placed on the economics of the colonies and their role as "bread baskets" or "granaries" enabled the planners to cast the colonies with respect to what they could economically, politically, and morally bestow upon the *métropole*. In spite of its phantasmic decor and presentation, the architecture of the International Colonial Exposition was ultimately utilitarian. However, within this utilitarianism, architecture was able to evoke fantasy and pleasure in its (re)production of colonial myths. Joan Copjec has stressed that there was no hard and fast distinction between utilitarianism and pleasure as long as pleasure "could be used."[91] With respect to the architecture of the Colonial Exposition, pleasure and utility merged to create multifarious dimensions of the colonies that were produced by decor, exhibition, and the experience of walking through and seeing the photographs, informational graphics, objects, and people on display.

Given the messy clash of the religious, the political, the economic, the useful, and the pleasurable, it seems that the fundamental nature of the French Equatorial Pavilion is not quite as exotic as it appears to be. By the time of the larger world's fairs and expositions, domes had come to be widely used in the design of government buildings and religious ones, emphasizing the psychic relationship between god and the state. With respect to the expositions, those buildings most reproduced were temples, mosques, and indigenous *domed* houses, further emphasizing the conflation of the religious and the political in the overall representation of the French colonies. The teleuk was a precedent for a pavilion in 1931, but the houses of the Bamiléké, who live in the Cameroon Grasslands, were the prototype for the Cameroon and Togo Pavilion (fig. 68). The "domed" roof of the Bamiléké house is strongly vertical, and, in a similar fashion to the Mousgoum structure, invokes the same response from the Westerner. Thus, the appropriation of forms in the Colonial Exposition is centered around structures that can be molded into a Western form and thus made translatable, hence taking a role in assuaging Western anxieties surrounding the "darkness" or untranslatability of the African other. Moreover, in this translation, the reconstituted African persona, as it were, became an intense mediation on the European self.

Conclusion

In the architecture of the 1931 International Colonial Exposition, the French Equatorial Africa complex was a sign of distance and, more importantly, of modernity. In its appropriation, it illustrated the distinction between the *métropole*

FIGURE 68. Bamiléké Chefferie at Bandjoun, Cameroon, photographed July 19, 1994.

and the colonies. In its inclusion of Africans and copies of African sculpture, it was able to denote an image of the noble savage, serving to remind the civilized European of her or his own bucolic past and her or his own Garden of Eden. In its display of the civilizing mission, it was able to show the role of France in taking an active stance in simultaneously displaying difference and its rhetorical diminution through the benefits bestowed by the colonizers onto the colonized. In reality, the colonial pavilions become Western containers that held the indigenous flora, fauna, and people of the colonies within its confines. They were devices that assisted in the bolstering of French national identity.

Perhaps most importantly, the French Equatorial Africa Pavilion showed the necessity of racialism in exhibiting the advantages of civilization and whiteness.[92] In this sense, the International Colonial Exposition showed the paramount importance of the colonized in the understanding of the modern world and the paramount place of the colonized in the ideological construction of a twentieth-century European national identity. Ultimately, the 1931 International Colonial Exposition was an intense meditation on a collective national psyche that simultaneously attempted to reinscribe an unquestioned consciousness of white superiority.

Present Tense

In Africa, an elder who dies is a library that burns.
AMADOU HAMPÂTÉ BÂ, *Aspects de la civilization africaine*

4

In one of the interviews that were the staple of my field research in Pouss, my research assistant Hamat Gring invoked the above assertion. He was talking to Azao Dogo, considered by many to be the village historian. Gring asked, "If we do not know our elders, will our culture be on its knees?" The image raised by the discussion between Gring and Dogo painted a vivid portrait of fears surrounding the relationship between the past and the present as well as their belief that to survive in the present, one must know one's past. Gring's invocation of Bâ presented a poignant, complex set of relationships around which are centered Mousgoum cultural knowledge and identity.

For the Mousgoum, as for many cultures around the globe, art and architecture have become important vehicles for sustaining—in tangible, visible forms—a knowledge of the past that is embedded in ideas about cultural heritage. In that sense, Bâ's elder and the teleuk share much in common. The Mousgoum teleuk was said to have been disappearing as early as the 1930s—through the combination of forced labor under French colonialism, Mousgoum emigration, changes in societal structures, illness, and death. Indeed, during my preliminary fieldwork in and around Pouss in 1994, I saw few teleukakay still standing.

However, since 1995 there has been a resurgence in the building of the teleuk. Nearly twenty new ones stand today in Pouss and its environs (fig. 69 and plate 5). Alongside this development, the end of 1995 saw a virtual explosion in wall painting, and much of this work depicts the teleuk (plate 6). Fundamentally, the contemporary revival of the teleuk and its mural imagery shows how Mousgoum historical consciousness has been informed by the fear of irrevocable cultural loss, by the acutely understood importance of the connection between architecture and cultural heritage, and by the Cameroonian government's and the West's regard for the teleuk. At the end of the twentieth century, this structure has become a syncretic form—indigenous in its genesis and charged with a Mousgoum comprehension and interpretation of outside ideas. It is this crossroads of mean-

FIGURE 69. Enclosure consisting of teleukakay built by (left to right) Math Perleh, Afti Doupta, Idrissa Sonmaye, and Apaïdi Toulouk, Mourlà, Cameroon, 1995.

ing at what I call the "new fin de siècle" that serves as the foundation for this examination of the contemporary revival of the Mousgoum teleuk.

Bâ, Gring, and Dogo's conceptions about the preservation of cultural heritage—and their fear of losing it—underscore the importance of the roles that histories play within the constructions of contemporary identities. In a similar vein, Greg Dening explains:

> Histories, transformations of the past into expressions, clothe, constitute, *are* a present social reality. Histories always have this *double entendre*. They refer to a past in making a present. The knowledge of the past that re-presents the past in story or account makes the structures of the present—such as class or identity—in the expressing . . . . Histories are fictions—something made of the past—but fictions whose forms are metonymies of the present (emphasis in original).[1]

These historical metonymies, these symbolic moments that translate history from a series of events to symbols in an individual or group psyche, reverberate in the contemporary art and architecture of the Mousgoum. The new teleuka-kay, wall painting, and performances constitute visual and kinesthetic histories, reaching back to the past in ways that aid in the constitution of a present reality. In this sense, the past as articulated by the Mousgoum becomes a codified set of texts and imagery read as ancestral symbol and contemporary identity.

Mousgoum Self-Reinvention

The apotheosis of this inquiry is the celebration of the opening of the 1996 tourist season in northern Cameroon, which took place in Pouss on December 30, 1995. The event was, literally and symbolically, the meeting of the local and the national, the "traditional" and the "(post) modern," the past and the present and the Mousgoum and the Western tourist. In front of Lamido Mbang Yaya Oumar's palace, a stage was created, bounded by a permanent hangar on the right and a temporary one on the left. That on the right was reserved for Lamido Mbang Yaya Oumar; his brother, the lamido of Katoa, a small Chadian village about three miles to the southeast; the lamido of Guirvidig, a Mousgoum village about fifteen miles to the southwest; and other Mousgoum dignitaries (fig. 70). The hangar on the left provided shade for the Association of Elites for the Development of Maga, Cameroonian government officials, and Western tourists (fig. 71). In a semicircle extending from one hangar to the other, facing the palace, crowds of Mousgoum people as well as members of other local cultures also watched the events.[2]

Throughout the morning, various Mousgoum, Massa, and Toupouri groups, cheered on by family, friends, and other residents of the region, performed historic dances (fig. 72).[3] While music played to the enthusiasm of onlookers, many of whom were dancing and cheering, merchants handed out free samples of

FIGURE 70. Hangar in front of the palace of Lamido Mbang Yaya Oumar. Celebration of the opening of the 1996 Tourist season, Pouss, December 30, 1995.

FIGURE 71. Area reserved for tourists and government officials in front of the palace of Lamido Mbang Yaya Oumar. Celebration of the opening of the 1996 tourist season, Pouss, December 30, 1995.

Master's cigarettes, and workers placed posters advertising the beverages "33" Export, Castel, Beaufort, and D'jino around the center of activity.[4] Representatives from Cameroon Airlines gave out stickers and taped one of their advertising posters onto the lamido's palace. As the dancing and festivity continued, a stream of Peugeots, land vehicles, minivans, buses, and bush taxis came into the village center, releasing neighbors, visiting relatives, Cameroonian government officials, and tourists from Europe and the United States. At 11:30 a.m., a horn was sounded. The dancers stopped, and the chaotic, frenzied atmosphere immediately became still. Everyone went to her or his assigned place, and the procession of the Mousgoum lamidos began.

First came the cortege of Lamido Mbang Yaya Oumar of Pouss (fig.73). Under a bouncing, twirling bright blue umbrella, he was surrounded by a group of thirty-seven soldiers and some musicians. The soldiers rode horses lavishly decorated in reds, oranges, and blues. The ruler himself rode a steed clad in silver. One member of the procession carried a flywhisk, the rest held spears and swords—all symbols of the power of the sultanate. Musicians played horns and

FIGURE 72. Mousgoum dance. Celebration of the opening of the 1996 tourist season, Pouss, December 30, 1995.

drums around the entourage. The lamido and his retinue wore ceremonial Muslim dress—the soldiers wore brightly colored, richly embroidered *boubous*; the lamido wore a white *boubou* (white being a sign of Islamic piety), dark sunglasses, and a turban with an embroidered band around it. When seen under the blue umbrella and atop his highly decorated horse, the lamido's costume effectively distinguished him from his multicolored entourage. Moreover, the sunglasses and turban nearly covered the lamido's face, further serving to separate the ruler from the others.

In various African contexts, these royal trappings—the umbrella, the horses, the lavish costume, musicians, flywhisk, and weapons—contribute to the creation of a rich iconographic program that expresses the status, wealth, and power of the ruler. What is striking here is the similarity between the lamido's entourage and that of the Bagirmi ruler Gauaronga, whose court Olive MacLeod visited in 1911 (fig. 74). The Mousgoum had a contentious relationship with the Bagirmi kingdom, at times being in alliance with it, at others being dominated by it. MacLeod describes a scene she witnessed during the Bagirmi Fête du Mouton:

FIGURE 73. Lamido Mbang Yaya Oumar. Celebration of the
opening of the 1996 tourist season, Pouss, December 30, 1995.

Gauaronga appeared in state upon his war-horse. A huge tent-like umbrella,
symbolic of royal power, was held over him. He was magnificently mounted,
and jewels flashed from his high native saddle. This was of silver, covered with
repoussé work . . . It was impossible to judge of the man, for his mouth was
shrouded in a turban that came down over his forehead to where large black
goggles continued the concealment.[5]

André Gide notes the appearance of the Mousgoum general Patcha Alouakou's entourage during his 1926 visit to Pouss:

And sure enough, we could see on the shore in the distance a stupendously
big, fat man, surrounded by a numerous escort; he was underneath an immense canopy—a gigantic umbrella, like the awning spread over a merry-go-
round, and striped alternately in red, green, and yellow.[6]

Such similar regalia, like the Bagirmi-inspired architecture of the lamido's palace itself, speaks to the past connections between the two cultures and illustrates
how outside symbols of royalty and status have been assimilated by Mousgoum
rulers for their own iconographic program. Moreover, Mousgoum cosmopolitanism itself articulates royal status.

As the royal entourage arrived, the crowds bowed and cheered. They then opened up the semicircle to allow the procession to enter the center arena. Following this procession came that of the lamido of Katoa. His soldiers surrounded him. His regalia was similar to that of his brother.[7] He appeared under a bouncing, twirling umbrella in alternating stripes of red and green. The lamido of Guirvidig followed, driven to the celebration in his black Peugeot 504.

Once the procession had ended, there were speeches by the mayor of the nearby village of Maga as well as representatives of the provincial minister of tourism and the provincial governor. After these speeches, dancing continued, and the newly completed Mousgoum Cultural and Tourist Center was officially inaugurated.

On the stage created by the Lamido's palace and the hangars on both sides, "culture" and "tradition" were performed through music, dance, and ceremonial. The presence of the newly painted palace murals added to this spectacle, making art and architecture an important part of the festival. This fact was not lost on those present. Marcel Doubla, the mayor of Maga, noted, "I will cite [among other tourist sites] the beautiful palace of the sultan of Pouss, which in itself constitutes a tourist trump card."[8] The representative of the provincial minister of tourism added, "Thanks to the beauty of the palace of the sultan [which recalls] the brilliant civilization of the Sao people, Pouss is genuinely a tourist village."[9] The combination of speeches, the aforementioned advertisements, and a model

FIGURE 74. Bagirmi Mbang Gauaronga. Photographer: Olive MacLeod, 1910.
Source: MacLeod, *Chiefs and Cities of Central Africa*, 1912.

of a Cameroon Airlines 747 jet that sat on a small table by the speakers' microphone highlighted connections between indigenous performances, art, and architecture and contemporary realities that are, in part, couched within the framework of the economic development engendered by international tourism.

The celebration was a multilayered borderland where performance, art, and architecture expressed messages whose meanings differed depending upon the observer's position. For the Mousgoum it was a production and articulation of their cultural heritage, a celebration of Mousgoum agency that merged with the presence of outsiders. For the Western tourists, who were brought in by the dozens, it was the opportunity to see the practices and images of an "authentic" African "tribe." For the Cameroonian officials it was an expression of a small part of what defines modern-day Cameroon. And for the itinerant researcher it was an incredible opportunity for analysis and an unbelievably lucky break. During this daylong celebration, the Mousgoum were defining themselves to themselves and the outside world.

The process of defining oneself is relative, weaving the threads of the past and the present and the self and non-self into a unitary cloth. For the Mousgoum, it is not only their own past, but also that of the West that has figured in their contemporary self-representation. One of the threads in this cloth is Gide's renowned 1925 journey to Central Africa. Indisputably the best-known Westerner to visit the Mousgoum (whom he identifies as "Massa," a neighboring people), as discussed in chapter two, Gide wrote an extraordinary passage on the teleuk that is the most often quoted text on the structure:

> The Massa's hut, it is true, resembles no other; but it is not only strange, it is *beautiful*; and it is not its strangeness so much as its beauty that moves me. A beauty so perfect, so accomplished, that it seems natural. No ornament, no superfluity. The pure curve of its line, which is uninterrupted from base to summit, seems to have been arrived at mathematically, by ineluctable necessity; one instinctively realizes how exactly the resistance of the materials must have been calculated . . . [Its easy spring terminates] in the circular opening that alone gives light to the inside of the hut, in the manner of Agrippa's Pantheon. On the outside a number of regular flutings give life and accent to these geometrical forms and afford a foothold by which the summit of the hut . . . can be reached; they enabled it to be built without the aid of scaffolding; this hut is made by hand like a vase; it is the work, not of a mason, but of a potter. Its colour is the very colour of the earth—a pinkish-grey clay, like the clay of which the old walls of Biskra are made (emphasis in original).[10]

The Mousgoum themselves have used Gide's description of the teleuk to attract attention to their Cultural and Tourist Center, and the French association Patrimoine sans Frontières (Heritage without Borders) has also used the author's words in its brochures as a means of gaining financial support to rebuild teleukakay in and around Pouss.[11] Gide's passage is an extraordinary example of a Westerner's simultaneous identification with and disavowal of the "primitive" other, achieved through the marriage of the languages of high modernism and primitivism. While Gide marvels at the teleuk's technological sophistication and "classical" form, it is not, as would be the case with a Western edifice, the product of architectural genius (coded as European and male); rather it is that of potters, who for Gide, can only imitate that which their ancestors had already been doing for centuries. Such a view implies not only that the teleuk is "craft," as opposed to "architecture," but also that its makers, masons who are almost exclusively men, are somehow "female."

Nevertheless, perhaps the attraction of this passage for the Mousgoum is embedded in the ways in which outside factors affect one's perception of oneself. V. S. Naipaul articulates this idea in his novel *A Bend in the River*:

> Small things can start us off in new ways of thinking, and I was started off by the postage stamps of our area. The British administration gave us beautiful stamps. These stamps depicted local scenes and local things; there was one called "Arab Dhow." It was as though, in those stamps, a foreigner had said, "This is what is most striking about this place." Without that stamp of the dhow I might have taken the dhows for granted. As it was, I learned to look at them. Whenever I saw them tied up at the waterfront I thought of them as something peculiar to our region, quaint, something the foreigner would remark on.[12]

With respect to the Mousgoum and the formation of contemporary identities, the views of those non-Mousgoum—conveyed in texts and ephemera—serve as a powerful means of reevaluating the self. Gide's passage reintroduces the teleuk to the Mousgoum. More closely related to Naipaul, the French government issued the first of a series of postage stamps featuring the teleuk in 1938. In a broad sense such things have played a part in making the house understood as the most extraordinary thing about Mousgoum country. And this understanding constitutes an important part of the structure's attraction for the Mousgoum and the Western traveler (or scholar, as the case may be).

In 1993 the Cameroonian poet Baskouda Shelley wrote *Kirdi est mon nom* (Kirdi is my name), a volume that extols the unique natures of the twenty-six cultures—including the Mousgoum—formerly grouped together under the problematic term "Kirdi." Europeans applied that designation to the various peoples of the area that had not converted to Islam at the time of colonization. Although the term today has pejorative connotations for some, Shelley, who is from the region and identifies himself as Kirdi, has reappropriated it for his book.

A highly complex text, merging indigenous oral history and beliefs with French language, French literature, and Nietzschean philosophy, *Kirdi est mon nom* attempts to rectify through writing what its author sees as "a [Kirdi] world often superficially approached and profoundly misunderstood."[13] Shelley views his tome as half poetry and half coat of arms, and the latter is especially important here. The coat of arms is usually defined as a design on a shield used as an emblem by a family, city, or institution. This emblem in turn is a symbol of identity, of a group's (or individual's) unique place in the world. It is with this understanding that Shelley frames his text, and invoking language as emblem, the writer seeks to "open a door into the immense and complex Kirdi universe" (5). This universe exists through a series of twenty-six odes that create portraits of each of the Kirdi cultures.

Each ode begins with the greeting "Ephata! My people Ephata! Kirdi is my name," and then a more specific declaration of Kirdi identity: "I am ———." The ode beginning "I am Mousgoum" (43) marks the commencement of a poetic history of this culture, starting with a myth of origin. In Shelley's account the Mousgoum were said to have come into being on the banks of the Logone as the result of a marriage between a Kotoko prince and a Massa woman.

After setting forth the myth of origin and Mousgoum perseverance in the face of adversity, the poet focuses on the relations between spouses and the way indigenous spirits aid in progeniture. The important issues here revolve around nobility and beauty. Besides conjugal relations and connections to spirits, the author uses the cleanliness and proper ritual and eating habits of the Mousgoum as tools to construct an image of them that is noble and humane. Expanding on such tropes, Shelley then asks:

> Do you know my celebrated Mousgoum house that is in the form of a
>   cylindrical obus?
> This house that displays the genius of Africa to the world?
> It is perfect, mathematically thought out, geometrically flawless.
> In the manner of the Pantheon of Agrippa, it exhibits a well-formed curve.
> As a beautiful vase, it is built without scaffolding.
> From the base to the summit, it carries an earthen color without paint.
> In the interior, its smooth, lustrous, glazed walls offer with grace,
> A rare sweet coolness that chases the heat and replaces it . . . (45)

Although the references in this ode to the Mousgoum are straight out of Gide, rhetorically they are vastly different. Shelley, like Gide, connects beauty to technology and classical form. For the Kirdi poet, however, this connection constitutes a source for celebrating the genius of the Mousgoum in particular and Africa in general. This genius is an integral part of Mousgoum identity, of what makes them unique among the twenty-six Kirdi cultures. In essence, Shelly has intervened in Gide's description of the teleuk. He has rewritten it, reordering its semantic underpinnings to reveal the arbitrary and mutable nature of the *teleuk-as-sign*. This reconfiguration gives the structure another signification, another underpinning ordered by a new voice. The dome, as a product of Mousgoum agency, now highlights the similarity between the role of the Mousgoum mason and that of the celebrated modernist architect. Moreover, Shelly's insistence on Mousgoum ownership of the teleuk removes it from the otherworldly, ambiguous territory of "nonpedigreed" architecture, de-exoticizes it, and places it within its own historical and contemporary cultural contexts.

In his preface, Shelley, invoking Aimé Cesaire, uses castration as a metaphor of oppression and psychic slavery (6, 9).[14] In tandem with a reconstitution of the self, an operation that Cesaire describes as "decastration"; the exaltation of genius enables psychic restoration. By being invoked as the display of genius and indigenous agency, the teleuk becomes not only a marker but also an aggressive symbol of contemporary identity, metaphorically and literally built through what Charles Binam Bikoï calls "the mastery of the verb."[15] This notion, for Bikoï, underscores the transmission of history and cultural values through oral means.

Moreover, the Mousgoum structure squarely confronts ingrained myths that insist upon African inferiority. Here, the deployment of the teleuk serves as an integral part of an African reference point in the operation of self-evaluation and reconstruction. Abiola Irele explains this process, with respect to the ways in which African reference points, put into the service of self-exploration, first constitute a polemic, a counternarrative fundamentally opposed to imperialist ideology. In this action, the teleuk allows the articulation of a cultural identity, one that is steeped in what Irele calls "counteracculturation." This identity exists in relation to imperialist ideology, simultaneously striving to divest it of its symbolic and psychic force.[16] Hence this new symbol, which helps Shelley reach an empowering catharsis, proclaims the two words that mark the completion of Shelley's—as well as the Kirdi's—healing process: "Homo sum" (82).

Tourism and the Making of Meaning

Dean MacCannell has convincingly argued, "Tourism today occupies the gap between primitive and modern, routinely placing modernized and primitive peoples in direct face-to-face interaction."[17] This interaction occurs in Pouss on an almost daily basis. Western tourists—guided by travel stories, travelogues, advertising, and images on ephemera such as postage stamps—arrive to see the teleukakay, visit Lamido Mbang Yaya Oumar, wander through the market, and go on "hippo watches" on the neighboring Logone or Lake Maga. After this brief sojourn, the travelers return to the Coca-Colas and Fanta sodas that await them in the well-equipped minivan and drive the sixty or so miles back to the city of Maroua, satisfied that Pouss and its environs are exactly as the travel guides had said they would be. While MacCannell rigorously explains and analyzes the often exploitative encounter between the tourist and what he calls the "ex-primitive," his account ignores that while the ex-primitive is, in a large sense, staging a performance predicated on Western perception and desire, it is possible that in the performance of dances, the staging of festivals, the construction of new teleu-kakay, and the appearance of figural wall painting, there is a rewriting of history not only for the Westerner but also for the Mousgoum themselves. This oversight in MacCannell's analysis robs non-Westerners of their agency and obscures the fact that many of these encounters have multiple layers of meaning.

Paul Lane, in his work on the Dogon of Mali, notes, "Despite a history of colonial administration, and, more lately, growing tourist activity, it would be entirely inappropriate to regard all these changes as comparable parts of Westernization." Within this framework, he writes that indigenous responses are viewed "at worst as . . . passive reception and at best as opportunistic adaptation to events beyond the control of local inhabitants."[18] MacCannell's overemphasis on outside forces of change in non-Western cultures and his failure to seriously consider indigenous agency cause his analysis to come dangerously close to reinscribing the very tropes he seeks to deconstruct.

Stephen Greenblatt has recognized the danger in such thinking about the meeting of non-Western and Western cultures. In his exploration of Europeans in the New World, he begins by noting his experience as a Western tourist on the island of Bali, witnessing the assimilation of Western technology by a group of local residents. He found that the VCR and the television monitor had become a powerful alternative of self-representation. Grennblatt then emphasizes the need to "resist what we may call an *a priori* ideological determinism, that is, the notion that particular modes of representation are inherently and necessarily bound to a given culture or class or belief system, and that their effects are unidirectional."[19] For Greenblatt it is important to acknowledge that people have powerful mechanisms for assimilating and recasting things from within and without.[20] His encounter also shows that the assimilation of things foreign serves at once those inside and those outside a culture. In this vein, the reappropriation of the teleuk and its representation by the Mousgoum have been neither passive responses to outside forces nor opportunistic means of accumulating wealth at the expense of the Western tourist: they are instead an active, powerful way of reinventing themselves for themselves.

Moreover, within many regions of Sub-Saharan Africa, the "gap" between the traditional and the modern has its genesis not only in tourism but also in traces of colonialism, in religious conversion, and in the connection of contemporary Africa to a global economy. Within all these factors, as well as the complexities surrounding the formation of national identities, many African cultures have sought to refashion themselves so that the past and the present are not in complete opposition to one another. Shelley's text is a dramatic form of this fashioning of the self, showing the self as having multiple reference points and constructing a modern Mousgoum (and African) person as a sentient, rational being who has a syncretic worldview. This self-fashioning has much resonance in architectural and visual realms as well.

The Palace Mural Decoration

When one comes to Pouss, one can easily find the palace of Lamido Mbang Yaya Oumar. His residence dwarfs those around it, and vivid paintings on its façade emphasize the centrality of the entrance. The palace was first painted in the early 1990s, but it was repainted in December 1995 to prepare for the aforementioned celebration marking the opening of the tourist season (fig. 75). Communities of women painted the palace's façade. Grouped by their neighborhoods, they were each given an area to paint. Groups from the eastern side of Pouss had the wall to the right of the entrance; those from Pouss Center (the area abutting the square in front of the palace) had the entrance, its immediate vicinity, and the interior court; and those from the western side of Pouss, the wall from the left of the entrance. For her work, each woman was paid 200 Central African francs (about 40 cents).

The teleuk is depicted on the two sides of the palace's entrance, among the array of representational and abstract images. Shelley celebrated the color of the house as being the same as that of the ground, but the teleukakay on the lamido's palace are a pastiche of colorful contrasts in paint and low-relief in clay. As with the Western representations of the teleuk, much attention is given to the pattern of its outer walls; however, these bas-reliefs' multicolored ovals give the houses a tactility and sumptuousness lacking in Western descriptions and images. As in Shelley's ode, the reappropriation of the teleuk transforms it into a sign that undeniably attests to the desire of the Mousgoum to portray their culture as vital and contemporary, and the position of the houses on the two sides of the

FIGURE 75. Wall mural, palace of Lamido Mbang Yaya Oumar, Pouss, 1995.

FIGURE 76. Official stamp of Lamido Mbang Yaya Oumar.

entrance calls attention to the ruler's power and wealth. The capacity of the teleu-kakay to relay such qualities is emphasized in the image on the lamido's official stamp, where the house appears under two swords (fig. 76). This pictogram identifies the lamido and his dominion. The words, "SULTAN MBANG YAYA OUMAR/ CANTON POUSS, MAGA" appear within the surrounding ring. Working as part of the frame itself, the written name of the lamido and the place ground the teleuk within a Mousgoum vocabulary of royal power.

The lamido's brother and spokesperson, Salman Mbang Oumar, called the teleuk the Mousgoum "symbol of tradition," adding that it is the "card of identity of the Mousgoum." The view of the house as a cultural symbol was echoed by many people in and around Pouss. Ousman Assoua was explicit about such a connection, insisting: "The appearance of the *teleuk*, a symbol of Mousgoum culture that is nearly lost, on the wall of the lamido not only stirs the curiosity of the Mousgoum but also attracts the attention of tourists for the sake of joy." Évélé Douniya contended that the construction of the new teleukakay articulates "the memory of the past." These connections are also found pictorially on the wall of Mme. Boukar Patcha Alouakou's house (she is a daughter-in-law of the despot Patcha Alouakou), where the word *symbole* is written above a drawing of a te-leuk (fig. 77). She states, "I have revived or drawn the *teleuk* on my wall because it is something from our tradition which is in the process of disappearing." As these references reveal, the teleuk's reappropriation and reinterpretation recall a Mousgoum past whose symbolic import is much a part of the present.

When I interviewed the lamido in 1995, he elaborated even further in his description of the teleuk, comparing it to writing. He also claimed that the Mous-goum are a people who "appeared on the earth several millions of years ago" and added, "They are a people who come from the Sudan; they are a civilized peo-ple *because* of having built the teleuk" (emphasis mine). In these statements, the lamido consciously attaches the teleuk to his own ideas of civilization, and with-in this connection, places emphasis upon Mousgoum ingenuity and agency, re-minding us once again of Bikoï's "mastery of the verb." In his novel *No Longer at Ease*, the celebrated Nigerian author Chinua Achebe writes:

> And the symbol of the white man's power was the written word, or better still, the printed word. Once before he went to England, Obi heard his father talk with deep feeling about the mystery of the printed word to an illiterate kinsman:
>
> 'Our women made black patterns on their bodies with the juice of the *uli* tree . . . but it soon faded . . . . But sometimes our elders spoke about *uli* that never faded, although no one had ever seen it. We see it today in the writing of the white man. If you go to the native court and look at the books which clerks wrote twenty years ago or more, they are still as they wrote them. They do not say one thing today and another tomorrow, or one thing this year and another next year . . . . In the Bible, Pilate said, "What is written is written." It is the *uli* that never fades.'[21]

FIGURE 77. Mme. Boukar Patcha Alouakou, wall mural, Pouss, 1995.

In these conscious connections of African forms to writing—indeed, these forms *as* writing—the lamido and Achebe each reveal a perception of civilization and power rooted in the written word, and for the Mousgoum this connection is part of the way the teleuk becomes product and symbol of not only the Mousgoum civilization in particular but also the idea of civilization in general.

Writing has many other meanings with respect to the construction of the self that are steeped in different ideas of "culture" and civilization. In a framework dictated by Hegelian notions of civilization and the self, writing—and, by extension, the book—became understood as the ultimate tool that Africans could deploy to eradicate the intellectual and cultural alienation resulting from the colonizer's denial of the particularities of African cultures and, moreover, of the colonizer's wholesale negation of African humanity. It is in this spirit that the Cameroonian scholar André-Marie Ntsobe passionately insists:

> The book is the universal word, the word of the man of culture. It offers him the ultimate privilege of becoming aware of the weakness of what has been said in the past, its contradictions and even its contingency. It enables him to have a history of vast dimensions, a definitive structure of his social organization, to take charge of his life and fix it in an immutable form. The new language permits him to formulate his ultimate goals explicitly, it is the liberating word, an [eruption] into the world and history. . . . By consigning their knowledge to the printed page they counteract the alienation of Cameroonians . . . Hence the book is a sacred heritage, since it is a means for Cameroon to conserve its cultural characteristics, a means of expression for restoring fullness and meaning to its culture, since it crystallizes the riches of the centuries.[22]

The issues articulated by Ntsobe also find expression in the provocative analogy the lamido draws between the teleuk and writing. It is explicitly that which, like the work of Shelley, connects the Mousgoum to history, civilization, and full personhood. Herbert Cole also addresses the link between art and writing in Africa, expounding on the importance of the word in showing the literacy of artists and rulers. According to him, the power of the word also amplifies the ruler's authority and prestige.[23] The teleuk, as structure and as representation in painting, like Achebe's written word and Ntsobe's books, assumes a position of permanence tantamount to a declaration of civilization and a résumé of history for the Mousgoum people.

Lamido Mbang Yaya Oumar is not only the political leader of the sultanate of Pouss but also the spiritual leader of its Muslims. The sultanate converted to Islam by the turn of the twentieth century under the influence and domination of the Bagirmi.[24] By the 1930s and 1940s a large proportion of the sultanate's subjects had converted as well. The crescent moon and star—one of the paradigmatic signs of Islamic affiliation as well as an allusion to beginnings and endings—appears on the façade of the palace, announcing the paramount importance of Islam as part of the lamido's identity. This symbol works with the other images to construct the representation of his power and dominion.

The symbols on the lamido's wall point to the spiritual dimension of his person and his power, which derive from his being seen by Muslims as the earthly representative of the Prophet, a characterization that legitimates his rule. Here the crescent and star bear a striking symbolic resemblance to the turban of the ruler. As one hadith said, "as long as the Islamic community wears the turban, it will not go astray."[25] Hence the spirituality of the cloth serves as a metaphor for the spirituality of the sultanate. The images on the wall articulate the same message.

However, the turban finds analogies not only in the symbol of the crescent and star but also in the teleuk and its image on the palace wall. As is the case with many architectural forms throughout the world, the parts of the teleuk serve as metaphors for parts of the human body, and within this framework, the head takes on paramount importance. As mentioned in chapter one, the covering for the hole at the top of the teleuk is called a "straw hat" (*gidigilik*). The architectural metaphors it engenders easily accommodate and assimilate Islamic practices and beliefs. Thus, the importance of the turban in dress and the head in Mousgoum architecture creates a milieu in which the teleukakay on the lamido's façade articulate similar functions within political and spiritual realms. The multicolored representations of the teleuk work along with this. The combination of the white background with the colored *aziy*, or "feet" of the house on the left finds its metaphor in the Mousgoum fantasia, a lavish event, usually performed during important holidays, in which the lamido displays his royal power. Highlights include elaborate costumes, for man and horse, and the shooting of guns (plate 7). In both cases, the contrast of white and color serves to highlight the power and importance of the ruler.

The ability of the teleuk to become a reflection of the present and a mnemonic key to the past is reinforced by other paintings on the palace façade, such as the images of the airplane and the map of Cameroon. With respect to the Western veneration of the teleuk and the move throughout Cameroon to develop tourism, the airplane serves to represent contemporary industry and modern transit.

The image of the airplane appears frequently in developing countries as a symbol of modernity. It would be shortsighted, however, to see it only as such. Susan Vogel has convincingly argued that images of airplanes, Mercedes-Benzes, and the like in contemporary African art can at times be understood as both "traditional" and "modern." Using as an example the Ghanaian artist Kane Kwei's 1989 *Airplane-Shaped Coffin*, Vogel stresses that the artist's work "permits his patrons to uphold traditional values publicly through a conspicuously untraditional means" (fig. 78).[26]

If we consider the airplane on the lamido's wall in tandem with his own ceremonial appearances on an elaborately outfitted horse, as well as the representation of the horse on the earlier and present façades, we can then see these two mural images as striking metaphors for the ruler. Cole emphasizes how the horse underscores the superiority of rulers, helping to fashion them as "aggrandized, forceful males." He suggests that they are "faster, richer, more visually and psychologically impressive, and thus in a more commanding position to lead." Cole then draws analogies to wheeled vehicles and their capacity to signify similar ideas of wealth and prestige.[27] The airplane calls to mind the same analogy. While this means of transport speaks to the present as symbol of tourism, or "modernity" itself, it is multifaceted, addressing at once the lamido's cosmopolitanism as well as his superiority and ability to rule his subjects.

Perhaps the façade's most obvious image suggestive of contemporary life and identity is the map and flag of Cameroon. On an earlier façade, a dot with a leader line showing the location of the Mousgoum—specifically the sultanate of Pouss—within the modern nation-state illustrated a Mousgoum concern with connecting themselves to a larger political entity and showing their allegiance to it (fig. 79). As Mme. Elhadj Abdramane said about the Cameroonian flag on her own wall, "The flag is [there] because I am in my country" (fig. 80). The idea of Cameroon as a unified polity is rooted in the nationalist movements for independence that developed throughout the African continent during the 1950s and 1960s. Cameroon gained independence in 1960, and creating a unified national identity in a country containing over one hundred different cultures is still a contested issue.[28] The 1,000 Central African franc note is an example of how

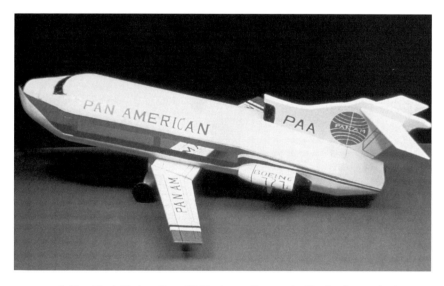

FIGURE 78. Kane Kwei, *Airplane-Shaped Coffin*, Accra, Ghana, 1989. Wood and enamel paint. Museum of International Folk Art, Santa Fe, New Mexico. Department of Cultural Affairs. Photo by: Herbert Lotz.

FIGURE 79. (*above*) Wall mural, detail, palace of Lamido Mbang Yaya Oumar, Pouss, c. 1991, photographed July 26, 1994.

FIGURE 80. (*below*) Mme. Elhadj Abdramane, wall mural, Pouss, 1995.

the Cameroonian government has used the teleuk to further this process (fig. 81). Considering that many of today's Mousgoum live in Chad, this alignment with Cameroon shows how, in postcolonial Africa, formerly arbitrary boundaries have helped constitute contemporary identities that are considered both viable and "real." On the lamido's wall, as in Shelley's work, there are multiple reference points: here they are not only ethnic and national but also connect to colonial and Western perception.

FIGURE 81. 1,000 Central African franc note, Bank of the States of Central Africa.

In this vein as well, the depiction of the map of Cameroon brings to the fore the relationship between the Cameroonian government and the sultanate of Pouss. In many regions of Cameroon, particularly the north, the nation-state allows many local chiefs to maintain their powers in their historical regions. In Pouss the power structure defined by the lamido and his guards has remained largely intact. People often go to the lamido—as opposed to Cameroonian governmental authorities—to solve their disputes. In many respects the government has allowed the northern sultanates to apply their own laws in their respective dominions, and in return the leaders of these ministates lend their support to national governmental structures.[29] Images of the map and flag allude to this reciprocity. Thus, we see not only an articulation of the sultanate's literal position within Cameroon, but also a symbol of the connectedness of local and national power.

Other depictions on the wall suggest how fully the image of the lamido in particular and the cultural identity of the Mousgoum more generally have been constituted here. Immediately to the right of the teleukakay, the airplane, the map, and the crescent moon and star, one finds representations of a lion, a teapot, and a giraffe eating the leaves from the top of a tree. These latter portrayals elucidate and amplify important qualities of the teleuk as well as important aspects of Mousgoum life.

In Mousgoum country, teapots are a staple of many homes. Certain ones are reserved for ritual ablutions before prayer; others are used for entertaining guests. A meeting of friends or associates at a home or in the market will often involve the sharing of tea. Through this act, old bonds are reaffirmed, and new ones are made. During my own stay in Pouss, the sharing of tea became one of the main ways I was able to extend friendship, respect, and appreciation to my Mousgoum family, friends, and associates. Embedded in this activity are tropes of goodwill and the social importance of "home." On the façade, the position of the teapot between the teleuk and the giraffe and tree creates an idea of "home" that is not only the house, but also the land, or, perhaps more appropriately, all Mousgoum country. This narrative of "home," however, expresses more than affiliation and belonging; it also declares ownership. As Abdoulaye Malbourg insisted, the things on the palace façade are those "which belong to the Mousgoum."

The animal images too evoke narratives of home and the self. They also appear, imbued with human attributes, in myths and fables, making them key agents in the teaching of indigenous manners and codes of behavior. They also play integral roles in stories that explain the world. The centrality of animals, for Salman Mbang Oumar, lies in the fact that in stories and myth, "the Mousgoum . . . can make animals and things speak and give them a description that is believed to be true."

The depiction of two men fishing to the left of the entrance, past the crescent moon and star, illustrates one of the primary occupations of the Mousgoum, an activity of the past that continues into the present day (fig. 82). This image of industriousness—echoed in various forms on walls throughout the village—also highlights indigenous agency. Here, male agency is represented as one of the things that ensure collective and familial well-being. This idea of well-being, couched in ideas of heritage and progeniture, is echoed by the appearance of a pot—an item made by women—on the wall (fig. 83).

FIGURE 82. Wall mural, detail, palace of Lamido Mbang Yaya Oumar, Pouss, 1995.

FIGURE 83. Wall mural, detail, palace of
Lamido Mbang Yaya Oumar, Pouss, 1995.

In a related context, some of the seemingly abstract images on the façade of
the lamido's palace express ideas of cultural survival. Moving left from the fishermen, one sees a number of shapes that look like two converging triangles (fig.
84). These signify the Mousgoum shield, an important item because of its ability to protect in war and to close off the teleuk to outside invaders. On another
wall, this abstract shape is given concrete form. The artist has painted a shape
in red ocher and black that is almost identical to the painted and raised abstract
images on the palace. Next to it is a smaller version of the image, above which
the artist has written the Munjuk word *gamar*, meaning "shield" (fig. 85). A spear
painted between the two like shapes underscores the importance of past warfare
in Mousgoum consciousness. In travelers' accounts and in field interviews, the
Mousgoum and war are often connected. In the past, Salman Mbang Oumar says,
"There was war. The Mousgoum often waged war." This attachment of warfare to
indigenous history and ideals about Mousgoum strength become part and parcel of the wall's imagery.

A bas-relief of an umbrella, lying under the scene of the fishermen, recalls the
fantasias and fêtes that are a staple of life in Mousgoum country (fig. 86). Like the
lamido's blue umbrella seen in the tourist celebration, the shields and other objects represented on the palace wall help to codify the umbrella's importance in
the presentation and definition of kingship. The umbrella, through its domical
associations, also finds analogy with the teleuk, each confirming the other's sta-

FIGURE 84. Wall mural, detail, palace of Lamido Mbang Yaya Oumar, Pouss, 1995.

FIGURE 85. Artist unknown, wall mural, Pouss, 1995.

FIGURE 86. Wall mural, detail, palace of Lamido Mbang Yaya Oumar, Pouss, 1995.

tus as part of the lamido's language of power. Ultimately, the palace façade in all its elements constructs a complex diagram not only of the lamido and his power in particular but of Mousgoum country more generally.

Building Teleukakay, Revising the Past

The Mousgoum Cultural and Tourist Center, officially inaugurated at the celebration of the opening of the 1996 tourist season, was built through a collaboration between the Youth Group of Pouss and the United States Peace Corps under the auspices of the Peace Corps partnerships (plate 8). Originally envisioned as a part of a larger project comprising a cultural heritage museum, an athletic court, and a community center, the immediate goals of the collaboration were the reconstruction of the nearly extinct teleukakay and the creation of a training program through which young men would be apprenticed to elder masons to learn how to build the structure. The project planners also saw the apprenticeship opportunities as a way to stem the exodus of young men, who were leaving the village for larger cities with more lucrative economic opportunities.

Under the Peace Corps Partnership Program, the local community is expected to raise at least 25 percent of a project's needed funds. At a total cost of $15,845, the Youth Group had planned to raise $4,983.[30] In lieu of money, the Mousgoum contribution came in the form of land given by the lamido and the labor supplied by Mousgoum men and women. The remaining funds were raised through application for foreign grants and requests for funding from private industry. Dana Goodhue, a returned Peace Corps volunteer who lived in Pouss in 1993–97, was instrumental in logistical and economic organization for the partnership.[31] During the four-month-long construction of the teleukakay that now constitute the Cultural and Tourist Center, twenty young men learned how to build the structures. Men and women decorated and painted the center in late December 1995.

Who conceived of building the Mousgoum Cultural and Tourist Center? The answer depends on whom one asks. Some, such as Mme. Abdramane, claimed that it was Goodhue who "inspired the young people to build the teleukakay." Others—both Mousgoum people and Westerners—insist that the Mousgoum themselves were the impetus behind the project. Either way, the Cultural and Tourist Center fulfills the desires of different constituencies. Like the painting of the lamido's palace, the reconstruction of teleukakay as a cultural and tourist center raises critical issues centering the intersection of the desire to preserve cultural heritage, economic necessity, community development, the salvage paradigm, and changes in the meaning of the Mousgoum teleuk. The Cultural and Tourist Center, like the teleukakay built in Mourlà by local residents in 1995, and like the teleukakay built, also in Mourlà, by the French group Patrimoine sans Frontières in 1997 all underscore changes in the teleuk's meaning. The house has been changed from its former status as a part of a homestead into the centerpiece of cultural heritage projects, and this change gives insight into the ways the Mousgoum have transformed architectural meaning in the late twentieth century. Moreover, this change allows another opportunity to explore the fusion of past and present and Mousgoum and Western agency in the built environment.

In the final stages of the Mousgoum Cultural and Tourism Center's construction, the Association of Elites for the Development of Maga, a group comprising primarily Mousgoum civil servants living in Yaoundé who originate from the village of Maga, in cooperation with Patrimoine sans Frontières, made plans to construct twelve teleukakay (in four enclosures of three teleukakay each) during the first half of 1997. This project, inspired by the fear that the few remaining teleukakay would disappear and with them the knowledge of building the structure, was conceived like that of building the Mousgoum Cultural and Tourist Center, but here there would be more houses and a budget projected at the equivalent of just over $52,000. The students in this project would consist not only of young Mousgoum men but also two European architecture students (one French and the other Spanish).[32]

The French group understood the transmission of knowledge through the apprenticeship as cultural salvage and as an opportunity to show Mousgoum architecture to a large Western public. Patrimoine sans Frontières has, in its own words, "started or carried out several *rescues*" (emphasis mine).[33] The association's brief statement brings to mind images of cultures on the brink of disaster. The trope of the dying culture, one that through change and *modernity* will be stripped of all its "tradition," is nothing new. Non-Western cultures have been represented in this way for decades. In a 1933 article, entitled "Dying Civilizations of Chad: The Mousgoum," Georges Geo-Fourrier characterized the Mousgoum and their neighbors as cultures that "appear to us as the descendents of very ancient civilizations that, degenerating, have actually reached a stage of evolution approximating a coma."[34] And the Mousgoum teleuk was dying too. Although Patrimoine sans Frontières's project was done in collaboration with a Mousgoum group, the association picks up Geo-Fourrier's rhetoric; underlying the teleuk is the assumption that the French group's participation is necessary, is critical to *save* the last vestiges of the teleuk and, by extension, a traditional, primordial Mousgoum existence.

Patrimoine sans Frontières's rescue mission also finds an analogy in "salvage" ethnography in which, as James Clifford points out, the disappearing object becomes the means through which the ethnographer can legitimate her or his right to "represent." Moreover, this "will-to-salvage" carries with it the assumption, in Clifford's words

> that the other culture is weak and "needs" to be represented by an outsider (and what matters in its life is its past, not present or future). The recorder and interpreter of fragile custom is custodian of an essence, unimpeachable witness to an authenticity. (Moreover, since the "true" culture has always vanished, the salvaged version cannot easily be refuted.)[35]

For Patrimoine sans Frontières, the representation of the Mousgoum is not in writing, but through the reconstruction of teleukakay and the filmic demonstration of the process.[36] In the film and in the world the two European students, through learning this "authentic," "primitive," and "endangered" means of building, can then go on to revive and reconstruct an extinct process, ultimately "saving" the Mousgoum teleuk, or at least a Western image of it.

However, as easy as it might be to merely accuse Patrimoine sans Frontières of practicing salvage ethnography, or, perhaps more appropriately, of creating salvage architecture, to do so would efface Mousgoum involvement and agency in this project. Neither this nor the Cultural and Tourist Center project are unidirectional undertakings in which Western ideals, perceptions, and desires have been simply, forcibly foisted upon the Mousgoum. These projects have meanings for the Mousgoum, meanings that are not based solely on those received from the West.

How do the Mousgoum understand the "process of cultural disappearance"? Many local residents, such as Gring and Dogo—not unlike more than a few Westerners—lamented the loss of ancestral knowledge among the Mousgoum; and many Mousgoum people understand the reconstruction of the teleukakay as the architectonic preservation of ancestral knowledge and cultural heritage. The fear of cultural loss is the primary impetus for the reconstruction of the house. Boukar Dadouazi remarked on this point explicitly, explaining that the new teleukakay in the Mousgoum Cultural and Tourist Center were built to "revive Mous-goum culture." Others echoed Dadouazi. Abba Mati, one of the young men who participated in the construction of the Cultural and Tourist Center, insisted that he took part in the project to "preserve and revive the culture that is in the pro-cess of disappearing." For Oumar Abedi, another young participant, the teleuk's form symbolizes strength, and he stressed that the house, through its form, "preserves the culture in the village." Time and again people stated similar views. Perhaps Mme. Djaoro Abourgadaï, a female mason from Mourlà and one of the few Mousgoum who still live in a teleuk, most explicitly articulated the role of the structure as an architectonic repository of Mousgoum history and memory. "I [will always live] in the teleuk in order to protect the authenticity, the memory of my parents. I use this teleuk as a kitchen, but I want [to ensure] that there will always be a teleuk in my homestead" (see plate 3).

The opinions and ways that the reconstruction of the teleukakay have been articulated finds analogy with the conversation among Gring, Dogo, and myself that opened this chapter. Unlike the salvage paradigm, the Mousgoum recon-struction of teleukakay is not the expression of a culture that seeks to relegate its own history to a permanent past, but rather one that seeks to use the past to inform the present and the future. It is one of the ways that Mousgoum ancestral knowledge will not die with the deaths of the elders. It is one of the ways that the Mousgoum will not, as Gring fears, become a culture on its knees. But what does the past hold for the present? How does the teleuk work within the dynamics of what Clifford calls has called "a present-becoming-future"?[37]

On a similar note Dogo eloquently speaks about the Mousgoum and the need to connect the present to the past, and the connection for him is the only way that the Mousgoum can maintain a meaningful sense of self. And for Dogo, the teleuk is the most obvious, most potent form to make such a bond. Dogo recog-nized such a need decades ago. "I started to build three teleukakay in 1968, [the purpose] was to encourage people to see [the teleukakay] and to carry on [fig. 87]. I have already given an example. Then we do not allow the disappearance of the past. There I make or see [a teleuk], and I continue. You also continue the re-search, continue the development." It is clear that the knowledge of the past, for Dogo, is a part of the ways in which one find grounding in the present. It is also clear that for Dogo the teleuk has emerged as the object most capable of fusing past, present, and future. The relationship between the past and the present ad-dressed by Dogo and other Mousgoum has also been articulated by Achebe. In his novel *Anthills of the Savannah* one of the elders of the Abazon people speaks:

> So why do I say that the story is chief among his fellows? The same reason I
> think that our people sometimes will give the name *Nkolika* to their daugh-
> ters—Recalling-Is-Greatest. Why? Because it is only the story that outlives
> the sound of war-drums and the exploits of brave fighters. It is the story,

FIGURE 87. Teleuk, part of an enclosure of three teleukakay built by Zigla Djimé,
Toussa Amidipini, and Évélé de Blali, garden of Azao Dogo, Pouss, 1968.

not the others, that saves our progeny from blundering like blind beggars
into the spikes of the cactus fence. The story is our escort; without it, we are
blind. Does the blind man own his escort? No, neither do we the story; rather
it is the story that owns and directs us. It is the thing that makes us different
from cattle: it is the mark on the face that sets one people apart from their
neighbors.[38]

The teleuk is a vehicle for connecting past and present; as such, it is imbued
by the Mousgoum with the qualities—progeniture, protection, etc.—that were
the same as those historically connected to the family homestead. However, the
teleuk as story, or as architectonic repository for the story, has been recast in a
role involving contemporary psychic and economic survival. This move marks
the Mousgoum as Mousgoum and makes the teleuk a powerful agent in the assertion of contemporary cultural identity.

Dogo acknowledges the attention foreigners have given to the teleuk in the
past and the present. Outsiders, in Dogo's mind, are a means of helping the
Mousgoum preserve their ancestral knowledge. Dogo believed that the presence
of Westerners—such as Goodhue and me—in Pouss aids in the preservation of
Mousgoum culture, for it focuses Mousgoum attention on their own history.[39]
Dogo and other Mousgoum understand in such deeds as revising and rebuilding
the teleuk, the structure has been changed from being merely a home or a place
in which everyday life is lived to a mnemonic symbol, a repository of cultural
patrimony and ancestral knowledge. It is the library that cannot burn.

The Mousgoum Cultural and Tourist Center was based in part on what was perceived as having been the paradigmatic Mousgoum family enclosure. Like many historic enclosures, or, more appropriately, memories of historic enclosures, the center's buildings are all teleukakay, and a granary is in the middle. Such enclosures were circular, and today one can see circular family compounds on the outskirts of Pouss and in smaller Mousgoum villages. However, the Cultural and Tourist Center, like the vast majority of contemporary family enclosures in Pouss, is rectangular.

Henri Lefebvre once wrote, "The adoption of another people's gods always entails the adoption of their space and system of measurement."[40] Pouss is no exception. Along with nearly a century of Islamicization in the region have come changes in residential planning and urbanism. The results of these changes in space have been the creation of new urban textures that strive to weave religion, politics, commerce, and domestic life into a tight fabric. While there still exists—in oral histories, travelers' accounts, images, and interviews—a paradigmatic circular homestead, in practice, and in contemporary quotidian life in Pouss, the paradigmatic family homestead has become rectangular, and the Mousgoum Cultural and Tourist Center reflects this fact (fig. 88). The center illustrates the marriage of Mousgoum and non-Mousgoum practices, a marriage

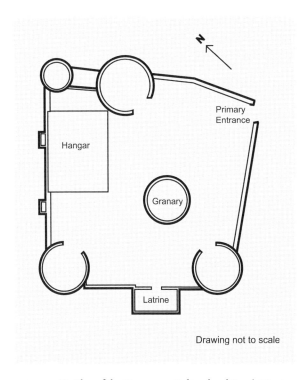

FIGURE 88. Plan of the Mousgoum Cultural and Tourist Center.

that has created a new, and indigenous, whole. Such a whole finds a potent analogy in Munjuk. As Muslims often define paradise in architectural terms, so do the Mousgoum. For them, paradise is "the homestead of Allah" (feŋ'alaw). Perhaps one could call the Mousgoum Cultural and Tourist Center "the homestead of the Mousgoum" (feŋ ni mpus).

Besides fusing things Mousgoum and non-Mousgoum, the center forcefully illustrates the merger of present realities and memories of the past. Like its neighbors, it is rectangular; like the enclosures of the master masons involved in the project, the center has a large granary in its center. These important, fundamental similarities are bridges that bind the past to the present, and they show the ability of the present teleukakay to become architectonic repositories, examples of Dening's assertion of history as a double entendre in which the past becomes a fiction put into the service of defining a present reality. The center also gives a three-dimensional shape and form to an articulation of syncretic histories, an articulation of "culture" as a process of understanding not only self and other but also the other within the self. Through the interrogation and construction of identity signified by the reconstruction of the teleuk, the Mousgoum are, in effect, negotiating difference in ways that are not predicated on binary divisions. They see the combination of ideas of different cultures and assimilation of different influences as a means of creating a coherent whole in a way that calls to mind the analytical strategies encouraged by Trinh T. Minh-ha:

> As notions that serve an analytical purpose, otherness and sameness are more useful when they are viewed not in terms of dualities or conflicts but in terms of degrees and movements within the same concept, or better, in terms of differences both within and between entities (differences between First and Third—if such boundaries can be temporarily fixed). Otherness *to* the outsider or insider is necessarily not the same as otherness *from* these positions, and in their encounter the two need not *conflict* with each other nor merely *complement* each other. Exploring oneself and one's culture in interaction with other selves and other cultures remains a vital process when *understanding is creating—is creation* (emphasis in original).[41]

In this act of creation, architecture, for the Mousgoum, is one of the key ways to explore the other within and the without. This other is constituted of multiple reference points: things non-Mousgoum, the Mousgoum past, Africa more generally, and Western ideas.

Architecture that uses ancestral knowledge in its construction has been advocated as one of the most effective means through which an ideologically and socially new "Cameroon" can be born. For the Cameroonian architect T.-A. Ebanda Mendunga, Mousgoum architecture is "certainly the most famous and impressive of all types of Cameroonian native architectures [sic]," noting that "critics, little inclined to praise, class it among the best architecture in the world."

Understanding indigenous architecture as a critical illustration of the genius of the Cameroonian people, he insists that the contemporary Cameroonian architect look at the forms of their ancestors in order "to propose an original synthesis with the modern world," concluding that "knowledge is power and you need it every hour."[42] In Pouss, the reconstruction and representation of teleukakay is predicated on the same view, revealing the importance as well as the conflation of architecture and ancestral knowledge. The Mousgoum poet Claude Abanga, who in his personification of the teleuk as an ancestor in his "Case en obus mousgoum" calls the house "illustrious eternal memory," makes this connection even more explicit.[43] In the poem as in what can be called ancestral architecture, the understanding of the past, the utilization of old customs is a means of empowerment through agency as well as the reclamation and preservation of memory.

And it is this metonymic relationship between the teleuk and memory that is so important in the structure's reconstruction. During my stay in Pouss, people interviewed routinely made similar connections among the teleuk, symbol, and memory. These connections stress the ability of the teleuk not only to represent, but also to become memory, cultural heritage, and knowledge themselves.

The elder masons Golo Agonan, Mathala Minsing and Ousman of Gouvraye built three of the four teleukakay that make up the Mousgoum Cultural and Tourist Center. Apprentices built the remaining house as well as one that stands in the neighboring compound of Gring Alouakou.[44] As in times past, the act of building was communal. Under the direction of the elder masons, others—men and women—mixed the mud, grass, and animal excrement and went through the process of physically building the compound. Once the structures were completed—a process that took about three months—women covered their surfaces with a layer of mud to protect them from the rains. The women then communally—with a few young men—painted the surfaces.

While the physical significance of the Mousgoum Cultural and Tourist Center shows the assimilation of things both indigenous and non-indigenous in its form, and changes the physical teleuk from house to indigenous monument and tourist attraction, the Mousgoum *process* of building, described in detail in chapter one, has remained intact. Gender roles, that is, the perception that men build the houses while women cover them—with the notable exception of the young male artists—are indistinguishable from the perceived roles of the past. With respect to conceptions of knowledge surrounding cultural heritage or ancestry more generally, this is critical, for this continuity reveals the ways in which heritage and knowledge are understood by the Mousgoum as well as the ways in which they have been and are being transmitted from generation to generation.

The process of constructing teleukakay and the triggering of memory are then two ways that the Mousgoum express and preserve ancestral knowledge. Ancestral knowledge is mnemonic and, like the relationship between the family enclosure and dance addressed in chapter one, kinesthetic. Here, we are able to see what was an implicit form of learning—the actual process involved in the construction of teleukakay—as becoming explicit through the reconstruction and representation of the structure. While writing and orality are two important factors that can be mnemonic aids and keys to "history," in this context the *making* and *seeing* of the teleuk has a major importance as well. If we look at the Munjuk word *sidi* (to know), the reconstruction of the teleuk perhaps takes on an even more central role with respect to knowledge, for *sidi* also means "to see" and "to recognize." Building and seeing the teleuk, especially given its mnemonic role within the Mousgoum culture, incorporate all three of these meanings. The root of *sidi* (*si-*) means "the body of" or "to be close to."[45] All these would find expression through the contemporary reconstruction of the teleuk, thus highlighting the multiple ways in which the Mousgoum gain and transmit cultural knowledge.

Telling "Herstories?" Wall Painting, Architecture, and Gender

As discussed earlier, Mousgoum, men, by and large, have built homes while women have covered and decorated them. In the past, the outsides of Mousgoum family enclosures were not painted, but covered and decorated nonrepresentationally with mud. At times architectural details such as inner and outer doorframes would be elaborated. Women and men constructed granaries. The patriarch arranged the family homestead. Women covered and decorated the space so conceived. While such gender roles have remained largely intact, the advent of exterior mural painting has brought with it a change in the Mousgoum woman's role. As the artists have explained, the act of painting for them is not inconsistent with the ways in which their mothers covered buildings with mud and decorated interiors. That is to say, many of the women see this change as being a process of evolution in house decoration. Throughout Mousgoum country, men articulate values in three dimensions; women articulate them in two.

While knowledge is preserved through the almost seamless continuity of labor in the building and decoration in and around Pouss, the advent of figural painting on the outsides of homes demands an examination of the changes in the role of the artist within existing social constructions. These new murals contain scenes that articulate the values of their creators in particular and Mousgoum cultural concerns more generally. The iconography of the walls in and around Pouss has rich motifs. Through these compositions, the artists attempt to articulate important cultural values and to attract the attention of passersby. Understanding this change in artistic practice as a complex process that weaves together the threads of the past and the present as well as an individual and the community, I would like to turn to the mural of Mme. Daniel Mainiazanga, exploring what such a change means with respect to gender relations and the primacy of the seemingly all-pervasive male voice among the Mousgoum (fig. 89).

FIGURE 89. Mme. Daniel Mainiazanga, wall mural, Pouss, 1995.

Within such an investigation, the sudden change in murals from being merely the "clothing" worn by architecture to tableaux of cultural history and memory, Mousgoum women take on a new role in Mousgoum culture; this new role insists, however tacitly, on the subjectivity of women in the reconstruction of Mousgoum history and cultural identity.

In a large composition that extends the expanse of her family enclosure, Mme. Mainiazanga has painted a mural that articulates Mousgoum concerns and connects past and present. As we have seen in other projects in and around Pouss, the artist has put history into the service of defining the present.

While the central section of Mme. Mainiazanga's wall first attracts the viewer's attention. I would like to begin at the left-hand side of the tableau (figs. 90, 91). Here, there is an abstracted floral motif flanked by a crocodile. To the right of the animal is another abstracted plant. Continuing to move to the right, there is a teleuk depicted in black, white, and red ocher. Connected to the teleuk is a man, wearing only shorts, who, seated on a stool, smokes a pipe. To the right, two elephants make a meal out of a tree. Again, there is a plant, and to its right, a cross, which articulates the family's Christianity. The bottom of the left-hand side of the wall is painted gray, and this border serves to anchor the objects represented. Directly to the right of the doorway stands a lion, who appears ready to pounce or attack.

Mme. Mainiazanga has painted another teleuk at the top of the central section of her wall (plate 9). As in the one to the left, the teleuk is depicted as the center of activity. Instead of a man smoking a pipe, we see a woman preparing food for her family. The relation of the woman, house, tree, and chickens below emphasizes the domesticity of the scene. Mme. Mainiazanga has placed the teleuk in a concrete, contemporary atmosphere. Moving to the lower half of the wall, the artist again addresses food. The image of three men fishing places food

FIGURE 90. Mme. Daniel Mainiazanga, wall mural, detail, Pouss, 1995.

FIGURE 91. Mme. Daniel Mainiazanga, wall mural, detail, Pouss, 1995.

into a masculine context. Fishing is one of the primary occupations of the Mousgoum; it plays a primary role in feeding the family. Here, one sees a man fishing by the shore; the other two are in a pirogue, working in either the Logone or on Lake Maga (this compound is quite near the shore of the lake). As in the scene at the top, trees and plants serve to elaborate the scene below.

FIGURE 92. Mme. Daniel Mainiazanga, wall mural, detail, Pouss, 1995.

FIGURE 93. Mme. Daniel Mainiazanga, wall mural, detail, Pouss, 1995.

The right-hand section of the wall is predominantly figural (figs. 92, 93). First two women pound millet. To their right is a war scene in which a man on horse-back engages in battle with two men holding spears and shields. Above them, Mme. Mainiazanga has painted an airplane. Moving to the right, the viewer finds a family enclosure, and another teleuk stands in its center. Its color and design serve to set it off from the other homes that accompany it. Here, Mme. Mainia-zanga has also depicted two women working in the enclosure. At the far right stands a male figure, whose dress compared to the other men could be seen as "modern," waving his hands in the air as if to attempt to call upon a passer-by.

Unlike the walls of Lamido Mbang Yaya Oumar's palace or the Mousgoum Cultural and Tourist Center, the rich iconography of Mme. Mainiazanga's wall is the vision of one artist. (Mme. Mainiazanga did not participate in the group projects.) Moreover, her mural has a coherence that the communal ones do not. In designing the composition for her wall, Mme. Mainiazanga has thought in terms of three motifs. From left to right, they could loosely be termed as the natural sphere, comprising floral and animal motifs; the domestic sphere, comprising images of food preparation; and those of work and warfare, comprising a group of women at work and one of men at war. What is striking is the presence of "home" in all three tableaux, hence alluding to the importance of the domestic sphere in all the sections of the wall.

What we can ascertain through a reading of the wall is Mme. Mainiazanga's personal conception of the Mousgoum contemporary place with respect to the past and the present and their immediate physical surroundings. On the left, the appearance of the teleuk with the animal and plant world can be understood as the place of the Mousgoum among nature and in the northern floodplains. If one goes to Waza National Park, about forty miles to the west, one can see elephants, lions, and (it is said) crocodiles. They are local animals, and their appearance on Mme. Mainiazanga's wall echoes their appearance on other walls in and around Pouss. On the right, the family enclosure is part of the war scenario, positing that the reason for war is the protection of the home and, by extension, the family. But what of the metonymic connection between the past and the present? Perhaps Mme. Mainiazanga describes it best when she states, "The teleuk is a tradition of the country of the Mousgoum. I made it for beauty and in order to recall the old culture for the present generation. The man on the horse and the men with the spears are symbols of traditional war." For Mme. Mainiazanga, as for others, the teleuk and the war scene have the ability to connect past and present in a di-dactic fashion. This connection is also amplified by the appearance of the air-planes and the figure at the left-hand corner of the wall. The former, a reminder of modernity, melds with the war scene and the homestead on the left, making the implicit ties between present and past or, in this case, the traditional and the modern, explicit. Like the palace wall and the Mousgoum Cultural and Tourist Center, the mural also recalls Dening's assertion that the summoning of the past is invariably part of the construction of a present reality.

Mme. Mainiazanga has not simply made isolated pictures of the Mousgoum teleuk. She has contextualized it. In the house's three appearances, it is nev-er alone, but part of a larger scene. The teleuk, symbol of the "old culture," is merged with activities that take place on a daily basis, suggesting that the house is part and parcel of contemporary Mousgoum life and identity. Furthermore, the ways in which Mme. Mainiazanga explores gender relations allow a better understanding of the artist's move towards a reconciliation between past and present. Food preparation, a typically female activity that predominantly takes place in the home—past and present—is contrasted with the gathering of fish, typically done by males. The Mousgoum understand these activities as complementary ones that are critical for the survival of the family. Mme. Mainiazanga uses the flowers on the right to amplify the implicit allusion food makes to progeniture. In their appearance with the teleuk and the elder with a pipe, the flowers seem to refer to the prosperity that comes with fertility and the survival of a family lineage. This linkage between male and female, between flower as fertility and the elder at home, amplifies the figure of the teleuk as mediator between past and present.

The contextualization of the teleuk on Mme. Mainiazanga's wall is rare on Mousgoum murals, but these unique scenarios allow us to see how this wall might be what we could call a "woman's" history, that is, a history that highlights the primacy and the intelligence of Mousgoum women. Speaking to the ways in which women create the scene on their walls, Mme. Elhadj Abdramane explained, "There was no one who whispered the idea to me; I decided all alone to place the drawings in my wall" (see fig. 80). Mme. Arkali Adogoï insisted, "[The things on my wall] are in my head. I cannot look at the homes of my neighbors" (fig. 94). This idea of independence underscores the freedom women have in decorating their homes, highlighting the creativity and intelligence they see

FIGURE 94. Mme. Arkali Adogoï, wall mural, Pouss, 1995.

FIGURE 95. Mme. Ibrahim Nouhou, wall mural, Pouss, 1995.

as being necessary to do it well. Unlike in many cultures in Western and Southern Africa, the painting of private homes in and around Pouss is not a communal activity; it is individual, and thus these murals become intense reflections of their makers.

Moreover, the artists are utterly aware of this fact when they discuss either their inspiration or the reasons that they painted their walls. Mme. Mainiazanga is explicit on this point. "I made [my mural] for beauty and in order to recall the old culture for the present generation." The artist's succinct sentence holds a complex set of relations that speak to how Mme. Mainiazanga understands the reasons for painting and her keen awareness of the mural's function. During my research, I often heard that such and such a thing was done for beauty, and in this context, beauty in and of itself has many important social meanings in Mousgoum country. Mme. Adogoï informed me, "I make a painting on the wall, and when my husband goes for a walk, one often says that he is beautiful because my wall is beautiful." Salman Mbang Oumar noted, "A concession that is beautiful ... shows the good morality of its occupants. A woman who has a beautiful house ... [that is where] strangers will go." To reiterate, beauty is not seen as simply a physical attribute, but also one that is intrinsically social and the outer expression of one's inner qualities.[46]

Beauty has the capacity to show the morality of a woman and, by extension, her family. Beauty is also a critical part of how the mural will interact with a viewer. Moreover, it is an unstated part of the articulation of Mousgoum history, memory, and identity that has always been seen as being the work of women. In the words of Mme. Adogoï, "In former times, if men did not make beautiful things it is only because they were closed, ignorant. There was not the evolution of modernism. Today, the young men have gone to school, they have seen drawings in books and a bit everywhere. With the young now, it is a time of revolution." As Mme. Adogoï suggests, the creation of something beautiful is a sign of a woman's intelligence. The exhibition of intellectual acuity is implicit in Mme. Mainiazanga's wall; on others it is explicit. Mme. Ibrahim Nouhou insists, "The Mousgoum or the black man has the capacity, the idea, and the imagination to draw art objects in the ways of Westerners." On her own wall, she sees the image of the horse as something she painted from her knowledge of Western imagery (fig. 95).

Writing on walls also constitutes a means through which Mousgoum women artists assert their intelligence and literacy. Mme. Boukar Patcha Alouakou, in painting the word *symbole* over the teleuk on her wall, shows her understanding of the teleuk as cultural icon in a manner that also shows her literacy (see fig. 77). Many other walls merge images and words, and Mme. Adoum Maïmouna's wall, which depicts two peacocks, is just one example. Above the peacock the artist has written, among other things, "*les oiseaux rares*" (rare birds), a reference to the lamido's peacock, a bird that is free to wander about the royal court (fig. 96). Like images of barber boards and contemporary African painting, these images highlight the literacy of their makers, flying in the face of many writings about African wall painting that chose to characterize such practices as being instinctual.[47] Here, Mousgoum women are cognizant about their goals and strive to show their artistic and intellectual acuity through their work.

FIGURE 96. Mme. Adoum Maïmouna, wall mural, Pouss, 1995.

FIGURE 97. Mousgoum *bawa* dance, Pouss, photographed April 20, 1996.

Within a context where women are still charged with making "beauty," as it were, the advent of figural wall painting has brought about a fascinating change within existing gender roles in Mousgoum building and house decoration. These two-dimensional representations are the first that the visitor—indigenous or otherwise—sees upon entering a "male-ordered" space. Within this paradigm, Mousgoum women now have the opportunity to define cultural identity and articulate their histories. As artists who communicate cultural histories, these women are striking counterparts to male griots or village historians. If we briefly look back at Mme. Mainiazanga's wall, we can see that in her historical narrative the composition privileges the duties of women. One such example is the scene of the women pounding millet in front of the central teleuk. This tableau is the first in the mural to attract the viewer's attention. The image calls to mind Mousgoum weddings in which women celebrate through a gathering that incorporates music, dance, and the pounding of millet for the three-day long wedding feast (fig. 97). Additionally, in the murals of the Mousgoum Cultural and Tourist Center, the nonabstract imagery highlights the teleuk as sign of tradition, but it also gives primacy to women, here embedded in the life-sized figure of a woman carrying water on her head (fig. 98). Artists depicted neither men nor symbols

FIGURE 98. Mousgoum Cultural and Tourist Center, Pouss, 1995.

of warfare on the center's walls. While women routinely tell stories to their children in the privacy of the family home, these murals make their voices public, blurring the boundaries between domestic and public identity. Furthermore, in a culture that has been trying to preserve its ancestral knowledge in a period of rapid social change, women's art has changed as well and has assumed a major role in the public sphere.[48]

Visually, this means that women, in a culture where they enjoy few privileges in relation to men, define contemporary Mousgoum cultural identity, and these new identities in many ways exhibit an understanding of the ability of the walls to affect perception as well as to display the primacy of female intellect and subjectivity. Moreover, the use of text and the understanding of imagery created by Mousgoum women demand that we expand the ways in which we interpret wall painting more generally. While it is common to see African wall murals as projections and reflections of the domestic sphere, it is also critical to see them as active tableaux and to understand the ways in which their production has the capacity to create spaces in which women, however tacitly or subtly, have the power to subvert, resist, and circumnavigate male voices.

Conclusion

In the realm of the (post)modern, in a village where art and architecture at once assert a cultural identity and give the tourist an "authentic" experience, the Mousgoum can counteract what many in Pouss see as a loss of culture and ancestral knowledge. Here, loss is perceived not only as the break between heritage and contemporary life, but also the migration of young men to the larger cities of Cameroon and Chad to find gainful employment. Again, the *process* of building and painting becomes as important as the thing itself. Here, we are reminded of Évélé Douniya's characterization of the construction of the new teleukakay as "the memory of the past." In the best of worlds, the apprenticeships with the elder masons would prepare the young for employment in and around the village and ultimately make it economically feasible for more of them to remain. Mme. Mainiazanga admits that one of the considerations of the way in which she designed and painted her wall was the possibility of economic gain and its preservation of Mousgoum history. Ultimately, it is not only the thing in itself, but also the *process*, the *savoir-faire*, that is a critical part of the Mousgoum cultural heritage, part of the preservation of and making a connection—real or imagined—with the past.

Hence, the Mousgoum connection with the past and the tourist who may well feel that she or he has stepped into the past are intertwined in this network. A good example of this is the village prayer that takes place at the end of Ramadan and during the Fête du Mouton. During the Ramadan prayer, Western tourists were bussed in to view a "timeless," "authentic" experience. Simultaneously, the Mousgoum felt a connection to a—revised—past. Like the celebration for the opening of the 1996 tourist season, this event was part indigenous Mousgoum consciousness and practice and part live tourist attraction. However, there is an important distinction between the two religious celebrations. The celebration of the end of Ramadan, which was viewed by many outsiders, was not as elaborate as was the Fête du Mouton, which took place during the April hot season—a time when few tourists venture to northern Cameroon. In the latter, the celebration was neither truncated nor amended as it had been at the end of Ramadan.

For the Mousgoum, tourism has worked neither as a means to salvage a dying form nor as a jolt to jump-start a timeless culture. While images, postcards, and souvenirs appeal to the Western tourist—myself included—and become records of experience, they also open a space for the Mousgoum to reappropriate their own cultural imagery, re-creating it in ways that articulate their own ideas of their past and their own perception of their present. The imagery simultaneously validates the fascination and satisfies the expectation of the Western tourist, enabling us to appropriate again the teleuk—also available in souvenir miniatures—and other items as a record, not of the Mousgoum, but of ourselves (fig. 99). And it is the ability of the teleuk to signify multiple meanings simul-

FIGURE 99. Mousgoum and other African souvenirs, acquired by Steven Nelson, 1994–96.

taneously that has been at the fore of the ways in which the Mousgoum have understood the relationship between themselves and the house; moreover, this ability is also a key factor in the ways in which the Mousgoum have understood the West and our relationship to the structure. Such a vast array of interpretive possibilities, centered in the teleuk, have allowed the Mousgoum to reinvigorate the form on their own terms as a means to construct their cultural identity at the new fin de siècle.

As stage of quotidian life, locus of living history, sign of authenticity, architectonic ancestor, home of cannibals, repository for experience, sign of empire, perfect tectonic statement, perfect fusion of form and function in an "unselfconscious culture," product of centuries of imitation, mark of African genius, stay against cultural loss, relic of antiquity, womb and tomb, sexual symbol, expression of cultural identity, articulation of the modern nation-state, the Mousgoum teleuk beautifully underscores architecture's preeminent place in representation. While this book has explored how the teleuk has been (and continues to be) submitted to culturally specific modes of interpretation, it has also attempted to tease out the critical point that these modes, while certainly specific, are not mutually exclusive. All of this book's interlocutors, be they Mousgoum or Western, have come to the house armed with some kind of prior knowledge (or cultural baggage) that affected (and continues to affect) their interpretation of the teleuk. In fact, the dependence on earlier accounts of the domed house in the construction of meaning often has been more significant in the ongoing interpretation of the teleuk than actually having seen the building with one's own eyes.

A few examples explicitly underscore the mining of accounts of the domed house. When André Gide came upon the teleuk in 1926, part of his writing about the form was to ignite a conversation with what others had already written about it. To reiterate, "I am astonished that the few rare travellers who have spoken of this country and of its villages and huts have only thought fit to mention their 'strangeness.' The [Mousgoum] hut, it is true, resembles no other; but it is not only strange, it is *beautiful*" (emphasis in original).[1] Gide's 1927 *Voyage au Congo* would affect, more than any description or representation of the teleuk, the reception of the structure. Ozenfant, who had never set foot in Africa, used Allégret's photograph of the village of Musgum, Chad, in his 1928 *Foundations of Modern Art*.[2] At the same time, Léon Fichet—having read travelers' accounts of the teleuk, perhaps having seen the dome used in previous expositions, having seen photographs of the house in French colonial publications, and having read Gide—appropriated the structure for the French Equatorial Africa Pavilion at the 1931 International Colonial Exposition in Paris. In the rebuilding of contemporary teleukakay in Pouss and its environs, the Mousgoum planners and masons cited the attention that André Gide had given to the structure, and, in fact, one can read his text while visiting the Mousgoum Cultural and Tourist Center.

One of the paramount qualities of the teleuk is its status as a unique object, as something special. It is also something seen as something endangered, something on the brink of extinction. Because of this, Mousgoum people and Westerners have attempted to "save the dome." At the same time the unique—and endangered—status of the teleuk has situated Pouss and its environs as a destination for international tourists, and Pouss-as-destination has been amplified by travel guides and travel posters (fig. 100). Travel posters advertising Cameroon as a tourist destination routinely feature the Mousgoum teleuk as one of the profound, spectacular things to see in the contemporary nation-state. Furthermore, the rebuilding of teleukakay and the 1995 tourist celebration have marked Pouss and its environs as a place that codifies and produces difference in tandem with the heritage and experience industries. One of the most compelling aspects of the transformation of Mousgoum country from place to destination is the preeminent role that the teleuk plays in these enterprises.

However, if we think of the destination as that which carries meanings not only for those who live in it, but also for those who visit it, what has been accomplished in Pouss is a reconstellation of architecture—both through literal revival and representation—that strongly suggests a highly complex terrain of seemingly disparate desires and agendas. Contemporary Mousgoum country with its reconstituted teleukakay and wall murals is the product of a literal reconstruction; the effect is that of a series of symbolic reconstitutions of architectural form. In the process of reconstruction, the house has become the preeminent articulation of heritage, a concrete translation of the past. Barbara Kirshenblatt-Gimblett has written, "While it looks old, heritage is actually something new. Heritage is a mode of cultural production in the present that has recourse to the past. Heritage thus defined depends on display to give dying economies and dead sites a second life as exhibitions of themselves."[3]

As heritage, the Mousgoum teleuk has indeed become part of the tourist and experience industries. Tourists can visit northern Cameroon and go, in the words of Jonathan Gregson, "hunting for [teleukakay]—the strange, domed clay houses found only in this region."[4] Heritage resuscitates the teleuk, and under its aegis, the dome experiences a new life as a structure invested with contemporary value. Moreover, this new home is no longer a home, but it stands as an exhibition of itself under the network of tourism and economies of experience. While tourism and heritage have brought the house back to life, the surviving domes constitute a conscious revision of history. While they ostensibly "illustrate" the

FIGURE 100. Poster, Cameroon Airlines.

past, as a representation—perhaps even a simulacrum—of itself, the teleuk is something new. As Kirshenblatt-Gimblett insists, the success of the destination depends on its unique nature. Difference is key to its survival.[5] Gregson's "hunt" underscores such a requirement, for besides its exoticism for the tourist, the most compelling thing about the Mousgoum teleuk is its unique nature. One can find the house only in northern Cameroon.

Such meanings, even the simple representation of the teleuk as something unique, as something endangered call up what I have called salvage architecture.

In such a paradigm to save the teleuk is to save the Mousgoum people. (Let us not forget that the Mousgoum have been characterized as a dying culture since the 1930s, the same decade that was identified by many—both Mousgoum and Western—as the beginning of the teleuk's decline.) What is complicated in such a scenario is the similarities to Western discourses that the Mousgoum themselves articulate in their concern with "saving" the domed house. Be that as it may, such desires speak to the importance of "living history," and, by extension, authenticity. Richard Handler and William Saxton define authenticity in part as "isomorphism between a living-history activity or event, and that piece of the past it is meant to re-create." In their minds, authenticity allows for what they understand as the perfect simulation of the past.[6] Susan Stewart and others also address authenticity, and what all of their definitions have in common is the ways in which the term routinely addresses the relation between the past and the present. Along such lines, to become witness to the authentic is to become witness to the past. Even beyond tourism and experience the contemporary Mousgoum teleuk, an oft-cited example of "architecture without architects," a phrase that itself denies coevalness, has often been understood as providing a link to prehistoric or ancient architecture. Such a connection transforms the building into what Fatimah Tobing Rony calls an "essential index of authenticity,"[7] an index that is routinely tied to Western desires for a connection with a past. When international tourism enters the arena, the authentic becomes a way in which we can both witness the past and psychologically travel to it, a phenomenon upon which rests the backbone of the exotic tourism industry, and a phenomenon upon which rests some measure of economic benefit to the people who live in such locales.

But our continued search for a past that is in many ways more real than it could ever have been at the time signals the persistence of nostalgia and the primitive, even in the transnational global village of the twenty-first century. Eco-tourism, primitive tourism, and/or exotic tourism are not ends in themselves, but rather provocative symptoms of Western alienation. In fact, some of the contemporary texts that attempt to lure tourists to exotic places highlight such symptoms. By way of finding an example, I found myself in the cybermall of wiredseniors.com, which contains a listing for Spector Travel of Boston, a travel agency that specializes in African tourism. Aimed at travelers who presumably have time to spare and cash to burn (or plastic to melt), Spector Travel offers what it describes as "primitive, cultural cutting edge adventure tours" to various locales on the continent. In this cacophony of exotic (and avant-travel) possibilities, Spector Travel has one eleven-day tour called, "Cameroon Pygmies and Lowland Gorillas," which promises the intrepid traveler a complete immersion into what the agency considers to be some of the most remote parts of Africa. The advertising copy reads, "The Pygmy (Baka), Koma, Mbororo, Fali, Mousgoum, Fulbe, and Kanuri people are considered some of the most untouched groups in

Africa. Their will to preserve their cultural identity and their own way of life has led them to the most remote areas of the region."[8]

However inaccurate Spector Travel's text may be, what is striking about it is the veracity of a Western romance with "primitive Africa." Although Pouss is a mere ninety-minute drive from one of Cameroon's largest cities (complete with one of the country's largest commercial airports), although many Mousgoum people listen to Western music on radios and tape players, although news reaches Mousgoum country as quickly as it does my Los Angeles home (I was living in Pouss when the 1996 O. J. Simpson not-guilty verdict was handed down, and I heard the news—in one of the *most remote* areas of Africa—less than three hours after it happened), although the Mousgoum postmaster in the nearby village of Maga wonders between incoming telephone calls whether Colin Powell will ever become president of the United States—in spite of all this, the West clings to the fantasy that there is some place out there that is untouched, unspoiled, by Civilization. To be in Pouss and see Mousgoum people in Western dress taking photographs or reading magazines or doing many of the things that we do in our quotidian existence and *still* consider ourselves experiencing "one of the most remote areas of Africa" takes a lot of work, and a stunning suspension of disbelief. It requires a willful blindness. But the traveler must perform such hard work, must suspend disbelief, and must become blind in order to see the past, in order to reverse her or his alienation. In undertaking such an experience, paradise, the exotic, the primitive, or the indigenous promises a return to the self, a return that, through an encounter with such pronounced difference, can enact a fantasy of completion. In this sense, to go away is to return to a home marked by its wholeness, its authenticity, its *pastness.*

If we understand, however problematically, leaving the West as being tantamount to going back in time, then one would expect that everything one sees would somehow fit into the category of pastness. However, the mechanisms of time in the travel experience can be more complicated. The encounters of the Western travelers examined in this text with the Mousgoum teleuk threw their notions of the "primitive" and the "savage" into disarray, for the dome threatened to become like them. For Heinrich Barth, this meant seeing traces of "art" in the structure. For Olive MacLeod, it meant seeing the dome's technological sophistication. For Gide, it meant understanding the dome as a Purist structure. In the meeting, the binaries between self and other were momentarily ruptured, and the travelers were reminded of themselves, or at least of Europe. Gunther von Hagen's response to the Mousgoum teleuk is particularly striking, and, quite frankly, absolutely fabulous:

> The most wonderful things in [Mousgoum country] are the houses. If one comes hither down the river from the Logone sultanate and sees the buildings for the first time, one would believe that he has been placed into a fairy-

land. It seems as if a magic hand had taken the domes of the Kremlin in Moscow and placed them here in the African steppe, where the red-hot tropical sun turned them brownish red.[9]

Even though Russia may have been exotic for the German anthropologist, its invocation in the middle of Africa is extraordinary, and it signals an unstable attachment between Africa and Europe engendered by the Mousgoum teleuk. And as in all of these travelers' observations the teleuk ceased to fit comfortably into the category of pastness.

In the ruptures produced by the meeting of the teleuk and the European travelers, the distance between the traveler's present and her imagined past threaten to collapse under the weight of the dome. Such ruptures occur at precisely the moment of recognition with the contemporary self. Along these lines, for Gide, the teleuk is an orderly prime number, a wonderful example of Purism in the architectural environment. Yet, such a nod to coevalness is quickly thwarted by the depiction of the Mousgoum dome as an Etruscan tomb, and as the product of "potters" who have been working in the same fashion, in Gide's opinion, for centuries.[10]

However, while the travelers' experiences point to ruptures that threaten to close the gap between a modern present and an imagined African past, the Mousgoum teleuk still had the ability to serve as a screen for the West's projections of its own romanticized past. Gide's rupture is smoothed by his retreat into such a paradigm. The dome may be Purist in sprit, it may be mathematically perfect, but it still reminds him of the Pantheon and an Etruscan tomb. In the 1931 International Colonial Exposition, the French Equatorial Africa Pavilion allowed for the entrance of "Pompeiian" motifs into the city of Paris, again serving as a reminder not of Africa, but of the West's own past and successful evolution into the present. Yet in such instances the dome gives form, like the image of Roland Barthes's mother, to nostalgia and absence. Specifically, the teleuk articulates a Western nostalgia for and loss of its own idyllic past.[11]

But the West does not corner the market on either authenticity or alienation. The Mousgoum, as well as non-Western peoples around the globe, have experienced similar things, and, like the West, they have attempted to find ways to "return" to themselves. The rebuilding of the teleuk is one example of such an impulse. As Azao Dogo explained in interviews, the rebuilding of teleukakay was attached to reestablishing cultural equilibrium. For him, as for others in Mousgoum country, to rebuild was understood as a means of not losing oneself, as a means of becoming reunited with one's cultural history, as a means of saving the knowledge of the past, and by extension, the past itself. Cultural equilibrium, for Dogo, was defined as having access—real and psychological—to a Mousgoum past in a Mousgoum present. The relationship between past and present in this scenario speaks of alienation, and it articulates a psychological split that is defined in terms of time. As site of the past, the teleuk is a mnemonic device capable of enacting cultural and individual memory, of closing the gap between present and past.

Thus, it not only Westerners who bring time to bear upon the Mousgoum teleuk. The Mousgoum themselves—both in the past and in the present—consciously and unconsciously brought together architecture and time in their built environment. The rebuilding of the teleuk and its representation on wall murals in Pouss and its environs is a conscious recollection of a revised past. These activities are also a conscious making of heritage. As a mnemonic touchstone to "history," they have become a critical component in the making of a contemporary reality. The rebuilding of teleukakay and the buildings' representation also signals the fact that while Westerners see the Mousgoum, the Mousgoum see Westerners seeing them. Through such encounters, the Mousgoum assimilate Western presence and Western responses to the teleuk in the service of their own cultural goals.

The domed house, in its reincarnation, gives recourse to the past. It holds forth the possibility of transcending alienation, for achieving a wholeness of the self. At the same time, the teleuk, as a tool for the construction of identity, remains, as it was in the past, a sign of social cohesion. What has changed, however, is the kind of social cohesion it engenders. As the form has evolved from home to monument and tourist attraction, it has been changed from a part of a larger complex that regulates quotidian social behavior to one that brings the Mousgoum together under the rubric of ethnic pride and cultural identity writ large. However, in the minds of the Mousgoum, that change matters little, what does matter is the idea that the "real" past still exists in the present. Hence, the teleuk is a symbol for Mousgoum society, it is a mark of tradition, and it gives form to a desire for and the success of Mousgoum social survival. Today's teleukakay and their representation, based on what is garnered through Mousgoum readings—the emphasis on indigenous agency, African genius, an illustrious heritage—is something *new*, an affirmative response that is recuperative, cathartic, and restorative. The appropriation of the teleuk as mark of heritage by the Cameroonian government follows the same lines.

I went to Japan to see Cameroon, and when I found it, I saw a teleuk invoked in the process of weaving a Cameroonian national fiction, and I realized how the histories of the house led the exhibition's organizers to believe in the success of the form in such an endeavor. These officials, understanding the histories of the teleuk, appropriated it for their own use, and they used it as a means of highlighting the ingenuity and agency of an African nation in the world arena. At the same time, the teleuk also lays out the hope, through tourism and trade, for economic development and foreign investment in Cameroon.

Notwithstanding, from all subject positions the reading of the Mousgoum teleuk posits that architecture is a tabula rasa. The teleuk's interpretations are testaments to the multifaceted ways in which such is the case through the reception of a single structure. While certain forms—most notably the dome—instill certain notions in the human psyche, the reading and reception of architecture illustrate the psychological transference of one's issues onto the built environment. The understanding of the teleuk as a tabula rasa and the examination of the myriad interpretations engendered by the domed house, both in and out of Africa, also reveal the ways in which meanings shift *and* remain stable over time. Such an understanding also exposes the teleuk not as a concrete symbol, but as an arbitrary, multivalent sign whose meanings depend on the viewers and users interacting with the structure and its representation. As tabula rasa, the Mousgoum teleuk also accommodates simultaneously a host of stories that articulate a vast range of human experience and cultural identities. However, within all of these arenas, what is most certainly true is the fact of the Mousgoum teleuk's tremendous impact on the ways that the Mousgoum people themselves have been (and continue to be) perceived by the West, and equally importantly, on the ways that the Mousgoum perceive themselves.

His Majesty Lamido Mbang Yaya
  Oumar
Mme. Elhadj Abdramane
Oumar Abedi
Bara Abourgadaï
Mme. Djaoro Bara Abourgadaï
Arkali Adogoï
Mme. Arkali Adogoï
Golo Agonan
Ousman Ahoudouk
Magra Akum
Mme. Boukar Patcha Alouakou
Gring Alouakou
Mme. Gring Alouakou
Ousman Assoua
Boukar Dadouazi
Azao Dogo
Évélé Douniya

Afti Doupta
Mme. Abdoulaye Ebéguedi
Mme. Assimini Évélé
Mamat Hamat
Mme. Mal Idrissa
Abba Madi
Mme. Adoum Maïmouna
Mme. Daniel Mainiazanga
Abdoulaye Malbourg
Mathala Minsing
Mme. Ibrahim Nouhou
Salman Mbang Oumar
Math Perleh
Mme. Hiri-Hiri Takao
Apaïdi Toulouk
Mme. Abezidi Wendi
Mamat Zigla

INTRODUCTION

1 Heinrich Barth, *Travels and Discoveries in North and Central Africa*, centenary ed. (London: Frank Cass & Co., 1965 [1857]), 3: 335.

2 Gunther von Hagen, "Einige Notizen über die Musgu," *Baessler-Archiv* 2 (1911): 120.

3 André Gide, *Travels in the Congo*, trans. Dorothy Bussy (Hopewell, NJ: Ecco Press, 1994 [1927]), 218–19.

4 Amedée Ozenfant, *Foundations of Modern Art* (New York: Dover, 1952 [1928]), 144.

5 Eduard F. Sekler, "Structure, Construction, and Tectonics," *Connection* (March 1965): 7.

6 Geoffrey Scott, *The Architecture of Humanism: A Study in the History of Taste* (London: Architectural Press, 1980 [1924]), 213.

7 See Sekler, "Structure," 7.

8 Mitchell Schwarzer, "Tectonics Unbound," ANY 14 (1996): 15.

9 Heinrich Wölfflin, *Prolegomena to a Psychology of Architecture*, in *Empathy, Form, and Space: Problems in German Aesthetics, 1873-1893*, trans. Harry Francis Mallgrave and Eleftherios Ikonomou (Los Angeles: Getty Center of the History of Art and the Humanities, 1994 [1886]), 152.

10 Patrick was quoted by Mertins. See Detlef Mertins, "Walter Benjamin's Tectonic Unconscious," ANY 14 (1996): 29.

11 Scott C. Wolf, "The Metaphysical Foundations of Schinkel's Tectonics: *Eine Spinne im eigenen Netz*," ANY 14 (1996): 17.

12 Ibid.

13 Sekler, "Structure," 5.

14 Ibid., 7.

15 Ibid., 4. Sekler also notes that empathy (*Einfühlung*) was elaborated by other nineteenth-century German architects and theorists, most notably Theodor Lipps.

16 Heinrich Wölfflin, *Prolegomena zu einer Psychologie der Architektur*, cited in Sekler, "Structure," 4-5.

17 Ibid., 7.

18 Dennis Sharp, "Earliest Architecture," Dennis Sharp, ed., *The Illustrated Encyclopedia of Architects and Architecture* (New York: Whitney Library of Architecture, 1991), 170–71.

19 Bernard Rudofsky, *Architecture without Architects: A Short Introduction to Non-pedigreed Architecture* (exhibition catalogue) (New York: Museum of Modern Art, 1965), n.p.

20 Ibid., n.p.

21 Peter Brooks, *Body Work: Objects of Desire in Modern Narrative* (Cambridge: Harvard University Press, 1993), 167.

22 Christian Seignobos, "Les Mbara et autres gens de la muraille et de fer dans l'interfleuve Chari-Logone," Henry Tourneux, Christian Seignobos, and Francine LaFarge, *Les Mbara et leur langue (Tchad)* (Paris: SELAF, 1986), 25–33.

23 Ibid., 27.

24 Gustav Nachtigal, *Sahara and Sudan III: The Chad Basin and Bagirmi*, trans. Allan G. B. Fisher and Humphrey J. Fisher (London: C. Hurst & Company, 1987 [1889]), 386. Nachtigal is reading from the Bagirmi king-list.

25 Ibid., 405. Nachtigal's history of the Bagirmi also mentions a village named Musgugu that had been subjugated by Mbang Abdullah (1568–1608). If this is another name, albeit a distorted one, for Mousgoum, it would seem that some group related to the Mousgoum may have been in the area by the sixteenth century or even earlier. See ibid., 402. He also suggests that a village named Gamda, which he claims is Mousgoum, was already in the region in the seventeenth century. Nachtigal notes in his account of the kingdom of Bornu that the "country of Logon"—which could have comprised Mousgoum people—was a vassal country of the Bornu sultanate. See ibid., 166.

26 Ibid., 418.

27 Ibid., 254, 275, 283; von Hagen, "Einige Notizen," 117. Von Hagen suggests that Islamic models influenced these walls, which were between sixteen and nineteen feet high. One also has to entertain the possibilities that these walls had indigenous referents that may have been utilized or that they were derived from both models.

28 Barth, *Travels*, 2: 347, 410.

29 Nachtigal, *Sahara and Sudan*, 258. In a note on the same page Allan G. B. Fisher and Humphrey J. Fisher, the translators of Nachtigal's travelogue, citing Arnold Schultze's account of the kingdom of Bornu (*The Sultanate of Bornu* [London: H. Milford, 1913], 192), write, "The Puss were described as one of the two best known of a number of sub-tribes of the Musgo."

30 *Mbang* is a Bagirmi term that designates the sovereign. In the Bagirmi kingdom, the *Mbang* was synonymous with the sun and, as such, the term *Mbang* carried the same connotations. The ruler's court was referred to as his planets. See S. P. Reyna, *Wars without End: The Political Economy of a Pre-colonial African State* (Hanover, NH: University Press of New England, 1990), particularly 92–118. The royal court of the newly formed sultanate of Pouss used the same model as well as the same terms. Eventually, the Siakou family adopted the term *Mbang* as its surname, and this remains in use today. Mbang Mati's rule began in Lium, Chad, in 1900. At the time of the sultanate's relocation to Pouss in 1911, the Germans and French were renegotiating colonial boundaries. At this time, the area of Lium, along with other territories between the Logone and Chari Rivers, passed from German to French rule. Although Mbang Mati was perceived as having been loyal to the French (see "Sultanat de Pouss," 1932–33, Document APA 11834/G, National Archives, Yaoundé, Cameroon), Dana Goodhue suggests that this move was precipitated by the ruler's possible fears of French support for the Bagirmi,

whose political domination he sought to escape. See Dana Goodhue, "The Mousgoum of Pouss," unpublished manuscript, 1995, 3–4.

31 Seignobos, "Les Mbara," 31–33, notes that Islamicization and "Bagirmization" went hand in hand in a brutal fashion. On the creation of Mousgoum royalty, see ibid., 17.

32 Henry Tourneux examines how this difference in the time of religious conversion has affected the Guirvidig and Pouss dialects of Munjuk. See Henry Tourneux, "Les emprunts en Musgu," E. Wolff and H. Meyer-Bahlburg, eds., *Studies in Chadic and Afroasiatic Linguistics* (Hamburg: Helmut Buske Verlag, 1983), 447.

33 Baskouda J. B. Shelley, *Kirdi est mon nom* (Yaoundé: Imprimerie Saint-Paul, 1993), 43–44. A similar version of this story was recited by an old man in Mala to Marc Allégret during his 1926 visit to Mousgoum country. See Marc Allégret, "Notes sur les Massa-Mousgoum," *Carnets du Congo: voyage avec André Gide* (Paris: CNRS Editions, 1993), 269–70.

34 The French founded SEMRY in 1954. SEMRY II opened in Maga in 1978; it was fully operational by 1984.

35 See von Hagen, "Einige Notizen," 117.

36 Christian Mousgoum people no longer practice polygamy.

37 Allégret, "Notes," 270.

38 In Mousgoum and Massa contexts, Seignobos sees the dowry cattle as a metonym for the bride herself. Seignobos, "Les Mbara," 65.

39 The prefix *Mu-* (alternately seen as *Ma-* and *M-*) refers to humans. See Henry Tourneux, "Les emprunts," 442.

40 Tourneux postulates that the Munjuk word "Alaw" is derived from "Allah." See "Les emprunts," 448. The word also appears in Barth's Munjuk word lists from the 1850s. See P. A. Benton, *Notes on Some Languages of the Western Sudan* (London: Henry Frowde, 1912), 95. My research assistant Hamat Gring suggests, "[Alaw] has a name similar to that of God." Mme. Abezidi Wendi claims that Alaw is both masculine and feminine.

41 Von Hagen has assumed, extrapolating from a talisman made of hippopotamus skin, that either Maana or Gangan was believed to have taken the form of the large animal. I did not hear this during my field research. See von Hagen, "Einige Notizen," 119.

42 Ernst Heims, "Through the Land of the Musgums to Lake Chad," Adolph Friedrich, *From the Congo to the Niger and the Nile: An Account of the German Central African Expedition of 1910–1911* (London: Duckworth & Co., 1913), 126.

43 See, for example, René Gardi, *Indigenous African Architecture*, trans. Sigrid MacRae (New York: Van Norstrand Reinhold Co., 1973), 91–95. Moreover, G. Geo-Fourrier claimed in 1933 that the Mousgoum themselves were a dying culture. See his "Civilisations agonistes du Tchad: Les Mousgou," *Nature*, no. 2918 (December 1933): 486–89.

44 Information from the field is similar to that found in colonial documents. See "Sultanat de Pouss," 1932–33, Document APA 11834/G, National Archives, Yaoundé, Cameroon.

CHAPTER ONE: PERFORMING ARCHITECTURE

1 James Clifford, "On Ethnographic Allegory," James Clifford and George E. Marcus, eds., *Writing Culture: The Poetics and Politics of Ethnography* (Berkeley: University of California Press, 1986), 98–121.

2 See Jean-Paul Bourdier and Trinh T. Minh-ha, *Drawn from African Dwellings* (Blooming-ton: Indiana University Press, 1996), ix.

3 Labelle Prussin has also noted the importance of process in the analysis of nomadic architecture. See her "When Nomads Settle: Changing Technologies of Building and Transport and the Production of Architectural Form among the Gabra, the Rendille, and the Somalis," Mary Jo Arnoldi, Christraud M. Geary, and Kris L. Hardin, eds., *African Material Culture* (Bloomington: Indiana University Press, 1996), 74.

4 In 1910, Olive MacLeod described Musgum as being "about two miles in circumference, and . . . enclosed by a 40-feet high wall." She also found that the village was crowded, noting that "farther on the street [a large open space] degenerated into a series of by-ways, where there was only just room to pass between the houses." See Olive Mac-Leod, *Chiefs and Cities of Central Africa* (Freeport, NY: Books for Libraries Press, 1971 [1912]), 111. Only a couple of months later, in early 1911, Ernst Heims wrote that the family enclosures in Musgum were "so close together that the streets are only wide enough to allow one man to pass at a time." See Ernst Heims, "Through the Land of the Musgums to Lake Chad," in Adolph Friedrich, *From the Congo to the Niger and the Nile: An Account of the German Central African Expedition of 1910–1911* (London: Duckworth & Co., 1913), 126. Gunther von Hagen noted the crowding of houses in Musgum and Mala. In his opinion the other Mousgoum villages he saw were basically "a disorderly pile of farms." See Gunther von Hagen, "Einige Notizen über die Musgu," *Baessler-Archiv* 2 (1911): 117.

5 According to Mme. Arkali Adogoï, thorn walls were first used to enclose the homestead. Walls of clay later served the same purpose.

6 Von Hagen, "Einige Notizen," 121.

7 Later images of homesteads also showed a diverse range of houses; however, images of strictly the teleuk far outnumber these.

8 Henry Tourneux, "Les emprunts en Musgu," E. Wolff and H. Meyer-Bahlburg, eds., *Studies on Chadic and Afroasiatic Linguistics* (Hamburg: H. Buske Verlag, 1983), 446. Tourneux also suggested that the word *teleuk* is not a standard word in Munjuk, but he is not sure of its origin. Conversation with Henry Tourneux, October 1995.

9 Given that most Mousgoum houses consist of one room, the conflation of "house" and "room" is not surprising, for in many compounds, they are in effect one and the same. To designate a particular room, one would make a phrase that takes its functions under account. The kitchen is referred to as either a "room for making fire" (*delemiy zi afu*) or a "room for making a ball" (*delemiy zi bek*). Bek refers to balls of either millet or rice.

10 It is unclear in conceptions of *fen* whether the idea of the homestead and village is derived from those of the family or vice-versa. Tourneux's Munjuk lexicon implies that the term as "family" was derived from that of "compound." However, the notion of family is central to the ways in which the Mousgoum conceive of certain parts of the body. A finger (and a bicep) is literally called the "child of the hand" (*ahiy-tiy*); a toe is literally "the child of the foot" (*ahiy-ni aziy*). Given the relationship here, and given that humans psychologically conceive of themselves as the center of their worlds, I wonder if it is possible that the *fen* as "concession" and "village" may have been in actuality derived from "family." See Henry Tourneux, *Lexique practique du Munjuk des rizières* (Paris: ORSTOM, 1991).

11 There is no Munjuk word for architect.

12 Mme. Hiri-Hiri Takao notes that she saw female masons when she was a child.

13 Mme. Abourgadaï's kitchen is a teleuk; Agonan lives in one.

14 For an important discussion of the relationships between architecture and the body in an African context, see Suzanne Preston Blier, *The Anatomy of Architecture: Ontology and Metaphor in Batammaliba Architectural Expression* (Chicago: University of Chicago Press, 1994 [1987]), especially chap. 4, "Houses are Human: Architectural Self-Images," 118–39. See also Jean-Paul LeBeuf, *L'habitation des Fali* (Paris: Librairie Hachette, 1961).

15 When someone refers to a window in a modern house, particularly one with a tin roof, Munjuk has borrowed the French word *fenêtre* (*feneeter*).

16 See Henri Lefebvre, *The Production of Space*, trans. Donald Nicholson-Smith (Oxford: Blackwell Publishers, 1991 [1974]), 139–40.

17 Claude Abanga, "Case en obus mousgoum," unpublished poem, n.d.

18 Labelle Prussin, *Hatumere: Islamic Design in West Africa* (Berkeley: University of California Press, 1986), 38.

19 Prussin explains this practice as making up for the reduction in the dome's ability to transmit horizontal and vertical stresses to the ground. Ibid., 40.

20 Ibid., 43.

21 John Miller Chernoff, *African Rhythm and African Sensibility: Aesthetic and Social Action in African Musical Idioms* (Chicago: University of Chicago Press, 1979), 144.

22 André Gide, *Travels in the Congo*, trans. Dorothy Bussy (Hopewell, NJ: Ecco Press, 1994 [1927]), 222–23.

23 Azao Dogo, Hamat Gring, and Mme. Gring Alouakou described these to me.

24 Susanne K. Langer, *Feeling and Form* (New York: Charles Scribner's Sons, 1953), 174.

25 Some claimed that children were buried in the houses of their respective mothers; others said that they were buried in gardens outside of the homestead.

26 Françoise Dumas-Champion, *Les Masa du Tchad: bétail et société* (Paris: Fondation de la Maison des sciences de l'homme, 1983), 58–61.

27 To picture this, one must have the same orientation in the two scenarios: therefore, I am reversing Dumas-Champion's left and right and am considering them as if facing the respective houses.

28 Christian Seignobos, "Les Mbara et autres gens de la muraille et de fer dans l'interfleuve Chari-Logone," Henry Tourneux, Christian Seignobos, and Francine LaFarge, *Les Mbara et leur langue (Tchad)* (Paris: SELAF, 1986), 25–33.

29 I am arriving at this conclusion based in part on the importance the Mousgoum give to the height of the teleuk and to the spirit Bangui, who is conceived of as being a star in the night sky.

30 This is similar in Massa contexts. See Dumas-Champion, *Les Masa*, 69.

31 Mikhail Bakhtin, *Rabelais and His World*, trans. Hélène Iswolsky (Bloomington: Indiana University Press, 1984 [1965]), 281.

32 Labelle Prussin, "West African Mud Granaries," *Paideuma* 18 (1972): 160.

33 See ibid., 161–64.

34 If there was not a granary in the middle of the homestead, he was still buried in that location.

35 Prussin, *Hatumere*, 34. She also noted the resemblance between termite hills and mosques in northern Ghana. See Labelle Prussin, *Architecture in Northern Ghana* (Berkeley: University of California Press, 1969), 69.

36 Bakhtin, *Rabelais*, 282–83.

37 One can hypothesize a relationship between Mousgoum architecture and dance through issues of time as well. As Prussin has observed (*Hatumere*, 71), life activities in much of West Africa—planting, harvesting, and building—are dependent upon time. In Munjuk, "time" and "place" are expressed by the word *halay*, and *kasku* means both "market" and "week." In this fashion, the connection that can be postulated among time, place, architecture, and dance is an interesting possibility.

38 Prussin has briefly talked about the strength of the termite hills of the African savannah. *Hatumere*, 32. Von Hagen suggests, like Perleh, that the teleuk's form may have been derived from the termite hill. See von Hagen, "Einige Notizen," 121.

39 While the termite hill is a model of invincibility, the termite is one of the few things that could destroy a teleuk.

40 Salman Mbang Oumar, "Le conte d'un a jeune homme capricieux voulant épouser une femme qui doit ressembler à sa mère" (unpublished manuscript, 1996).

41 Heims, "Through the Land," 125. Allégret notes that the two "artistic manifestations" of the Mousgoum occur in architecture and drawing. Marc Allégret, *Carnets du Congo: voyage avec André Gide* (Paris: CNRS Editions, 1993), 287.

42 MacLeod, *Chiefs and Cities*, 105.

43 Olive MacLeod, "My Journey through the German Kameruns," *New York Times*, June 18, 1911, SM2.

44 MacLeod, *Chiefs and Cities*, 113–14. She also notes that the paints were obtained from reeds. Salman Mbang Oumar stated that the red ocher is from a particular soil, the black from grasses, and the white from shells.

45 See Suzanne Preston Blier, "Moral Architecture: Beauty and Ethics in Batammaliba Building Design," Jean-Paul Bourdier and Nezar AlSayyad, eds., *Dwellings, Settlements, and Traditions: Cross-Cultural Perspectives* (New York: Lanham, 1989), 335–55; Sylvia Ardyn Boone, *Radiance from the Waters: Ideals of Feminine Beauty in Mende Art* (New Haven: Yale University Press, 1986); Harris Memel-Fotê, "The Function and Significance of Negro Art in the Life of the Peoples of Black Africa," paper delivered at a colloquium on Function and Significance of African Negro Art in the Life of the People and for the People, First World Festival of Negro Arts, Dakar, April 1–24, 1966; Susan Mullin Vogel, *African Aesthetics: The Carlo Monzino Collection* (New York: Center for African Art, 1986), and Vogel, *Beauty in the Eyes of the Baule: Aesthetics and Cultural Values* (Philadelphia: Institute for the Study of Human Values, 1980).

46 Boone, *Radiance from the Waters*, 89.

47 Memel-Fotê, "The Function and Significance," 48–50.

48 See Blier, "Moral Architecture," 338; and Memel-Fotê, "The Function and Significance," 56.

49 See Boone, *Radiance from the Waters*, 81–152.

50 Blier, "Moral Architecture," 343–50.

51 Rudolf Arnheim, *Art and Visual Perception: A Psychology of the Creative Eye* (Berkeley: University of California Press, 1974 [1954]), 149.

52 Robert P. Morgan, "Musical Time/Musical Space," W. J. T. Mitchell, ed., *The Language of Images* (Chicago: University of Chicago Press, 1980), 264–65.

53 Theo van Doesburg, "The Significance of Colour for Exterior and Interior Architecture," Joost Baljeu, *Theo van Doesburg* (New York: Macmillan, 1974 [essay first published 1923]), 139–40.

54 Prussin, following D. Zahan, has suggested that Mousgoum interior door decoration is sexually symbolic. See Prussin, "West African Mud Granaries," 155, n29.

CHAPTER TWO: PARABOLIC PARADOXES

1 See Ida Vera Simonston, "Housekeeping in Africa: Savage Servants and Dangers Make the Domestic Problem Difficult," *Delineator* 75, no. 4 (April 1910): 319.

2 See Hal Foster, "'Primitive' Scenes," *Critical Inquiry* 20, no. 1 (autumn 1993): 69–102.

3 Anthony Kirk-Greene, "Heinrich Barth: An Exercise in Empathy," Robert I. Rotberg, ed., *Africa and Its Explorers: Motives, Methods, and Impact* (Cambridge: Harvard University Press, 1970), 19.

4 Heinrich Barth, *Travels and Discoveries in North and Central Africa*, centenary ed. (London: Frank Cass & Co., 1965 [1857]), 1: xxv. All page references are to this edition and appear in parentheses in the text.

5 Richardson died March 4, 1851, Overweg September 27, 1852.

6 Actually, there was a great deal of difference in the popularity of Barth's and Livingstone's texts. Anthony Kirk-Greene points out that of the original 1857 Longman's edition, only 2,250 copies of volumes 1 through 3 were printed, and this was followed by fewer than 1,000 copies of volumes four and five. See A. H. M. Kirk-Greene, "Heinrich Barth: A Biographical Note," in Barth, *Travels*, 1: xvi.

7 Augustus Petermann, "Expedition to Central Africa," *New York Daily Times*, March 27, 1855, 8 (reprinted from the *London Athenaeum*). See also Petermann, "Expedition to Central Africa," *New York Daily News*, December 17, 1852, 8 (reprinted from the *London Times*, November 22, 1852), and "The Expedition to Central Africa, *New York Times*, August 18, 1853, 8 (reprinted from the *London Athenaeum*).

8 *London Times*, April 4, 1855, 10.

9 Charles H. Brigham, "Recent Researches in Africa," *North American Review* 86, no. 179 (April 1858): 532.

10 See John Dodds, *The Age of Paradox: A Biography of England 1841–1851* (New York: Rinehart, 1952), 429, 431.

11 See Annie Coombs, *Reinventing Africa: Museums, Material Culture, and Popular Imagination in Late Victorian and Edwardian England* (New Haven: Yale University Press, 1994), 63–83.

12 For a discussion on the Hottentot Venus, see Sander L. Gilman, "Black Bodies, White Bodies: Toward an Iconography of Female Sexuality in Late Nineteenth-Century Art, Medicine, and Literature," in Henry Louis Gates, Jr., ed. *"Race," Writing, and Difference* (Chicago: University of Chicago Press, 1986), esp. 231–39.

13 Brigham, "Recent Researches," 533–34.

14 Ibid., 530–31.

15 Mary Louise Pratt, "Scratches on the Face of the Country; or What Mr. Barrow Saw in

the Land of the Bushmen," Gates, ed. *"Race,"* 153.

16 See ibid., 142–53.

17 Sigmund Freud, *Civilization and Its Discontents*, trans. James Strachey (New York: W. W. Norton, 1961), 13.

18 Ibid., 44, 34.

19 See Sylvia Lavin, *Quatremère de Quincy and the Invention of a Modern Language of Architecture* (Cambridge: MIT Press, 1992), 61.

20 Karl Otfried Müller, *Manual of the Archaeology of Art*, trans. John Leitch (London: A. Fullarton, 1850 [1830]), 34.

21 Ibid., 288.

22 See Joseph Rykwert, "Thinking and Doing," *On Adam's House in Paradise: The Idea of the Primitive Hut in Architectural History* (New York: Museum of Modern Art, 1972), 13–28.

23 E. Baldwin Smith, *The Dome* (Princeton: Princeton University Press, 1950), 4.

24 Marianna Torgovnick, *Gone Primitive: Savage Intellects, Modern Lives* (Chicago: University of Chicago Press, 1990), 83.

25 John Wood, *The Origin of Building; or the Plagiarism of the Ancients Detached* (Bath, U. K., 1741), 71f., cited in Joseph Rykwert, *The Dancing Column: On Order in Architecture* (Cambridge: MIT Press, 1996), 27–29.

26 See Gerald Needham, *19th Century Realist Art* (New York: Harper & Row, 1988), 9–32.

27 For a discussion of the relationship between image and text in the travelogue, see Christopher B. Steiner, "Of Drums and Dancers," *Harvard Review* 1, no. 1 (fall 1986): 104–29, esp. 111–14.

28 Sigmund Freud, "Symbolism and Dreams," *Introductory Lectures on Psycho-analysis*, trans. James Strachey (New York: W. W. Norton, 1966), 188–95.

29 Hal Foster, *Compulsive Beauty* (Cambridge: MIT Press, 1993), 23.

30 Joseph Thomson, "The Results of European Intercourse with the African," *Contemporary Review* 57 (March 1890): 339.

31 H. H. Johnston, *The Opening Up of Africa* (London: Williams and Norgate, 1911), 9.

32 Review of Olive MacLeod, *Chiefs and Cities of Central Africa*, *Times Literary Supplement*, May 9, 1912, 193.

33 The first headline appeared in the *Gazette Times Home Journal*, 1911, the second in the *Western Morning News*, Plymouth, February 27, 1911, cited in Alexander, *Whom the Gods Love*, 281.

34 *London Times*, February 27, 1911, 8. This rumor was again discredited on March 7 and 8 and April 3.

35 *London Times*, May 10, 1911, 7.

36 For a discussion of photographic postcards in French Colonial Senegal, see David Prochaska, "Fantasia of the *Photothèque*: French Postcard Views of Colonial Senegal," *African Arts* 24, no. 4 (October 1991): 40–47+.

37 J. Thompson in E. A. Reeves, *Hints to Travellers, Scientific and General*, 2 vols., 10th ed. (London: Royal Geographic Society, 1921), 2: 51.

38 Olive MacLeod, *Chiefs and Cities of Central Africa* (Freeport, NY: Books for Libraries Press, 1971 [1912]), 2. All page references are to this edition and appear in parentheses in the text.

39 Letter from Olive MacLeod to Herbert Alexander, June 13, 1911, cited in Alexander, *Whom the Gods Love*, 286. Joan Alexander's account of MacLeod's journey to Africa (277–90) is the sentimental love story as told by one of Boyd Alexander's descendants.

40 Mary H. Kingsley, *Travels in West Africa*, 3rd ed. (London: Frank Cass, 1965 [1897]), xxiii.

41 See Joan Copjec, *Read My Desire: Lacan against the Historicists* (Cambridge: MIT Press, 1994), 16–19.

42 Review of MacLeod, 193. See MacLeod, *Chiefs and Cities*, 10.

43 Review of Olive MacLeod's *Chiefs and Cities of Central Africa*, *Bookman* 42, no. 249 (June 1912): 140.

44 See Cheryl McEwan, *Gender, Geography, and Empire: Victorian Women Travelers in West Africa* (Aldershot: Ashgate, 2000), 4.

45 Waldram notes that the MacLeod's pictures appeared in *London Magazine*. Percy J. Waldram, *The Principles of Structural Mechanics* (London: B. T. Batsford, 1912), 308–9.

46 Marcel Griaule, "Dictionnaire," *Documents* 1, no. 7 (1929): 381.

47 Michel Leiris, "Dictionnaire," *Documents* 1, no. 7 (1929): 381–82.

48 For an illuminating discussion of the *informe*, see Yve-Alain Bois, "Introduction: The Use Value of 'Formless,'" Yve-Alain Bois and Rosalind E. Krauss, *Formless: A User's Guide* (New York: Zone Books, 1997), 13–40.

49 Georges Bataille, "Dictionnaire," *Documents* 2, no. 5 (1930): 298–300.

50 Freud, *Civilization*, 39–40.

51 Mary Douglas, *Purity and Danger* (London: Frederick A. Praeger, 1966), 2.

52 André Gide, *Travels in the Congo*, trans. Dorothy Bussy (Hopewell, NJ: Ecco Press, 1994 [1927]), 3. All page references are to this edition and appear in parentheses in the text.

53 "André Gide Journeys to Central Africa," *New York Times Book Review*, May 12, 1929, 7.

54 André Gide, *The Counterfeiters* with *Journal of the Counterfeiters* (New York: Vintage, 1973 [1927]), 439.

55 See, for example, *Illustrated London News*, January 15, 1927, 92–93; *La nouvelle revue française*, December 1, 1927, 723–46, January 1, 1928, 28–54, and February 1, 1928, 177–204; *L'Illustration*, March 5, 1927, 236–37; *Le monde colonial illustré*, no. 45, May 1927, 107; *Cahiers d'art*, no. 7/8 (1927), 262–65; and *Les cahiers de Belgique*, no. 4, 138–43.

56 Gide, *Journal of the Counterfeiters*, 439.

57 Tzvetan Todorov, *On Human Diversity: Nationalism, Racism, and Exoticism in French Thought*, trans. Catherine Porter (Cambridge: Harvard University Press, 1993 [1989]), 345.

58 Gide, *Amnytas*, trans. Richard Howard (New York: Ecco Press, 1988 [1906]), 79.

59 The Galápagos was a focus of Charles Darwin, who closely studied the biological life of the archipelago. See his *On the Origin of Species* (Cambridge: Harvard University Press, 1964 [1859]), 388–406.

60 *New York Times Book Review*, May 12, 1929, 7.

61 Gide, *The Journals of André Gide*, vol. 1, 1889–1924, trans. Justin O'Brien (Evanston: Northwestern University Press, 1987), 266.

62 Gide, *Journals*, 1: 231, 284. Gide had begun to translate Conrad's work by 1916.

63 Gide, *Amnytas*, 88.

64 Todorov, *On Human Diversity*, 265.

65 Le Corbusier, *Towards a New Architecture*, trans. Frederick Etchells (New York: Dover, 1986 [1923]), 170, 49.

66 Ozenfant, *Foundations of Modern Art*, trans. John Rodker (New York: Dover, 1952 [1928]), 144.

67 Ibid., 17–18, 41, 212.

68 Daniel Durosay, "Introduction," Marc Allégret, *Carnets du Congo: voyage avec André Gide* (Paris: CNRS Editions, 1993), 48.

69 Gide, *The Counterfeiters*, 187.

70 Rosalind E. Krauss, "No More Play," *The Originality of the Avant-Garde and Other Modernist Myths* (Cambridge: MIT Press, 1986), 42–85.

71 This photograph was published backwards in *Cahiers d'art*. See Gide, "Architectures négres," *Cahiers d'art*, no. 7/8 (1927): 262.

72 Allégret, *Carnets*, 210, 213. There are two versions of notes on the Mousgoum/Massa in the Rosch-Allégret Archives. One is reproduced as "Note sur les Massa-Mousgoum," *Carnets*, 267–89.

73 Ibid., 214.

CHAPTER THREE: A PINEAPPLE IN PARIS

1 "Josephine Baker Honored," *New York Times*, March 11, 1931, 8.

2 Jacques Mauny, "The Colonial Exhibition," *New York Times*, May 3, 1931, sec. 8, p. 11.

3 Gaston Donnet, "The French Colonial Craze," *Fortnightly Review* 70 (December 1898): 869 (originally published as "L'exaggeration coloniale," *Revue Blue*, September 24, 1898).

4 "Exotic Life of the Colonies to Be Reproduced," *New York Times*, Feb. 1, 1931, sec. 8, p. 16.

5 See Paul Greenhalgh, "Imperial Display," *Ephemeral Vistas: The Expositions Universelles, Great Exhibitions, and World's Fairs, 1851–1939* (Manchester, England: Manchester University Press, 1988), 56–57, 64.

6 "France's Far-flung Colonial Domain," *Literary Digest* 72, no. 6 (February 11, 1922): 27.

7 Toni Morrison, *Playing in the Dark: Whiteness and the Literary Imagination* (Cambridge: Harvard University Press, 1992), 17.

8 Jean Suret-Canale, *French Colonialism in Tropical Africa, 1900–1945*, trans. Till Gottheimer (London: C. Hurst, 1971 [1964]), 146.

9 A. Adu Boahen, ed., *General History of Africa*, vol. 7, *Africa under Colonial Domination 1880–1935* (Paris: UNESCO, 1990), 15.

10 Suret-Canale, *French Colonialism*, 71.

11 Patrick Manning, *Francophone Sub-Saharan Africa 1880–1985* (Cambridge: Cambridge University Press, 1988), 13.

12 Suret-Canale, *French Colonialism*, 84.

13 William B. Cohen, *The French Encounter with Africans: White Response to Blacks, 1530–1880* (Bloomington: Indiana University Press, 1980), 231.

14 Louis Faidherbe, *Essai sur la langue poul* (Paris, 1975), 14, cited in Cohen, *The French Encounter*, 231.

15 Tzvetan Todorov, *On Human Diversity: Nationalism, Racism, and Exoticism in French Thought*, trans. Catherine Porter (Cambridge: Harvard University Press, 1993 [1989]), 258.

16 Todorov, *On Human Diversity*, 258–59.

17 H. Labouret, *A la recherche d'une politique indigène dans l'Ouest africain* (Paris: Editions du Comité de l'Afrique française, 1931), 13, cited in Suret-Canale, *French Colonialism*, 84–85.

18 Manning, *Francophone Sub-Saharan Africa*, 16.

19 Recorded in "Sultanat de Pouss," 1932–33, Document APA 11834/G, National Archives, Yaoundé, Cameroon.

20 For more on Lyautey, see Patricia A. Morton, *Hybrid Modernities: Architecture and Representation at the 1931 Colonial Exposition, Paris* (Cambridge: MIT Press, 2000), and Gwendolyn Wright, *The Politics of Design in French Colonial Urbanism* (Chicago: University of Chicago Press, 1991).

21 André Gide, *Travels in the Congo*, trans. Dorothy Bussy (Hopewell, NJ: Ecco Press, 1994 [1927]), 241.

22 Ibid., 295.

23 *Le domaine colonial français* (Paris: Les Éditions du Cygne, 1929), 2: 426.

24 Dr. Georges Papillault, in Marcel Olivier ed., *Exposition coloniale internationale de Paris, Rapport général* (Paris: Imprimerie Nationale, 1932–34), 5, part 1: 52–53.

25 Morton, *Hybrid Modernities*, esp. 176–215.

26 Suret-Canale, *French Colonialism*, 80–81.

27 Recorded in M. Robin, "Rapport de tourneé," dated 25 August 1932, in "Sultanat de Pouss," 1932–33, Document APA 11834/G, National Archives, Yaoundé, Cameroon.

28 Recorded in "Sultanat de Pouss."

29 Report #216, Yagoua, 23 December 1932, in "Sultanat de Pouss."

30 *Patcha* is a Mousgoum/Bagirmi term translated as "general." In the Bagirmi court, the *mbang* was the sun. The *patcha*, whose position was of slave origin, was considered to be the "sun of the night," or the moon. As S. P. Reyna explains, the *patcha* was in many ways a surrogate *mbang*. See S. P. Reyna, *Wars without End: The Political Economy of a Precolonial African State* (Hanover, NH: University Press of New England, 1990), 115–18. Azao Dogo talked about the ways in which Patcha Alouakou played a large part in illegally taking taxes from Mousgoum villagers.

31 Dana Goodhue, "The Mousgoum of Pouss," unpublished manuscript, 1995, 4–5.

32 Report of the Governor-General W. Ponty to the Council of Government, 20 June 1910, *Bulletin du Comité de l'Afrique française*, no. 7, July 1910, cited in Suret-Canale, *French Colonialism*, 78.

33 Suret-Canale, *French Colonialism*, 60–61.

34 Norman Dwight Harris, *Europe and Africa Being a Revised Edition of Intervention and Colonization in Africa* (New York: Negro Universities Press, 1969 [1927]), 145–46.

35 Paul Fierens, "Colonial Exhibit Proves to Be a Superb Spectacle," *Art News* 29 (May 31, 1931): 6.

36 Jean Bourdon, "Colonies françaises et population," *Mercure de France*, no. 798 (September 15, 1931): 513.

37 *New York Times*, May 6, 1931, 8.

38 "French Exposition Popular," *New York Times*, June 6, 1931, 20.

39 *Rapport général* 3: 570. The 1900 Paris Universal Exposition attracted 48.4 million, and the 1889 Paris Universal Exposition attracted 32.4 million. The population of Paris in 1930 was roughly 2.8 million.

40 *Rapport général* 5, part 2, 365–75.

41 Ibid., 369.

42 Ibid., 360.

43 Ibid., 366–67.

44 Ibid., 376.

45 "L'urbanisme en Afrique Equatoriale Française: considérations générales," in Jean Royer, ed., *L'urbanisme aux colonies et dans les pays tropicaux* (Paris: Les Editions de l'Urbanisme, 1935), 2: 158.

46 "La Ville de Pointe Noire au point de vue de l'hygiène et de l'urbanisme," in Royer, 2: 168.

47 Labelle Prussin, *Hatumere: Islamic Design in West Africa* (Berkeley: University of California Press, 1986), 11–13.

48 Pierre Courthion, "L'architecture à l'exposition coloniale," *Art & Decoration*, no. 60 (August 1931): 37.

49 Ibid., 38–39.

50 Ibid., 52.

51 Ibid., 45.

52 Ibid., 52.

53 Ibid., 54.

54 Yvanhoé Rambosson, "Le mouvement des arts appliqués," *Le bulletin de l'art*, no. 776 (March 1931): 124.

55 Rambosson, "Le mouvement des arts appliqués," *Le bulletin de l'art*, no. 783 (December 1931): 472.

56 *Rapport général* 5, part 2, 366.

57 Ibid., 368.

58 Georges Hardy, "L'Exposition Coloniale, moment historique," *L'Europe Nouvelle* 14, no. 697 (20 June 1931): 868.

59 Roland Barthes, "Myth Today," *Mythologies*, trans. Annette Lavers (New York: Noonday Press, 1972 [1957]), 152.

60 *Rapport général* 5, part 2, 369.

61 Le Corbusier, *Towards a New Architecture*, trans. Frederick Etchells (New York: Dover, 1986 [1923]), 171.

62 Gide, *Travels*, 217.

63 For an example see Maurice Besson, *La tradition coloniale française* (Paris: Gauthier-Villars et Cie, 1931).

64 Christian Norberg-Schulz, *Meaning in Western Architecture*, trans. Anna Maria Norberg-Schulz (New York: Praeger Publishers, 1975 [1974]), 100.

65 Ibid., 100.

66 Suetonius, *The Lives of the Caesars*, ed. and trans. J. C. Rolfe (Cambridge, MA: Loeb Classical Library, 1979), 2:135–37, cited in Oleg Grabar, "From Dome of Heaven to Pleasure Dome," *Journal of the Society of Architectural Historians* 49, no. 1 (March

1990): 15.

67 Grabar, "From Dome of Heaven," 15–16.

68 Ibid., 16.

69 *Rapport général* 5, part 1, 391–92.

70 Johannes Fabian, *Time and the Other: How Anthropology Makes Its Object* (New York: Columbia University Press, 1983), 18.

71 Ibid., 17–18.

72 *Rapport général* 5, part 2, 368–69.

73 Carol Duncan, "Art Museums and the Ritual of Citizenship," Ivan Karp and Steven D. Lavine, eds., *Exhibiting Cultures* (Washington: Smithsonian Institution Press, 1991),91.

74 Donna Haraway, *Primate Visions: Gender, Race, and Nature in the World of Modern Science* (New York: Routledge, 1989), 27.

75 For a fruitful account of the column and its importance in architectural discourse, see Joseph Rykwert, *The Dancing Column: On Order in Architecture* (Cambridge: MIT Press, 1996).

76 P. J. Philip, "Great French Show to Open This Week," *New York Times*, May 3, 1931, sec. 3, 3.

77 *Rapport général* 5, part 2, 371.

78 See Duncan, "Art Museums," 93–94.

79 See Guide des colonies françaises, *Afrique française: Afrique occidentale française, Afrique équatoriale française, Togo et Cameroun* (Paris: Société d'Editions Géographiques, Maritimes et Coloniales, 1931).

80 *Rapport général* 5, part 2, 444.

81 Christopher B. Steiner, *African Art in Transit* (Cambridge: Cambridge University Press, 1994), 100–107.

82 Susan Stewart, *On Longing: Narratives of the Miniature, the Gigantic, the Souvenir, the Collection* (Durham: Duke University Press, 1984), 39.

83 James Clifford, "Of Other Peoples: Beyond the 'Salvage Paradigm,'" Hal Foster, ed., *Discussions in Contemporary Culture*, no. 1 (Seattle: Bay Press, 1987), 122.

84 Stewart, On Longing, 146.

85 John Frow, "Tourism and the Semiotics of Nostalgia," *October* 57 (summer 1991): 130.

86 Craig Owens, "The Allegorical Impulse: Toward a Theory of Postmodernism," *Beyond Recognition: Representation, Power, and Culture* (Berkeley: University of California Press, 1992), 54.

87 Ibid., 53.

88 Joseph Trillat, *L'Exposition coloniale de France* (Paris: Librairie des Arts Décoratifs, 1931), actually describes the exposition as a Garden of Eden.

89 *Rapport général* 5, part 2: 368.

90 See Annie Coombs, *Reinventing Africa: Museums, Material Culture, and Popular Imagination in Late Victorian and Edwardian England* (New Haven: Yale University Press, 1994), 7–28.

91 Joan Copjec, *Read My Desire: Lacan against the Historicists* (Cambridge: MIT Press, 1994), 82.

92 See Morrison, *Playing in the Dark*, 64.

1 Greg Dening, *Performances* (Chicago: University of Chicago Press, 1996), 37.

2 The Association of Elites for the Development of Maga is a Mousgoum group comprising civil servants living in Yaoundé and Douala, Cameroon, who are committed to engendering economic, social, and cultural development of the Maga region, which includes Pouss.

3 The Massa live among the Mousgoum; however, the largest numbers of them live around Yagoua, a city about forty miles south of Pouss. The Toupouri live primarily in the areas surrounding the villages of Guidiguis and Kaele, which are at the southernmost part of the Extreme North province. These cultures, like the Mousgoum, straddle the border between Cameroon and Chad.

4 "33" Export, Castel, and Beaufort are popular beers bottled in Cameroon. D'jino is a carbonated soft drink.

5 Olive MacLeod, *Chiefs and Cities of Central Africa: Across Lake Chad By way of British, French, and German Territories* (Freeport, NY: Books for Libraries Press, 1971 [1912]), 160–61.

6 André Gide, *Travels in the Congo*, Dorothy Bussy, trans. (Hopewell, NJ: Ecco Press, 1994 [1927]), 281.

7 The lamido of Katoa is actually the first cousin of the lamido of Pouss. In Mousgoum families, however, first cousins are referred to as siblings.

8 Speech given by Marcel Doubla at the celebration of the opening of the tourist season in the Extreme North province of Cameroon, December 30, 1995.

9 Speech given by the representative of the provincial minister of tourism for the Extreme North province of Cameroon at the celebration of the opening of the tourist season, December 30, 1995. The Mousgoum often claim that they are descendants of the Sao.

10 Gide, *Travels in the Congo*, 217–18.

11 See "Mousgoum Cultural Center," handout at the Mousgoum Museum and Community Center, Pouss, Cameroon, 1995. See also "Reconstruction de *teleukakay* au Cameroun et au Tchad: transmission du savior-faire des paysans mousgoums," brochure (Paris: Patrimoine sans Frontières, 1995), 2.

12 V. S. Naipaul, *A Bend in the River* (New York: Alfred A. Knopf, 1979), 15.

13 Baskouda J. B. Shelley, *Kirdi est mon nom* (Yaoundé: Imprimerie Saint-Paul, 1993), 5. Shelley does not tell his reader to which "Kirdi" culture he belongs. All page references are to this edition and appear in parentheses in the text.

14 See Aimé Cesaire, *Cahier d'un retour au pays natal* (Paris: Présence Africaine, 1983).

15 Charles Binam Bikoï, "The Literary Dimension of Cameroon Cultural Identity," Ministry of Information and Culture and the Department of Cultural Affairs, *The Cultural Identity of Cameroon* (Yaoundé: Ministry of Information and Culture, Department of Cultural Affairs, 1985), 92.

16 Abiola Irele, "Contemporary Thought in French Speaking Africa," Isaac James Mowoe and Richard Bjornson, eds., *Africa and the West: The Legacies of Empire* (Westport, CT: Greenwood Press, 1986), 124–25.

17 Dean MacCannell, *Empty Meeting Grounds: The Tourist Papers* (New York: Routledge, 1992), 17.

18 Paul J. Lane, "Tourism and Social Change among the Dogon," *African Arts* 21, no. 4 (August 1988): 66. See also Walter E. A. Van Beek, "Enter the Bush: A Dogon Mask Festival," Susan Vogel, *Africa Explores: 20th Century African Art* (New York: Center for African Art, 1991), 56–73.

19 Stephen Greenblatt, *Marvelous Possessions: The Wonder of the New World* (Chicago: University of Chicago Press, 1991), 3–4.

20 Ibid., 4.

21 Chinua Achebe, *No Longer at Ease* (New York: Astor-Honor, 1961), 126–27. Uli are the impermanent markings that some Igbo women of Nigeria paint onto their bodies.

22 André-Marie Ntsobe, "Cameroon's Cultural Identity and Book Production," Ministry of Information and Culture, *The Cultural Identity of Cameroon*, 234–35. In a response to Ntsobe, Joseph-Marie Essomba adds, "In books there are other aspects—pictorial, iconographical—that can bear witness to our culture." See *Cultural Identity of Cameroon*, 289.

23 Herbert M. Cole, *Icons: Ideals and Power in the Art of Africa* (Washington: Smithsonian Institution Press, 1989), 155.

24 Bertrand Lembezat, *Les populations païennes du Nord-Cameroun et de l'Amadaoua* (Paris: Presses Universitaires de France, 1961), 67. See also Dana Goodhue, "The Mousgoum of Pouss," unpublished manuscript, 1995, 3.

25 Quoted in Seyyed Hossein Nasr, *A Young Muslim's Guide to the Modern World* (Chicago: Kazi Publications, 1993), 112. Nasr points out that the turban signifies that one's head is straight and makes the male wearer remember his function as Allah's servant on earth. See ibid., 112–13.

26 Susan Vogel, *Africa Explores: 20th Century African Art* (New York: Center for African Art, 1991), 100.

27 Cole, *Icons*, 116.

28 For discussions about various aspects in the construction of a "Cameroonian identity," see the essays in Ministry of Information and Culture, *The Cultural Identity of Cameroon* (Yaoundé: Ministry of Information and Culture, Department of Cultural Affairs, 1985).

29 Amnesty International, Network Africa, and other local and international organizations have sharply criticized this policy, claiming that it has led to the abuse of power by local rulers. This abuse is allegedly ignored by the Cameroonian president Paul Biya, as it is claimed that he relies heavily on the influence and cooperation of traditional rulers in manipulating the electorate.

30 See "Mousgoum Cultural Center," 1 p. brochure, Pouss, Cameroon, 1996.

31 Much of the outside funding for the project came from Goodhue's home community and Rotary Club of Springfield, Massachusetts.

32 See Patrimoine sans Frontières, "Reconstruction de teleukakay au Cameroun et au Tchad" (brochure), 1995, 8, 9. Part of the goal of these brochures was the garnering of financial support from individuals and corporations.

33 Ibid., 12.

34 G. Geo-Fourrier, "Civilisations agonistes du Tchad: Les Mousgou," *Nature*, no. 2918 (December 1933): 486.

35 James Clifford, "On Ethnographic Allegory," James Clifford and George E. Marcus, eds.

Writing Culture: The Poetics and Politics of Ethnography (Berkeley: University of California Press, 1986), 112, 113.

36 Patrimoine sans Frontières planned, as part of this project, to produce a documentary, to be shown in the West, showing the process of rebuilding the teleukakay. See Patrimoine sans Frontières, "Reconstruction de *teleukakay*," 8.

37 James Clifford, "Of Other Peoples: Beyond the 'Salvage Paradigm,'" Hal Foster, ed., *Discussions in Contemporary Culture*, no. 1 (Seattle: Bay Press, 1987), 127.

38 Chinua Achebe, *Anthills of the Savannah* (New York: Doubleday, 1988), 114.

39 Although this is underaddressed here, I feel that the presence of the scholar in the field is an issue that needs much more attention than it is generally given. The researcher's presence affects the ways in which the residents of a place understand their world, and I believe that this should be acknowledged in our work. We are not invisible and we do not leave our respective places of research without having affected them in some manner. An example occurred shortly after the celebration of the 1996 tourist season, when, after I had spent the day taking pictures and taking notes, Salman Mbang Oumar inquired why I had not been under the hangar with Lamido Mbang Yaya Oumar and his retinue.

40 Henri Lefebvre, *The Production of Space*, trans. Donald Nicholson-Smith (Oxford: Blackwell, 1991 [1974]), 111.

41 Trinh T. Minh-ha, "Of Other Peoples: Beyond the 'Salvage Paradigm,'" in Hal Foster, ed., *Discussions in Contemporary Culture*, no. 1 (Seattle: Bay Press, 1987), 140.

42 T.-A. Ebanda Mendunga, "The Cultural Identity of Cameroon and Native Architecture," in Ministry of Information and Culture, *The Cultural Identity of Cameroon*, 501, 513–14.

43 Claude Abanga, "Case en obus mousgoum," unpublished poem, n.d.

44 The apprentices, according to Goodhue, were Mamat Hamat, Mahamat Ousman, Mahamat Oumar, Oumar Abedi, Boukar Ousman, Ousman Ahoudouk, Zacharia Oumar, Hamadou Baquit, Ali Mahamat, Hassane Kardri, Sali Zigla, Réné Louwang, Permanas Ndjidda, Awersing Mathieu, Mahamat Jean-Pierre, and Abba Mati. The actual building of the compound took place before my own residence in Pouss; however, the covering of its walls and its decoration were done while I was in engaged in fieldwork there.

45 The root *si-* is also the root for *sitirit*, which means "to learn" or "to study."

46 Lisa Aronson discusses the relationship among beauty, social networks, and wall painting among the Gurensi of northern Ghana. See her "Women in the Arts," in *African Women South of the Sahara*, Margaret Jean Hay and Sharon Stichter, eds. (London: Longman, 1994), 126.

47 See, for example, Paul Changuion, *The African Mural*, text by Tom Matthews and Annice Changuion (London: New Holland, 1989), 13.

48 Aronson, "Women in the Arts," 119.

AFTERWORD: DESTINATION CAMEROON

1 André Gide, *Travels in the Congo*, trans. Dorothy Bussy (Hopewell, NJ: Ecco Press, 1994 [1927]), 217.

2 See Ozenfant, *Foundations of Modern Art* (New York: Dover, 1952 [1928]), 145.

3 Barbara Kirshenblatt-Gimblett, *Destination Culture: Tourism, Museums, and Heritage* (Berkeley: University of California Press, 1998), 6.

4 Jonathan Gregson, "Warthog à la crème," *Sunday Independent* (London), December 3, 1995, 69.

5 Kirshenblatt-Gimblett, *Destination Culture*, 152.

6 Richard Handler and William Saxton, "Dyssimulation: Reflexivity, Narrative, and the Quest for Authenticity in 'Living History,'" *Cultural Anthropology* 3, no. 3 (August 1988): 242.

7 Fatimah Tobing Rony, *The Third Eye: Race, Cinema, and Ethnographic Spectacle* (Durham: Duke University Press, 1996), 195.

8 See http://www.wiredseniors.com/mall-img/553.htm.

9 Gunther von Hagen, "Einige Notizen über die Musgu," *Baessler-Archiv* 2 (1911): 120.

10 Gide, *Travels in the Congo*, 218–19.

11 See Roland Barthes, *Camera Lucida: Reflections on Photography*, trans. Richard Howard (New York: Noonday Press, 1981 [1980]).

ACHEBE, CHINUA. *Anthills of the Savannah*. New York: Doubleday, 1988.

———. *No Longer at Ease*. New York: Astor-House, 1961.

———. *Things Fall Apart*. New York: Doubleday, 1994. First published 1959.

ALEXANDER, JOAN. *Whom the Gods Love*. London: Heinemann, 1977.

ALLÉGRET, MARC. *Carnets du Congo: voyage avec André Gide*. Paris: CNRS Editions, 1993.

ALTMAN, DENNIS. *Paper Ambassadors: The Politics of Stamps*. Auckland: Angus and Robertson, 1991.

ANZALDÚA, GLORIA. *Borderlands/La Frontera: The New Mestiza*. San Francisco: Spinsters| Aunt Lute, 1987.

APPIAH, KWAME ANTHONY. *My Father's House: Africa in the Philosophy of Culture*. Oxford: Oxford University Press, 1992.

APPADURAI, ARJUN, ed. *The Social Life of Things: Commodities in Cultural Perspective*. Cambridge: Cambridge University Press, 1986.

L'Architecture à l'Exposition Universelle de 1900. Paris: Librairies-Imprimeries Réunies, 1900.

ARNHEIM, RUDOLF. *Art and Visual Perception: A Psychology of the Creative Eye*. Berkeley: University of California Press, 1974. First published 1954.

———. *The Dynamics of Architectural Form*. Berkeley: University of California Press, 1977.

ARONSON, LISA. "Women in the Arts." In *African Women South of the Sahara*, ed. Margaret Jean Hay and Sharon Stichter, 119–38. London: Longman, 1994.

L'autre et nous: "scènes et types." Paris: ACHAC, 1995.

BÂ, HAMPÂTÉ AMADOU. *Aspects de la civilization africaine*. Paris: Présence Africaine, 1972.

BACHELARD, GASTON. *The Poetics of Space*. Trans. Maria Jolas. Boston: Beacon Press, 1994. First published 1958.

BAKHTIN, M. M. *Rabelais and His World*. Trans. Hélène Iswolsky. Bloomington: Indiana University Press, 1984. First published 1965.

BALJEU, JOOST. *Theo van Doesburg*. New York: Macmillan, 1974.

BARTH, HEINRICH. *Sammlungen und Bearbeitung Central-Afrikanischer Vokabularien*. Gotha: J. Perthes, 1862.

———. *Travels and Discoveries in North and Central Africa*. 3 vols. London: Cass, 1965. First published 1857.

BARTHES, ROLAND. *Camera Lucida: Reflections on Photography.* Trans. Richard Howard. New York: Noonday Press, 1981. First published 1980.

———. *Mythologies.* Trans. Annette Lavers. New York: Noonday Press, 1972. First published 1957.

BATAILLE, GEORGES. "Dictionnaire" *Documents* 2, no. 5 (1930): 298–300.

BATES, ROBERT H., V. Y. MUDIMBE, and JEAN O'BARR, eds. *Africa and the Disciplines.* Chicago: University of Chicago Press, 1993.

BARZUN, H. M. "France's African Empire." *Current History Magazine of the New York Times* 19 (November 1923): 230–36.

BASCOM, WILLIAM R., and MELVILLE J. HERSKOVITZ, eds. *Continuity and Change in African Cultures.* Chicago: University of Chicago Press, 1959.

BAUDRILLARD, JEAN. *Simulations.* Trans. Paul Foss, Paul Patton, and Philip Beitchman. New York: Semiotext(e), 1983. First published 1981.

BEAUPLAN, ROBERT DE. "La nuit merveilleuse." *L'Illustration*, no. 4616 (August 22, 1931): n.p.

BEAUTHEAC, NADINE, and FRANCOIS-XAVIER BOUCHART. *L'Europe exotique.* Paris: Chêne, 1985.

BENJAMIN, WALTER. *Illuminations: Essays and Reflections.* Trans. Henry Zohn. New York: Schocken Books, 1985. First published 1955.

———. *Reflections: Essays, Aphorisms, Autobiographical Writings.* Trans. Edmund Jephcott. New York: Schocken Books, 1986. First published 1978.

BENTON, P. A. *Notes on Some Languages of the Western Sudan.* London: Frowde, 1912.

BESSON, MAURICE. *La tradition coloniale française.* Paris: Gauthier-Villars et Cie, 1931.

BETTS, RAYMOND. *Assimilation and Association in French Colonial Theory, 1890–1914.* New York: Columbia University Press, 1961.

BHABHA, HOMI. *The Location of Culture.* New York: Routledge, 1994.

BIKOÏ, CHARLES BINAM. "The Literary Dimension of Cameroon Cultural Identity." In *The Cultural Identity of Cameroon*, ed. Ministry of Information and Culture and the Department of Cultural Affairs, 89–99. Yaoundé: Ministry of Information and Culture, Department of Cultural Affairs, 1985.

BIRKETT, DEA. *Spinsters Abroad: Victorian Lady Explorers.* Oxford: Basil Blackwell, 1989.

BJORNSON, RICHARD. *The African Quest for Freedom and Identity: Cameroonian Writing and the National Experience.* Bloomington: Indiana University Press, 1994.

BLANCHARD, PASCAL, and ARMELLE CHATELIER. *Images et colonies: iconographie et propagande sur l'Afrique française de 1880 à 1962.* Paris: ACHAC, 1993.

BLIER, SUZANNE PRESTON. *The Anatomy of Architecture: Ontology and Metaphor in Batammaliba Architectural Expression.* Chicago: University of Chicago Press, 1994. First published 1987.

———. "Moral Architecture: Beauty and Ethics in Batammaliba Building Design." In *Dwellings, Settlements, and Tradition: Cross-Cultural Perspectives*, ed. Jean-Paul Bourdier and Nezar AlSayyad, 335–55. New York: Lanham, 1989.

BOAHEN, A. ADU, ed. *General History of Africa*, vol. 7. *Africa under Colonial Domination 1880–1935.* Paris: UNESCO, 1990.

BOIS, YVE-ALAIN. "La Penseé Sauvage." *Art in America* 73, no. 4 (April 1985): 178–89.

———. *Painting as Model.* Cambridge: MIT Press, 1993.

BOIS, YVE-ALAIN, and ROSALIND E. KRAUSS. *Formless: A User's Guide.* New York: Zone Books, 1997.

BOONE, SYLVIA ARDYN. *Radiance from the Waters: Ideals of Feminine Beauty in Mende Art.* New Haven: Yale University Press, 1986.

BOURDIER, JEAN-PAUL, and NEZAR ALSAYYAD, eds. *Dwellings, Settlements, and Tradition: Cross-Cultural Perspectives.* New York: Lanham, 1989.

BOURDIER, JEAN-PAUL, and TRINH T. MINH-HA. *African Spaces: Designs for Living in Upper Volta.* New York: Africana Publishing, 1985.

———. *Drawn from African Dwellings.* Bloomington: Indiana University Press, 1996.

BOURDON, JEAN. "Colonies françaises et population." *Mercure de France,* no. 798 (September 15, 1931): 513–30.

BRAND, STEWART. *How Buildings Learn: What Happens after They're Built.* New York: Penguin Books, 1994.

BRAVMANN, RENE A. *Islam and Tribal Art in West Africa.* Cambridge: Cambridge University Press, 1974.

BRETON, ANDRÉ. *Manifestos of Surrealism.* Ann Arbor: University of Michigan, 1990.

BRIGHAM, CHARLES H. "Recent Researches in Africa." *North American Review* 86, no. 179 (April 1858): 530–63.

BROOKS, PETER. *Body Work: Objects of Desire in Modern Narrative.* Cambridge: Harvard University Press, 1993.

BRUEL, GEORGES. *La France Équatoriale Africaine.* Paris: Larose Éditions, 1935.

CADILLAC, PAUL-EMILE. "Promenade à travers les cinq continents." *L'Illustration,* no. 4603 (May 23, 1931): n.p.

———. "Un soir à l'exposition." *L'Illustration,* no. 4608 (June 27, 1931): n.p.

ÇELIK, ZEYNEP. *Displaying the Orient: Architecture of Islam at the Nineteenth-Century World's Fairs.* Berkeley: University of California Press, 1992.

CESAIRE, AIMÉ. *Cahier d'un retour au pays natal.* Paris: Présence Africaine, 1983.

CHANGUION, PAUL. *The African Mural,* text by Tom Matthews and Annice Changuion. London: New Holland, 1989.

CHERNOFF, JOHN MILLER. *African Rhythm and African Sensibility: Aesthetics and Social Action in African Musical Idioms.* Chicago: University of Chicago Press, 1979.

CLIFFORD, JAMES. "Of Other Peoples: Beyond the 'Salvage Paradigm.'" In *Discussions in Contemporary Culture,* no. 1, ed. Hal Foster, 121–30. Seattle: Bay Press, 1987.

———. "On Ethnographic Allegory." In *Writing Culture: The Poetics and Politics of Ethnography,* ed. James Clifford and George E. Marcus, 98–121. Berkeley: University of California Press, 1986.

———. *Predicament of Culture.* Cambridge: Harvard University Press, 1991.

CLIFFORD, JAMES, and GEORGE MARCUS, eds. *Writing Culture: The Poetics and Politics of Ethnography.* Berkeley: University of California Press, 1986.

COHEN, WILLIAM. *The French Encounter with Africans: White Response to Blacks, 1530–1880.* Bloomington: Indiana University Press, 1980.

COLE, HERBERT M. *Icons: Ideals and Power in the Art of Africa.* Washington: Smithsonian Institution Press, 1989.

COMTE, GILBERT. *L'empire triomphant 1871–1936.* Vol. 1. Paris: Denoël, 1988.

CONNELLY, A. P. *The Nineteenth Century.* Chicago: A. P. Connelly, 1898.

CONRAD, JOSEPH. *Heart of Darkness*. New York: W. W. Norton, 1988. First published 1902.

CONTE, ARTHUR. *Nostalgies françaises*. Paris: Librairie Plon, 1993.

COOMBS, ANNIE E. *Reinventing Africa: Museums, Material Culture, and Popular Imagination in Late Victorian and Edwardian England*. New Haven: Yale University Press, 1994.

COPJEC, JOAN. *Read My Desire: Lacan against the Historicists*. Cambridge: MIT Press, 1994.

COURTHION, PIERRE. "L'architecture à l'exposition coloniale." *Art & Decoration*, no. 60 (August 1931): 37–54.

DARWIN, CHARLES. *On the Origin of Species*. Cambridge: Harvard University Press, 1964. First published 1859.

DELAFOSSE, MAURICE. *Enquête coloniale dans l'Afrique française occidentale et équatoriale*. Paris: Société d'Éditions Géographiques, Maritimes et Coloniales, 1930.

DEMAISON, ANDRÉ. *Exposition coloniale internationale: "votre guide."* Paris: Editions Mayeux, 1931.

DENING, GREG. *Performances*. Chicago: University of Chicago Press, 1996.

DENYER, SUSAN. *African Traditional Architecture*. New York: Africana Publishing, 1978.

DESCHAMPS, HUBERT. *The French Union*. Paris: Editions Berger-Leverault, 1956.

DESCHAMPS, PAUL, et al. *Les colonies et la vie française pendant huit siècles*. Paris: Librairie de Paris, Firmin-Didot et Cie Editeurs, 1931.

DODDS, JOHN W. *The Age of Paradox: A Biography of England 1841–1851*. New York: Rinehart, 1952.

Le domaine colonial français. 4 vols. Paris: Les Éditions du Cygne, 1929.

DOMINGUEZ, VIRGINIA. "The Marketing of Heritage." *American Ethnologist* 13, no. 3 (1986): 546-55.

DONNET, GASTON. "The French Colonial Craze." *Fortnightly Review* 70 (December 1898): 864–71.

DOUGLAS, MARY. *Purity and Danger*. New York: Praeger, 1966.

DUMAS-CHAMPION, FRANÇOISE. *Les Masa du Tchad: bétail et société*. Paris: Fondation de la Maison des sciences de l'homme, 1983.

DUNCAN, CAROL. "Art Museums and the Ritual of Citizenship." In *Exhibiting Cultures*, ed. Ivan Karp and Steven D. Lavine, 88–103. Washington: Smithsonian Institution Press, 1991.

EDWARDS, ELIZABETH, ed. *Anthropology and Photography 1860–1920*. London: Royal Anthropological Institute, 1992.

ENWEZOR, OKWUI, OCTAVIO ZAYA, and OLU OGUIBE, eds. *In/Sight: African Photographers, 1940–Present*. Exhibition catalogue. New York: Guggenheim Museum, 1996.

ERRINGTON, SHELLY. *The Death of Primitive Art and Other Tales of Progress*. Berkeley: University of California Press, 1998.

D'ESME, JEAN. "Au coeur de l'Afrique française." *L'Illustration*, no. 4603 (May 23, 1931): n.p.

ETIENNE-NUGUE, JOCELYNE. *Crafts and the Arts of Living in the Cameroon*. Baton Rouge: Louisiana State University Press, 1982.

EXPOSITION COLONIALE DE PARIS 1931. *Histoire militaire de l'Afrique équatoriale française*. Paris: Imprimerie Nationale, 1931.

EZRA, ELIZABETH. *The Colonial Unconscious: Race and Culture in Interwar France.* Ithaca: Cornell University Press, 2000.

FABIAN, JOHANNES. *Remembering the Present: Painting and Popular History in Zaire.* Berkeley: University of California Press, 1996.

———. *Time and the Other: How Anthropology Makes Its Object.* New York: Columbia University Press, 1983.

FANON, FRANTZ. *Black Skin, White Masks.* New York: Grove Press, 1967. First published 1952.

———. *The Wretched of the Earth.* New York: Grove Press, 1963. First published 1961.

FIERENS, PAUL. "Colonial Exhibit Proves to Be a Superb Spectacle." *Art News* 29 (May 31, 1931): 3+.

FINDLING, JOHN E., ed. *Historical Dictionary of World's Fairs and Expositions, 1851–1988.* Westport, CT: Greenwood Press, 1990.

FLITTSCHEN, KLAUS. "Karl Otfried Müller zum 150. Todestag: Ansprache anläßlich der Gedenkfeier am 25. Oktober 1990." *Mitteilungen des Deutschen Archaeologischen Instituts: Athenische Abteilung* 106 (1991): 1–7.

FOSTER, HAL. *Compulsive Beauty.* Cambridge: MIT Press, 1993.

———. "'Primitive' Scenes." *Critical Inquiry* 20, no. 1 (autumn 1993): 69–102.

———. *Recodings: Art, Spectacle, Politics.* Seattle: Bay Press, 1985.

FOUCAULT, MICHEL. *Discipline and Punish: The Birth of the Prison.* Trans. Alan Sheridan. New York: Vintage Books, 1979. First published 1975.

FRAMPTON, KENNETH. *Studies in Tectonic Culture: The Poetics of Construction in Nineteenth and Twentieth Century Architecture.* Cambridge: MIT Press, 1995.

"France's Far-flung Colonial Domain." *Literary Digest* 72, no. 6 (February 11, 1922): 26–27.

FRASER, DOUGLAS. *Village Planning in the Primitive World.* New York: George Braziller, 1968.

FREUD, SIGMUND. *Civilization and Its Discontents.* Trans. James Strachey. New York: W. W. Norton, 1961. First published 1930.

———. *Introductory Lectures on Psycho-analysis.* Trans. James Strachey. New York: W. W. Norton, 1966. First published 1916–17.

———. *The Standard Edition of the Complete Psychological Works.* 23 vols. Trans. James Strachey. London: Hogarth Press, 1953–74.

FRIEDRICH, ADOLPH, DUKE OF MECKLENBURG. *From the Congo to the Niger and the Nile: An Account of the German Central African Expedition of 1910–1911.* 2 vols. London: Duckworth, 1913.

FRITSCH, PIERRE. "Aspects géographiques des plaines d'inondation du Nord-Cameroun." *Cameroun Agricole, Pastoral et Forestier,* June 1973, 22–23; November 1973, 22–28.

FROW, JOHN. "Tourism and the Semiotics of Nostalgia." *October* 57 (summer 1991): 123–51.

GARDI, RENÉ. *Indigenous African Architecture.* Trans. Sigrid MacRae. New York: Van Norstrand Reinhold, 1973. First published 1973.

GARINE, IGOR DE. *Les Massa du Cameroun.* Paris: Presses Universitaires de France, 1964.

GATES, HENRY LOUIS, JR. *The Signifying Monkey: A Theory of African-American Literary Criticism.* Oxford: Oxford University Press, 1988.

————, ed. *"Race," Writing, and Difference*. Chicago: University of Chicago Press, 1986.

GEARY, CHRISTRAUD M. "Missionary Photography: Public and Private Readings." *African Arts* 24, no. 4 (October 1991): 48–59+.

————. "Old Pictures, New Approaches: Researching Historical Photographs." *African Arts* 24, no. 4 (October 1991): 36–40+.

GEHRKE, HANS-JOACHIM. "Karl Otfried Müller und das Land der Greichen." *Mitteilungen des Deutschen Archäologischen Instituts: Athenische Abteilung* 106 (1991): 9–35.

GEO-FOURRIER, G. "Civilisations agonistes du Tchad: Les Mousgou." *Nature*, no. 2918 (December 1933): 486–89.

GIDE, ANDRÉ. *Amnytas*. Trans. Richard Howard. New York: Ecco Press, 1988. First published 1906.

————. "Architectures nègres." *Cahiers d'art*, no. 7/8 (1927): 262–65.

————. *The Counterfeiters* with *Journal of "The Counterfeiters."* Novel trans. Dorothy Bussy; journal trans. Justin O'Brien. New York: Vintage Books, 1973. Novel first published 1927.

————. *The Immoralist*. Trans. Richard Howard. New York: Vintage Books, 1996. First published 1901.

————. *The Journals of André Gide*. 2 vols. Trans. and ed. Justin O'Brien. Evanston: Northwestern University Press, 1987. First published 1947–51.

————. *Si le grain ne meurt*. Paris: Editions Gallimard, 1955. First published 1921.

————. *Strait Is the Gate*. Trans. Dorothy Bussy. New York: Vintage Books, 1952. First published 1909.

————. "Sur le Logone." *La nouvelle revue française*, no. 171 (December 1, 1927): 723–46; no. 172 (January 1, 1928): 28–54; no. 173 (February 1, 1928): 177–204.

————. *Travels in the Congo*. Trans. Dorothy Bussy. Hopewell, NJ: Ecco Press, 1994. Translation of *Voyage au Congo: suivi du retour du Tchad* (1927), listed below.

————. "Les villages des tribus Massas." *L'Illustration*, no. 4383 (March 5, 1927): 236–37.

————. *Voyage au Congo: carnets de route*. Paris: Éditions de la Nouvelle Revue Française, 1927 (original edition of 1,163 imprints).

————. *Voyage au Congo: suivi de retour du Tchad*. Illustrated with 68 photographs by Marc Allégret. Paris: Gallimard, 1929. First published 1927.

————. *Voyage au Congo: suivi du retour du Tchad*. Paris: Gallimard, 1981.

GILMAN, SANDER L. "Black Bodies, White Bodies: Toward an Iconography of Female Sexuality in Late Nineteenth-Century Art, Medicine, and Literature." In *"Race," Writing, and Difference*, ed. Henry Louis Gates, Jr., 223–61. Chicago: University of Chicago Press, 1986.

GOMBRICH, ERNST. *Art and Illusion: A Study in the Psychology of Pictorial Representation*. Princeton: Princeton University Press, 1989.

GOODHUE, DANA. "The Mousgoum of Pouss." Manuscript, 1995.

GRABAR, OLEG. "From Dome of Heaven to Pleasure Dome." *Journal of the Society of Architectural Historians* 49, no. 1 (March 1990): 15–21.

————. *The Mediation of Ornament*. Princeton: Princeton University Press, 1992.

GRABURN, NELSON, ed. *Ethnic and Tourist Arts*. Berkeley: University of California Press, 1976.

GREENBLATT, STEPHEN. *Marvelous Possessions: The Wonder of the New World*. Chicago: University of Chicago Press, 1991.

GREENHALGH, PAUL. *Ephemeral Vistas: The Expositions Universelles, Great Exhibitions, and World's Fairs, 1851–1939.* Manchester, England: University of Manchester Press, 1988.

GRESWELL, WILLIAM. "Europe and Africa." *Blackwood's Edinburgh Magazine* 151 (June 1892): 843–52.

GRIAULE, MARCEL. "Dictionnaire." *Documents* 1, no. 7 (1929): 381.

GUIDE DES COLONIES FRANÇAISES. *Afrique française: Afrique occidentale française, Afrique équatoriale française, Togo et Cameroun.* Paris: Société d'Editions Géographiques, Maritimes et Coloniales, 1931.

VON HAGEN, GUNTHER. "Die Bana." *Baessler Archiv* 2 (1911): 77–116.

———. "Einige Notizen über die Musgu." *Baessler Archiv* 2 (1911): 117–22.

HANDLER, RICHARD, and WILLIAM SAXTON. "Dyssimulation: Reflexivity, Narrative, and the Quest for Authenticity in 'Living History,'" *Cultural Anthropology*, vol. 3, no. 3 (August 1988), 242–60.

HARAWAY, DONNA. *Primate Visions: Gender, Race, and Nature in the World of Modern Science.* New York: Routledge, 1989.

HARDY, GEORGES. "L'Exposition Coloniale, moment historique." *L'Europe Nouvelle* 14, no. 697 (June 20, 1931): 867–68.

HARRIS, NORMAN DWIGHT. *Europe and Africa Being a Revised Edition of Intervention and Colonization in Africa.* New York: Negro Universities Press, 1969. First published 1927.

HARROW, KENNETH W. *Faces of Islam in African Literature.* Portsmouth, NH: Heinemann, 1991.

HIBBERT, CHRISTOPHER. *Africa Explored: Europeans in the Dark Continent, 1769–1889,* Middlesex, England: Penguin Books, 1982.

HOBSBAWM, ERIC. *The Age of Empire, 1875–1914.* New York: Vintage Books, 1989.

HODNETT, EDWARD. *Image and Text: Studies in the Illustration of English Literature.* London: Scolar Press, 1982.

HODEIR, CATHERINE, and MICHEL PIERRE. *L'Exposition Coloniale.* Brussels: Editions Complexe, 1991.

HOFFMANN, CARL. "The Personal Pronoun in Musgum." *Research Notes from the Department of Linguistics and Nigerian Languages, University of Ibadan* 3, no. 1 (March 1970).

HUSSEY, CHRISTOPHER. *The Picturesque: Studies in a Point of View.* London: Archon Books, 1967. First published 1927.

ICHAC, PIERRE. "Carefree People of the Cameroons." *National Geographic* 91 (February 1947): 233–48.

IRELE, ABIOLA. "Contemporary Thought in French Speaking Africa." In *Africa and the West: The Legacies of Empire*, ed. Isaac James Mowoe and Richard Bjornson, 121–58. Westport, CT: Greenwood Press, 1986.

IRWIN-ZARECKA, IWONA. *Frames of Remembrance: The Dynamics of Collective Memory.* New Brunswick, NJ: Transaction Publishers, 1994.

JAMESON, FREDRIC. *The Political Unconscious: Narrative as a Socially Symbolic Act.* Ithaca: Cornell University Press, 1981.

JOHNSTON, H. H. *The Opening Up of Africa.* London: Williams and Norgate, 1911.

JULES-ROSETTE, BENETTA. *The Messages of Tourist Art: An African Semiotic System in Comparative Perspective.* New York: Plenum Press, 1984.

KAEPPLER, ADRIENNE L. "Memory and Knowledge in the Production of Dance." In *Images of Memory*, ed. Susan Küchler and Walter Melion, 109–20. Washington: Smithsonian Institution Press, 1991.

KAHN, ELY JACQUES. "Impressions of the Paris Colonial Exposition." *American Architect* 140 (October 1931): 34–39+.

KANE, CHEIKH HAMIDOU. *L'aventure ambiguë*. Paris: Gallimard, 1961.

KASFIR, SIDNEY L. "African Art and Authenticity: A Text with a Shadow." *African Arts* 25, no. 3 (April 1992): 40–53+.

KERN, STEPHEN. *The Culture of Time and Space 1880–1918*. Cambridge: Harvard University Press, 1983.

KEVLES, DANIEL J. *In the Name of Eugenics: Genetics and the Uses of Human Identity*. Cambridge: Harvard University Press, 1995. First published 1985.

KINGSLEY, MARY H. *Travels in West Africa*. 3rd ed. London: Frank Cass, 1965. First published 1897.

KIRK-GREENE, ANTHONY. "Heinrich Barth: An Exercise in Empathy." In *Africa and Its Explorers: Motives, Methods, and Impact*, ed. Robert I. Rotberg, 13–38. Cambridge: Harvard University Press, 1970.

KIRSHENBLATT-GIMBLETT, BARBARA. *Destination Culture: Tourism, Museums, and Heritage*. Berkeley: University of California Press, 1998.

KRAUSS, ROSALIND E. *L'Amour Fou: Photography and Surrealism*. Exhibition catalogue. Washington: Corcoran Gallery of Art, 1985.

———. *The Originality of the Avant-Garde and Other Modernist Myths*. Cambridge: MIT Press, 1986.

LABBÉ, EDMOND. *Exposition internationale des arts et techniques, rapport général*. 11 vols. Paris: Imprimerie Nationale, 1938–40.

LACAN, JACQUES. *Écrits: A Selection*. Trans. Alan Sheridan. New York: W. W. Norton, 1977. First published 1966.

LANE, PAUL J. "Tourism and Social Change among the Dogon." *African Arts* 21, no. 4 (August 1988): 66–69+.

LANGER, SUSANNE K. *Feeling and Form*. New York: Scribner's, 1953.

———. *Philosophy in a New Key: A Study in the Symbolism of Reason, Rite, and Art*. 3rd ed. Cambridge: Harvard University Press, 1957.

LAUDE, JEAN. *La peinture française 1905–1914 et "L'art nègre."* Paris: Editions Klinksieck, 1968.

LAVIN, SYLVIA. *Quatremère de Quincy and the Invention of a Modern Language of Architecture*. Cambridge: MIT Press, 1992.

LEBEUF, ANNIE, and JEAN-PAUL LEBEUF. *Les arts du Sao: Cameroun, Tchad, Nigeria*. Paris: Chêne, 1977.

LEBEUF, JEAN-PAUL. *L'habitation des Fali*. Paris: Librairie Hachette, 1961.

LE CORBUSIER. *Towards a New Architecture*. Trans. Frederick Etchells. New York: Dover, 1986. First published 1923.

LEFEBVRE, HENRI. *The Production of Space*. Trans. Donald Nicholson-Smith. Oxford: Blackwell, 1991. First published 1974.

Le Livre des Expositions Universelles 1851–1989. Paris: Editions des arts décoratives, 1993.

LEIRIS, MICHEL. "Dictionnaire." *Documents* 1, no. 7 (1929): 381–82.

LEMBEZAT, BERTRAND. *Kirdi: les populations païennes du Nord-Cameroun*. Yaoundé: Institut Français de l'Afrique Noire, 1950.

———. *Les populations païennes du Nord-Cameroun et de l'Amadaoua*. Paris: Presses Universitaires de France, 1961.

LES GUIDES BLEUS. *Afrique centrale: Les républiques d'expression française*. Paris: Librairie Hachette, 1962.

L'habitat au Cameroun. Paris: Éditions de l'Union Française, 1952.

LUCEY, MICHAEL. *Gide's Bent: Sexuality, Politics, Writing*. Oxford: Oxford University Press, 1995.

LUKAS, JOHANNES. *Deutsche Quellen zur Sprache der Musgu in Kamerun*. Berlin: D. Reimer, 1941.

———. *Zentralsudanische Studien: Wörterzeichnisse der Deutschen Zentral-Afrika-Expedition 1910-11, Nachgelassene Aufnamen von Gustav Nachtigal und eigene Sammlungen*. Hamburg: Friederischen, de Gruyter, 1937.

LYAUTEY, MARÉCHAL. "Le sens d'un grand effort." *L'Illustration*, no. 4603 (May 23, 1931): n.p.

MACCANNELL, DEAN. *Empty Meeting Grounds: The Tourist Papers*. New York: Routledge, 1992.

———. *The Tourist: A New Theory of the Leisure Class*. New York: Schocken Books, 1976.

MACLEOD, OLIVE. *Chiefs and Cities of Central Africa: Across Lake Chad by Way of British, French, and German Territories*. Freeport, NY: Books for Libraries Press, 1971. First published 1912.

———. "Lake Léré and the Discovery of the MacLeod Falls in the Mao Kabi." *Blackwood's Edinburgh Magazine* 190 (July 1911): 35–43.

MAIGRET, JULIEN. *Afrique Équatoriale Française*. Paris: Société d'Editions Géographiques, Maritimes et Coloniales, 1931.

MANNING, PATRICK. *Francophone Sub-Saharan Africa 1880-1985*. Cambridge: Cambridge University Press, 1988.

———. *Slavery and African Life: Occidental, Oriental, and African Slave Trades*. Cambridge: Cambridge University Press, 1990.

MCCLINTOCK, ANNE. *Imperial Leather: Race, Gender, and Sexuality in the Colonial Contest*. New York: Routledge, 1995.

MCEWAN, CHERYL. *Gender, Geography, and Empire: Victorian Women Travelers in West Africa*. Aldershot: Ashgate, 2000.

MENDUNGA, T.-A. EBANDA. "The Cultural Identity of Cameroon and Native Architecture." In *The Cultural Identity of Cameroon*, ed. Ministry of Information and Culture and the Department of Cultural Affairs, 493–514. Yaoundé: Ministry of Information and Culture, Department of Cultural Affairs, 1985.

MERTINS, DETLEF. "Walter Benjamin's 'Tectonic' Unconscious." *ANY* 14 (1996): 28–35.

MEYER-BAHLBURG, HILKE. *Studien zur Morphologie und Syntax des Musgu*. Hamburg: Helmut Buske Verlag, 1972.

———. "Texte in Musgu von Girvidik." *Afrika & Übersee* 56, no. 1/2 (1972): 61–71.

MILLER, CHRISTOPHER L. *Blank Darkness: Africanist Discourse in French*. Chicago: University of Chicago Press, 1985.

MINH-HA, TRINH T. "Of Other Peoples: Beyond the 'Salvage Paradigm.'" In *Discussions in Contemporary Culture*, no. 1, ed. Hal Foster, 138–41. Seattle: Bay Press, 1987.

MINISTRY OF INFORMATION AND CULTURE AND DEPARTMENT OF CULTURAL AFFAIRS, ed. *The Cultural Identity of Cameroon.* Yaoundé: Ministry of Information and Culture, Department of Cultural Affairs, 1985.

MITCHELL, W. J. T., ed. *Landscape and Power.* Chicago: University of Chicago Press, 1994.

———. *The Language of Images.* Chicago: University of Chicago Press, 1980.

MORAGA, CHERRÍE, and GLORIA ANZALDÚA, eds. *This Bridge Called My Back: Writings by Radical Women of Color.* New York: Kitchen Table: Women of Color Press, 1983.

MOREL, E. D. *The Black Man's Burden.* New York: Modern Reader Paperbacks, 1969. First published 1920.

MORGEN, C. VON. *Durch Kamerun von Süd nach Nord: Reisen und Forschlagen im Hinterlande 1889 bis 1891.* Leipzig: F. V. Brochthaus, 1893.

MORRISON, TONI. *Playing in the Dark: Whiteness and the Literary Imagination.* Cambridge: Harvard Belknap Press, 1992.

MORTON, PATRICIA A. "National and Colonial: The Musée des Colonies at the Colonial Exposition, Paris, 1931." *Art Bulletin* 80, no. 2 (June 1998): 357–77.

———. *The Civilizing Mission of Architecture: The 1931 International Colonial Exposition in Paris.* Ann Arbor: University Microfilms, 1994.

———. *Hybrid Modernities: Architecture and Representation at the 1931 Colonial Exposition, Paris.* Cambridge: MIT Press, 2000.

MOUSSET, PAUL. "L'Exposition Coloniale—un bilan." *Le Correspondant,* no. 1661 (December 10, 1931): 641–46.

MUDIMBE, V. Y. *Before the Birth of the Moon.* Trans. Marjolin de Jager. New York: Fireside, 1989. First published 1976.

———. *The Idea of Africa.* Bloomington: Indiana University Press, 1994.

———. *The Invention of Africa: Gnosis, Philosophy, and the Order of Knowledge.* Bloomington: Indiana University Press, 1988.

MÜLLER, FRIEDRICH. *Die Musuk-Sprache in Central Afrika: Nach den Aufzeichnungen von G. A. Krause.* Vienna: Carl Gerold's Sohn, 1886.

MÜLLER, KARL OTFRIED. *Ancient Art and its Remains or a Manual of the Archaeology of Art.* 2nd ed. Trans. Friedrich Gottlieb Welcker. London: A. Fullarton, 1850. First published 1830.

———. *Manual of the Archaeology of Art.* Trans. John Leitch. London: A. Fullarton, 1850. First published 1830.

NACHTIGAL, GUSTAV. *Sahara and Sudan III: The Chad Basin and Bagirmi.* Trans. Allan G. B. Fisher and Humphrey J. Fisher. London: C. Hurst, 1987. First published 1889.

NAIPAUL, V. S. *A Bend in the River.* New York: Alfred A. Knopf, 1979.

NASR, SEYYED HOSSEIN. *A Young Muslim's Guide to the Modern World.* Chicago: Kazi Publications, 1993.

NEEDHAM, GERALD. *19th Century Realist Art.* New York: Harper & Row, 1988.

NELSON, STEVEN. "'Savages' on the Seine: The Mousgoum Dome." *Annals of Scholarship: Art Practices and the Human Sciences in a Global Culture* 14, no. 1 (2000): 13–25.

———. "Site and Symbol: Framing Cultural Identities in Mousgoum Architecture." Ph.D. diss., Harvard University, 1998.

———. "Writing Architecture: The Mousgoum *Tòlék* and Cultural Self-Fashioning at the New *Fin de Siècle*." *African Arts* 34, no. 3 (autumn 2001): 38–49+

NORA, PIERRE, ed. *Les lieux de mémoire*. 3 vols. Paris: Gallimard, 1984.

NORBERG-SCHULZ, CHRISTIAN. *Existence, Space, and Architecture*. New York: Praeger Publishers, 1971.

———. *Meaning in Western Architecture*. Trans. Anna Maria Norberg-Schulz. New York: Praeger Publishers, 1975. First published 1974.

NTSOBE, ANDRÉ-MARIE. "Cameroon's Cultural Identity and Book Production." In *The Cultural Identity of Cameroon*, ed. Ministry of Information and Culture and the Department of Cultural Affairs, 231–37. Yaoundé: Ministry of Information and Culture, Department of Cultural Affairs, 1985.

OLIN, MARGARET. "Self-Representation: Resemblance and Convention in Two Nineteenth-Century Theories of Architecture and the Decorative Arts." *Zeitschrift für Kunstgeschichte* 49, no. 3 (1987): 376–97.

OLIVIER, MARCEL, ed. *Exposition coloniale internationale de Paris, Rapport général*. 7 vols. Paris: Imprimerie Nationale, 1932–34.

OUOLOGUEM, YAMBO. *Bound to Violence*. Trans. Ralph Manheim. New York: Harcourt, Brace Jovanovich, 1971. First published 1968.

OWENS, CRAIG. *Beyond Recognition: Representation, Power, and Culture*. Berkeley: University of California Press, 1992.

OZENFANT, AMEDÉE. *Foundations of Modern Art*. Trans. John Rodker. New York: Dover, 1952. First published 1928.

PARKENHAM, THOMAS. *The Scramble for Africa, 1876–1912*. New York: Random House, 1991.

PATTISON, JAMES WILLIAM. "The French Colonial Exposition at Marseilles." *World To-Day* 11 (November 1906): 1189–97.

PÈTRE, LÉON, and JOSEPH TRILLAT, *La France outre-mer*. Paris: Les Éditions Jos. Vermaut, c. 1930.

PEVSNER, NIKOLAUS. *Some Architectural Writers of the Nineteenth Century*. Oxford: Clarendon Press, 1972.

PHILLIPS, RUTH B. *Representing Women: Sande Masquerades of the Mende of Sierra Leone*. Los Angeles: UCLA Fowler Museum of Cultural History, 1995.

PIETERSE, JAN NEDERVEEN. *White on Black: Images of Africa and Blacks in Western Popular Culture*. New Haven: Yale University Press, 1992.

POLLOCK, GRISELDA. *Avant-Garde Gambits 1888–1893: Gender and the Color of Art History*. London: Thames and Hudson, 1992.

PRATT, MARY LOUISE. "Scratches on the Face of the Country; or What Mr. Barrow Saw in the Land of the Bushmen." In *"Race," Writing, and Difference*, ed. Henry Louis Gates, Jr., 138–62. Chicago: University of Chicago Press, 1986.

PRICE, SALLY. *Primitive Art in Civilized Places*. Chicago: University of Chicago Press, 1989.

PROCHASKA, DAVID. "Fantasia of the *Photothèque*: French Postcard Views of Colonial Senegal." *African Arts* 24, no. 4 (October 1991): 40–47+.

PRUSSIN, LABELLE. *Architecture in Northern Ghana*. Berkeley: University of California Press, 1969.

———. *Hatumere: Islamic Design in West Africa.* Berkeley: University of California Press, 1986.

———. "West African Mud Granaries." *Paideuma* 18 (1972): 144–69.

PYNE, WILLIAM HENRY. *Etching of Rustic Figures of the Embellishment of Landscape.* London: M. A. Nattali, 1819.

———. *Picturesque Views of Rural Occupations in Early Nineteenth-Century England.* New York: Dover Publications, 1977. First published 1824.

RAMBOSSON, YVANHOÉ. "Le mouvement des arts appliqués." *Le bulletin de l'art,* no. 776 (March 1931): 122–27.

———. "Le mouvement des arts appliqués." *Le bulletin de l'art,* no. 778 (May 1931): 211–18.

———. "Le mouvement des arts appliqués." *Le bulletin de l'art,* no. 783 (December 1931): 467–72.

"Réflexions d'architects sur l'architecture colonial." *Le bulletin de l'art,* no. 783 (December 1931): 473–76.

REYNA, S. P. *Wars without End: The Political Economy of a Precolonial African State.* Hanover, NH: University Press of New England, 1990.

REEVES, E. A. *Hints to Travellers, Scientific and General.* 2 vols. 10th ed. London: Royal Geographic Society, 1921.

RICHARDSON, JAMES. *Narrative of a Mission to Central Africa.* 2 vols. London: Chapman and Hill, 1853.

ROBERTS, ANDREW, ed. *The Colonial Moment in Africa: Essays on the Movement of Minds and Materials 1900–1940.* Cambridge: Cambridge University Press, 1986.

ROBERTSON, GEORGE, et al., eds. *Travellers' Tales: Narratives of Home and Displacement.* New York: Routledge, 1994.

ROBINSON, RONALD, and JOHN GALLAGHER. *Africa and the Victorians: The Climax of Imperialism.* Garden City, NY: Anchor Books, 1968. First published 1961.

ROBINSON, SIDNEY K. *Inquiry into the Picturesque.* Chicago: University of Chicago Press, 1991.

ROBIN, M. "Rapport de tourneé." 25 August 1932, in "Sultanat de Pouss," 1932–33, Document APA 11834/G. National Archives, Yaoundé, Cameroon.

RONY, FATIMAH TOBING. *The Third Eye: Race, Cinema, and Ethnographic Spectacle.* Durham: Duke University Press, 1996.

ROUSSEAU, JEAN-JACQUES. *The Social Contract and Discourse on the Origin of Inequality.* New York: Simon and Schuster, 1967.

ROYCE, ANYA P. *The Anthropology of Dance.* Bloomington: Indiana University Press, 1977.

ROYER, JEAN, ed. *L'urbanisme aux colonies et dans les pays tropicaux.* 2 vols. Paris: Les Editions de l'Urbanisme, 1932, 1935.

RUSKIN, JOHN. *The Seven Lamps of Architecture.* New York: John Wiley & Son, 1874. First published 1849.

RUSSELL, MARY. *The Blessings of a Good Thick Skirt: Women Travellers and Their World.* London: Collins, 1986.

RYKWERT, JOSEPH. *On Adam's House in Paradise: The Idea of the Primitive Hut in Architectural History.* New York: Museum of Modern Art, 1972.

———. *The Dancing Column: On Order in Architecture.* Cambridge: MIT Press, 1996.

RYDELL, ROBERT W. *All the World's a Fair: The Century of Progress Expositions.* Chicago: University of Chicago Press, 1993.

SAID, EDWARD. *Culture and Imperialism.* New York: Knopf, 1993.

———. *Orientalism.* New York: Vintage, 1978.

SCHNEIDER, WILLIAM. *An Empire for the Masses: The French Image of Africa, 1870–1900.* Westport, CT: Greenwood Press, 1982.

SCHWARZER, MITCHELL. "Ontology and Representation in Karl Bötticher's Theory of Tectonics." *Journal of the Society of Architectural Historians* 52 (September 1993): 267–80.

———. "Tectonics Unbound." *ANY* 14 (1996): 14–15.

SCOTT, GEOFFREY. *The Architecture of Humanism: A Study in the History of Taste.* London: Architectural Press, 1980. First published 1924.

SEIGNOBOS, CHRISTIAN, and FABIEN JAMIN. *La case obus: histoire et reconstitution.* Marseilles: Éditions Parenthèsis—Patrimoine sans Frontières, 2003.

SEKLER, EDUARD F. "Structure, Construction, and Tectonics." *Connection,* March 1965, 2–11.

SHELLEY, BASKOUDA J. B. *Kirdi est mon nom.* Yaoundé: Imprimerie Saint-Paul, 1993.

SILVER, KENNETH E. *Esprit de Corps.* Princeton: Princeton University Press, 1989.

SIMONSTON, IDA VERA. "Housekeeping in Africa: Savage Servants and Dangers Make the Domestic Problem Difficult." *Delineator* 75, no. 4 (April 1910): 319+.

SMITH, E. BALDWIN. *The Dome: A Study in the History of Ideas.* Princeton: Princeton University Press, 1950.

SMITH, VALENE, ed. *Hosts and Guests: The Anthropology of Tourism.* Philadelphia: University of Pennsylvania Press, 1977.

SOLOMON-GODEAU, ABIGAIL. "Going Native." *Art in America* 77, no. 7 (July 1989): 118–29+.

SONTAG, SUSAN. *On Photography.* New York: Dell Publishing, 1973.

SOYINKA, WOLE. *Art, Dialogue, and Outrage: Essays on Literature and Culture.* New York: Pantheon, 1993.

SPECTOR, JACK J. *Surrealist Art and Writing, 1919–1939.* Cambridge: Cambridge University Press, 1997.

SPENCER, PAUL, ed. *Society and the Dance.* Cambridge: Cambridge University Press, 1985.

STAFFORD, BARBARA. *Voyage into Substance: Art, Science, Nature, and the Illustrated Travel Account, 1760–1840.* Cambridge: MIT Press, 1984.

STEINER, CHRISTOPHER B. *African Art in Transit.* Cambridge: Cambridge University Press, 1994.

———. "Of Drums and Dancers: Convention and Reality in Portrayals of Non-Western Peoples in European Accounts of Discovery and Exploration." *Harvard Review* 1 (1986): 104–29.

STEWART, SUSAN. *On Longing: Narratives of the Miniature, the Gigantic, the Souvenir, the Collection.* Baltimore: Johns Hopkins University Press, 1984.

STROTHER, Z. S. *Inventing Masks: Agency and History in the Art of the Central Pende.* Chicago: University of Chicago Press, 1998.

"Sultanat de Pouss," 1932–33, Document APA 11834/G. National Archives, Yaoundé, Cameroon.

SURET-CANALE, JEAN. *French Colonialism in Tropical Africa 1900–1945.* Trans. Till Gott-heimer. London: C. Hurst, 1971. First published 1964.

TALBOT, D. AMAURY. *Women's Mysteries of a Primitive People: The Ibibios of Southern Nigeria.* London: Frank Cass, 1968. First published 1915.

TALBOT, P. AMAURY. *The Peoples of Southern Nigeria: A Sketch of their History, Ethnology and Languages with an Abstract of the 1921 Census.* 4 vols. London: Frank Cass, 1969. First published 1926.

———. *Tribes of the Niger Delta: Their Religions and Customs.* London: Frank Cass, 1967. First published 1932.

THOMAS, JEAN. *A travers l'Afrique équatoriale sauvage.* Paris: Larose, 1934.

THOMSON, JOSEPH. "Results of European Intercourse with the African." *Contemporary Review* 57 (March 1890): 339–52.

TODOROV, TZVETAN. *On Human Diversity: Nationalism, Racism, and Exoticism in French Thought.* Trans. Catherine Porter. Cambridge: Harvard University Press, 1993. First published 1989.

TORGOVNICK, MARIANNA. *Gone Primitive: Savage Intellects, Modern Lives.* Chicago: University of Chicago Press, 1990.

———. *Primitive Passions: Men, Women, and the Quest for Ecstasy.* Chicago: University of Chicago Press, 1998.

TOURNEUX, HENRY. "Les emprunts en Musgu." In *Studies in Chadic and Afroasiatic Lin-guistics,* ed. E. Wolff and H. Meyer-Bahlburg, 441–77. Hamburg: H. Buske Verlag, 1983.

———. *Lexique pratique du Munjuk des rizières, Dialect de Pouss.* Paris: ORSTOM, 1991.

———. *Le mulwi ou vùlùm de Mogron (Tchad).* Paris: SELAF, 1978.

TOURNEUX, HENRY, CHRISTIAN SEIGNOBOS, and FRANCINE LAFARGE. *Les Mbara et leur Langue (Tchad).* Paris: SELAF, 1986.

TRILLAT, JOSEPH. *L'Exposition coloniale de France.* Paris: Librairie des Arts Décoratives, 1931.

TROY, NANCY J. *The De Stijl Environment.* Cambridge: MIT Press, 1983.

TURNER, VICTOR. *The Anthropology of Performance.* New York: PAJ Publications, 1986.

———. *The Forest of Symbols: Aspects of Ndembu Ritual.* Ithaca: Cornell University Press, 1967.

VALÉRY, PAUL. *Reflections on the World Today.* Trans. Francis Scarfe. New York: Pantheon, 1948. First published 1945.

VAN DOESBURG, THEO. "The Significance of Colour for Exterior and Interior Architec-ture." In Joost Baljeu, *Theo van Doesburg,* 137–40. New York: Macmillan, 1974.

VAN WYK, GARY N. *African Painted Houses: Basotho Dwellings of Southern Africa.* New York: Abrams, 1998.

VARENNE, GASTON. "Le musée permanent des colonies." *Art & Decoration,* no. 60 (Au-gust 1931): 59–68.

VATIN-PÉRIOGON, E. "L'Exposition Coloniale." *Le Correspondant,* no. 1651 (July 10, 1931): 33–44.

VIOLLET-LE-DUC, EUGÈNE-EMMANUEL. *Lectures on Architecture.* 2 vols. Trans. Ben-jamin Bucknall. New York: Dover, 1987. First published 1872.

VOGEL, SUSAN. *Africa Explores: 20th Century African Art.* New York: Center for African Art, 1991.

WALDRAM, PERCY J. *The Principles of Structural Mechanics.* London: B. T. Batsford, 1912.

WOLF, SCOTT C. "The Metaphysical Foundations of Schinkel's Tectonics: *Eine Spinne im eigenen Netz.*" ANY 14 (1996): 16–21.

WÖLFFLIN, HEINRICH. *Prolegomena to a Psychology of Architecture.* In *Empathy, Form, and Space: Problems in German Aesthetics, 1873–1893.* Trans. Harry Francis Mallgrave and Eleftherios Ikonomou, 149–90. Los Angeles: Getty Center of the History of Art and the Humanities, 1994. First published 1886.

WRIGHT, GWENDOLYN. *The Politics of Design in French Colonial Urbanism.* Chicago: University of Chicago Press, 1991.

YATES, FRANCES A. *The Art of Memory.* London: Pimlico, 1994. First published 1966.

YOUNGS, TIM. *Travellers in Africa.* Manchester, England: Manchester University Press, 1994.

Page numbers in italics refer to figures.

colonialism: European, 3, 19, 82, 114, 141, 158. *See also* France

colonized, 108, 109, 111, 113, 114, 132, 133, 140, 142, 146

colonizer, 109, 140, 142, 146, 162

color, 159, 163, 181

columns, 116, 137, 138, 139

commerce, 52, 55, 118, 142, 175

commercial issues, 3

commodities, 143, 144

compound. *See* family compound

concession. *See* family compound

Congo, 82, 115

Conrad, Joseph, 51, 55, 86, 87; *Heart of Darkness*, 50, 69, 86, 87; *Typhoon*, 86

construction: and dance, 40; and subjectivity, 6; of the teleuk, 28–31, 177–78, 188. *See also* coil-pottery technique

contradiction, 67, 68, 90, 96, 107, 108, 140, 144, 162

Coombs, Annie, 53

Copjec, Joan, 73, 145

Corbusier, Le, 89, 133, 134, 138, 139

cosmopolitanism, 152, 164

costumes, 151, 163

Counterfeiters, The (Gide), 90

Courthion, Pierre, 126, 128, 132, 138, 142

cows, 20, 42

craft, 95, 96

creativity, 206n41. *See also under* gender

crescent moon and star, 162–63, 166

crocodiles, 179, 182

cultural: advancement, 9, 56; heritage, 4, 154, 167, 170, 171, 172, 177, 188, 192, 197; knowledge, 147, 171, 172, 173, 174, 176, 177, 187, 188, 191, 196; loss, 147, 160, 171, 172, 173, 188, 191, 194; relativism, 108; survival, 4, 168; symbol, 160, 161; transformation, 111, 112, 113, 187; values, 157. *See also* civilization; culture; evolution; nature

culture, 55, 56, 63, 84, 85, 96, 104, 142, 153, 162, 176. *See also* civilization; cultural: advancement; evolution; France; nature

cupola, 133, 135

Dadouazi, Boukar, 172, 173

Dakar, 107

dalam (compound), 24

dance, 19, 31, 32, 34, 36, 37, 38, 149, 151, 158, 177, 186. *See also* architecture: and dance; *individual dances*

death, 18, 37, 53, 58, 61, 66, 84, 86, 94, 95, 96. *See also* architecture: and death; funerals; funerary practices

decomposition, 80. *See also* body: deformation

decoration. *See* ornament; murals; wall painting

delemiy (house), 23, 24, 25, 204n9. *See also* *feɲiy*; house types

Dening, Greg, 148, 176, 182

De Stijl, 89

destination, 192

desublimation, 67, 68, 80. *See also* sublimation

difference, 8, 61, 67, 77, 88, 89, 104, 108, 138, 146, 176, 192. *See also under* gender

dirt, 80, 81, 82, 95

disappearance (of the teleuk). *See* cultural: loss; extinction

distance, 145; geographic, 8, 104; psychological, 54–55, 58–59, 73, 74, 80, 81, 87, 95, 96, 104, 136, 140, 142; temporal, 143, 196

diviner, 39

Documents (journal), 80

Dodds, John, 53

Dogo, Azao, 34, 43, 112, 147, 148, 172, 173, 196, 211n30; teleukakay of, 174

Dogon, 158

domaine coloniale français, Le, 99, 109, 110, 123

Donnet, Gaston, 98

Douala (people), 111

Doubla, Marcel, 153

dougate (Mousgoum dance), 31, 32, 35

Douniya, Évélé, 160, 188

Doupta, Afti, 25, 26

dourmalaye (Mousgoum dance), 38

drawings, 71, 120, 206n41
Dumas-Champion, Françoise, 32
Duncan, Carol, 137, 141
Durand, J. N. L., 60
Durosay, Daniel, 90
"Dying Civilizations of Chad: The Mous-
    goum" (Geo-Fourrier), 171–72

earth, 30. *See also* clay
economic: benefit, 194; development, 154,
    171, 197; opportunity, 170; resources,
    22–23; structure, 13–14; value, 144
ego, 68
Egypt, 137, 138, 139
elephants, 42, 179, 182
empathy, 7, 8, 62, 63, 67, 68, 74, 97, 201n15
empire, 75, 191. *See also* France;
    imperialism
enclosure. *See* family compound
engravings, 65–66, 70, 71, 120
Enlightenment, 66
Essomba, Joseph-Marie, 215n22
Ethiopia, 106
ethnoarchaeology, 6
ethnography, 6, 122, 124
European: domination, 111; nationalism,
    105
Europe nouvelle, L', 98
evolution, 56, 57, 60, 61, 63, 85, 87, 89,
    107, 110, 136, 142. *See also* civiliza-
    tion; cultural: advancement; culture;
    nature
exotic, exoticism, 83, 87, 88, 95, 99, 134,
    135–36, 137, 139, 144, 195
exploration, 52, 53, 96
Expo 2005 (Aichi Province, Japan), 1–3
Exposition of Decorative Arts (Paris,
    1925), 120, 126, 137
expositions, 101. *See also individual
    expositions*
extinction (of the teleuk), 16–17, 113–14,
    147, 171–72, 192, 194

Fabian, Johannes, 136
face (*aray*), 28

Faidherbe, Louis, 106, 107, 108
Fali, 194
family compound, 3, 8, 14, 19, 20, 22,
    24, 25, 32, 35, 36, 37, 38, 39, 40,
    41, 44, 46, 47, 48, 65, 66, 67, 92,
    93, 94, 174, 178, 180, 181, 204n5,
    204n7; layout of, 19–23, 32–34, *33*,
    57, 175. *See also* architectural plan;
    Atuisingué, Lawane: com-
    pound of
family enclosure. *See* family com-
    pound
family homestead. *See* family com-
    pound
Fanon, Frantz, 140
fantasia, 163, *plate 7*
fantasy, 145; metropolitan, 144; of travel,
    141; Western, 115
father of the house. *See* patriarch
feŋ (compound), 24, 204n10
feŋiy (house), 23, 24. See also *delemiy*;
    house types
feŋ ni mpus (homestead of the Mous-
    goum), 176
fertility, 15, 35, 183. *See also* birth; preg-
    nancy; progeniture
Fête du Mouton, 151–52, 188
fetishization, 92
Fichet, Léon, 101, 120, 121, 132, 133, 134,
    136, 139, 144, 191–92
Fierens, Paul, 114
fishing, 13, 15, 167, 179, 180, 183
Five Weeks in a Balloon (Verne), 69
flywhisks, 150, 151
food, 34, 36, 37, 47, 48, 68, 92, 94, 179, 182.
    See also millet; rice
forced labor. *See under* labor
forgetfulness, 83, 84, 87
Fort Archambault, 86
Foster, Hal, 68
Foucault, Michel, 73
Foulbe, 12, 13, 194
Foundations of Modern Art (Ozenfant),
    89, 121
Frampton, Kenneth, 5